MILITARY NECESSITY

MILITARY NECESSITY

Civil-Military Relations in the Confederacy

PAUL D. ESCOTT

In War and in Peace: U.S. Civil-Military Relations
David S. Heidler and Jeanne T. Heidler, General Editors

Praeger Security International
Westport, Connecticut · London

Library of Congress Cataloging-in-Publication Data

Escott, Paul D., 1947–
    Military necessity : civil-military relations in the Confederacy / Paul D. Escott.
        p.   cm.—(In war and in peace: U.S. Civil-military relations, ISSN 1556–8504)
    Includes bibliographical references and index.
    ISBN 0–275–98313–7 (alk. paper)
  1. Confederate States of America—Politics and government.   2. Confederate States of
America—Military policy.   3. Civil-military relations—Confederate States of America.   4.
Confederate States of America—Social conditions.   5. United States—History—Civil War,
1861–1865—Social aspects.   I. Title.   II. Series.
    E487.E83   2006
    973.7'13—dc22   2005020945

British Library Cataloguing in Publication Data is available.

Library of Congress Catalog Card Number: 2005020945
ISBN: 0–275–98313–7
ISSN: 1556–8504

First published in 2006

Praeger Security International, 88 Post Road West, Westport, CT 06881
An imprint of Greenwood Publishing Group, Inc.
www.praeger.com

Printed in the United States of America

The paper used in this book complies with the
Permanent Paper Standard issued by the National
Information Standards Organization (Z39.48–1984).

10 9 8 7 6 5 4 3 2 1

We are not yet fully awake to the extent to which we have abdicated popular Government. . . . The plea of military necessity has been presented in all its bearings, and its demands set forth in plain, candid words. The urgency of the plea has been acknowledged by us, and . . . we have willingly and cheerfully surrendered one privilege of freemen after another.

Daily Richmond Enquirer,
November 19, 1864

Contents

Illustrations

PLATES

MAPS

Series Foreword

No other aspect of a nation's political health is as important as the relationship between its government and its military. At the most basic level, the necessity of protecting the country from external and internal threats must be balanced by the obligation to preserve fundamental civil liberties. The United States is unique among nations, for it has successfully maintained civilian control of its military establishment, doing so from a fundamental principle institutionalized in its Constitution and embraced by its citizens. The United States has thus avoided the military coup that elsewhere has always meant the end of representative government and the extinguishing of individual freedom. The American military is the servant of their citizens, not their master.

This series presents the work of eminent scholars to explain as well as assess civil-military relations in U.S. history. The American tradition of a military controlled by civilians is venerable—George Washington established it when he accepted his commission from the Continental Congress in 1775—but we will see how military leaders have not always been sanguine about abdicating important decisions to those they regard as inexperienced amateurs. And while disagreements between the government and the military become more likely during wars, there is more to this subject than the institutional arrangements of subordination and obedience that mark the relationship of government authorities and the uniformed services. The public's evolving perception of the military is also a central part of this story. In these volumes we will explore the fine line between dissent and loyalty in war and peace and how the government and the armed forces have balanced civil liberties against national security. From the years of the American Revolution to the present, the resort to military justice has always been an option for safeguarding domestic welfare, but it has always been legally controversial and generally unpopular.

The United States relies on civilians to serve as most of its warriors during major conflicts, and civilian appreciation of things military understandably changes during such times. Opinions about the armed services transform accordingly, usually from casual indifference to acute concern. And through it all, military and civilian efforts to sustain popular support for the armed forces and mobilize enthusiasm for its operations have been imperative, especially when the military has been placed in the vague role of peacekeeper far from home for extended periods. The changing threats that America has confronted throughout its history have tested its revered traditions of civil-military relations, yet Americans have met even the most calamitous challenges without damaging those traditions. The most successful representative democracy in the world has defended itself without losing its way. We are hopeful that the volumes in this series will not only explain why but will also help to ensure that those vital traditions Americans rightly celebrate will endure.

David S. Heidler and Jeanne T. Heidler, General Editors

Preface

The Civil War was the most destructive and exhausting war in United States history. In that painful cataclysm, citizens of the Confederacy suffered disproportionately. Outnumbered and less provided with material resources, southerners had to join the army in greater percentages, innovate more rapidly, and make deeper sacrifices than their opponents if they hoped to sustain a conflict with the more powerful North. Yet most white southerners initiated this fateful conflict with excitement and high hopes.

Proud—even boastful—of their statesmanship and military prowess, they declared their independence and established a separate republic. It was to be a government centered not on the hopes and dreams of the Founding Fathers but on their eighteenth-century compromises and concerns. Thus, it would be a government less centralized, more constrained, more respectful of slavery and of state and individual rights than the federal government that had developed. In this corrected, southern version of the United States, states would have more power, Congress would be more influential relative to the executive branch, and opportunities for military glory would unfold within a context of civilian supremacy over the military and of representative government dominated by slaveholding interests.

The leaders of the slave South were revolutionaries, but they sought conservative, not revolutionary, ends. Driven by fear of what the Republican Party might do, they took preemptive action, forcing a change in government in order to protect their social system, and slavery, from change. They believed that they knew where they were going, and they recognized that they would have to rely on their military to achieve their aims. But war follows its own terrible arithmetic and remorseless logic. Events soon demonstrated that the South's leaders had profoundly underestimated both the role of their military and the forces of change that they had unleashed.

The fate of the Confederacy was to be engulfed in a vortex of change. The Civil War remade the Confederacy into a nation that many of its founders could not recognize, as the realities of conflict transformed the economy, the government, the society, and even the landscape. A rural, agricultural region spawned growing cities and raced to develop manufacturing industries. Power flowed to the central government instead of to the states and to the executive branch instead of to Congress. The influence of the military grew without interruption until military commanders were infringing civil liberties, seizing resources, conducting dragnets over the countryside, and influencing policy in ways never before imagined. Thus, the story of the Confederacy contains revealing chapters on civil-military relations in American history. The Confederacy's story also is a cautionary tale about the power of war to remake society and alter its traditions and values.

For the South the Civil War was a severe test that revealed hidden social realities. Among the sobering truths that came to light were many that apply to the experience of the United States in general and to other periods of its history. War brings the question of survival into play, and to the extent that a society faces this ultimate question, military necessity gains coercive power. As the crisis of the Confederacy deepened, "the plea of military necessity" became more irresistible. Hallowed traditions were overturned. Values so important that they had become shibboleths were abandoned. Civil liberties became expendable. The interests of the nation took precedence over the rights of the individual. Measures necessary to reach military goals prevailed over accustomed norms, beliefs, and political philosophy. A central lesson from the Confederate experience is that war is a potent, corrosive agent of societal change that gains in power as the scope of fighting on the battlefield increases.

Only the deepest values of a society whose survival is threatened can endure. In the South the imperatives of national survival almost trumped both the tradition of civilian supremacy over the military and the political system's dedication to constitutionalism. In the last, desperate days of the Confederacy, these traditions were severely questioned, but they remained viable, a fact that may offer some encouragement to accompany the sobering evidence of change and dissolution. The Confederacy's experience also revealed that the fundamental pillars of social power resist change to the end, and for Confederate legislators human slavery proved to be one of those pillars. The story of civil-military relations in the Confederacy is an important and instructive tale. In many ways it is also a profoundly unsettling one.

I gratefully acknowledge the work, support, and help of many scholars and individuals who have made this book possible. Among historians, those who have been particularly helpful to me in my career include Robert F. Durden, Raymond Gavins, Jeffrey J. Crow, Bell Wiley, and Emory Thomas. In exploring the work of the many military historians who focus on the Civil War, I have especially enjoyed and benefited from the scholarship of Thomas Connelly, Archer Jones, Steven Woodworth, and William C. Davis. My sincere thanks go to David S. Heidler and Jeanne T. Heidler for inviting me to contribute this volume to the Civil-Military Relations in U.S. History series and to Provost William Gordon of Wake Forest University, whose kindness and support allowed me the time to finish writing it.

MILITARY NECESSITY

1

Traditions for a New Nation

In 1861 white Southerners made a new beginning. On February 4 delegates from the seceded states of the lower South met in Montgomery, Alabama, to organize the Confederate States of America. In only four days they hammered out a Provisional Constitution, and barely a month later they completed work on the Permanent Constitution for their new nation. Yet much of what they were doing was not new, and despite such apparent decisiveness, fundamental disagreements lay beneath the surface appearance of consensus. The Confederacy was a new government but not a government unburdened by the past. It carried military and civil traditions that were both potent and complex. History's legacy to Confederates influenced them in differing directions.

Politically and culturally, the South had been part of the United States through generations of cooperation as well as sectional conflict. The region shared the history and values of the United States—including those governing civil-military relations—while it also prized its own record of increasingly fierce dissent. White Confederates honored many American traditions. Indeed, they tended to see themselves as upholding and preserving the legacy of the Founding Fathers, which they accused Northerners of violating. Yet they also had broken away from the United States, and their leaders burned with zeal to pursue an agenda defined in years of sectional conflict.

Thus, the government of the Confederacy labored under strong societal expectations that it would live up to a fabled past *and* improve on it. The South's political heritage moved elected officials to revere much of the American government while rebelling against it. Their cultural heritage was deeply American but also distinctly and defiantly Southern. Tradition would influence the leaders of this new nation in different ways, depending on how they interpreted their past. Such differences frequently led to conflict and to an incipient Confederate tradition that was different in many ways from what anyone had expected.

In the view of many scholars, part of the South's distinctive character was its devotion to a strong military tradition. For example, historian Robert D. Meade argued that in the Mexican War "the South supplied over 46,000 troops, or twice as many as did the North" and "almost all the outstanding Generals." In fact, a disproportionate number of famed nineteenth-century generals came from the state of Virginia alone. Meade's analysis of prominent families in Virginia and Massachusetts demonstrated that the profession of arms held far more appeal to southerners than to New Englanders. Another scholar, political scientist Samuel P. Huntington, believed that the conservatism of Southern thought "channeled the military concern aroused by the other aspects of Southern life into an active recognition of the nature of the military profession and a preference for that profession as a career." Between 1832 and 1846 U.S. Army officers produced a body of scholarly writing on war that Huntington has called the "American Military Enlightenment," and this scholarship was dominated by southern writers. Moreover, Southerners enrolled in West Point in considerable numbers, and in the 1850s two Southerners served as secretary of war—Jefferson Davis of Mississippi (West Point class of 1828) and John B. Floyd of Virginia. During the antebellum period, three Virginians—General in chief Winfield Scott, Adjutant General Roger Jones, and Quartermaster General T. S. Jesup—held senior posts in the regular army for a total of eighty-two years.[1]

These and other writers saw southern culture as nurturing ways of thinking that supported the military. Southern society was overwhelmingly rural, compared to the North, and most Southerners were accustomed to using firearms. The prevalence of slavery also meant that the use of force to subdue revolts or enforce plantation discipline was always a possibility. A culture of assertiveness that often expressed itself in a hair-trigger resort to violence reigned among men of the elite, while boisterous conflict, brawling, or eye-gouging were elements of manliness among the common folk who lived closer to the frontier. Ideas of chivalry and romanticism about medieval knights and tournaments lent additional support to an ethos of combat.[2]

Marcus Cunliffe has challenged these arguments and attempted to put the idea of a Southern military tradition in better perspective. He noted that many features of Southern life—from military publications to medieval-style tournaments—were not unique to the South. Moreover, though Southerners may have entered West Point in large numbers, many did not graduate, and Southern products of the academy did not stay in the army with greater frequency than men from other parts of the country. Only in the cavalry were Southern officers in the majority, while a "large majority" of enlisted men in the regular army were Northerners.[3] The U.S. Army's staff and line officers numbered 950 in 1860, and of these 555 (or 58.4 percent) came from free states compared to 395 from the slave states (including those that never joined the Confederacy). Two hundred and thirteen of the 395 Southern officers resigned their commissions in order to join the Confederate war effort—fewer than one might imagine from the prominence given to a few significant examples, such as Robert E. Lee. Of 76 field grade officers in the U.S. Army in 1860—men who might be expected to earn quick promotion to general during war—only 30 were from the South. Thus the Confederate army did not have a marked advantage in professionally trained military leadership. In fact, only 146 of the Confederacy's 425 generals were graduates of West Point, and 226 of those who earned the rank of general could claim no previous military experience at all. Cunliffe concluded that "the semi-legendary version of a Cavalier or militant South" was largely a postwar creation of both North and South.[4]

Nevertheless, it is undeniable that many Confederates went into the Civil War valuing military prowess very highly. Martial ardor animated many parts of the South in the wake of secession. Southerners were overly optimistic about their chances in the coming conflict, and some young blades did, in fact, boast that they would be able to whip the Yankees in only a few months' time. Even older newspaper editors, who should have been wiser, shared this exaggerated confidence. "Our raw troops are far superior to the raw troops of the United States," proclaimed the *Charleston Mercury*.[5] It is true that relatively few Southerners were unfamiliar with a rifle, although many were quite new to military training. And if Southerners did not prove to be clearly superior soldiers, they were superior cavalrymen, at least in the first years of the war.[6]

The hunger for glory on the battlefield affected many leading Confederates and not always positively. Senator Robert Toombs of Georgia quickly became a general and almost as quickly resigned in disgust that his military capacities were not going to win him the kind of prominence that his political abilities had earned.[7] He was only one of many "political" generals whose prominence sometimes gained them a rank that exceeded their skill. But the professional generals who came out of West Point also yearned for glory. They measured their aspirations against a historical standard, and—given the prominence in previous wars of Southerners such as George Washington, Andrew Jackson, Zachary Taylor, and Winfield Scott—it was natural for the Confederacy's professional soldiers to have great ambitions. To distinguish themselves, they would have to meet the high standard that Southern generals had set in the past. Thus, a historical legacy may have contributed to the burning ambition and enormous egos that sometimes impaired the efficiency of the Confederate command structure.

Equally important to the civil-military relations of the Confederacy was the fact that Jefferson Davis, president of the Confederacy, was a professional soldier by training. After graduating from West Point in 1828, Davis served for six and a half years in the regular army. His resignation in 1835 probably had more to do with his desire to marry Colonel Zachary Taylor's daughter than with any dissatisfaction with his career. Because Taylor did not want his daughter to suffer the inconveniences of army life, Davis resigned his commission and followed his plan to become a planter in Mississippi, even after her sudden and untimely death. But financial and political success in the civilian world did nothing to lessen Davis' interest in things military. When the Mexican War began, he left his seat in Congress and broke a promise to his second wife, Varina Howell Davis, in order to become the colonel of a Mississippi regiment.[8]

After seeing action in the Battle of Monterrey (and basking in the praise of enthusiastic Mississippians), Davis and his men distinguished themselves in February 1847, at the Battle of Buena Vista. Facing a sudden onslaught from a formidable body of 2,000 cavalry, Davis quickly arranged his troops in a V and urged them to hold their fire until the Mexican cavalrymen entered the open angle. His troops waited with cool steadiness, and when they finally unleashed a salvo, their converging fire stopped the charge and sent the Mexican horsemen reeling. Shot in the ankle early in this battle, Davis nevertheless stayed on the field, winning great renown back home as the hero of a splendid victory. Enormously proud of his tactical innovation and its contribution to this victory, Davis spent many hours in later years answering questions about the battle and his V-formation. He also proved ready at all times to argue that his troops, not a unit from Tennessee, had been the first to capture a stone fort in the Battle of Monterrey.[9] Davis prized his reputation as a military hero. It strengthened him in politics and supplied a glory that evidently was very important to him.

After further success and some reverses in politics, Davis accepted Franklin Pierce's offer to become secretary of war. In this important post he confronted practical challenges and a major ambiguity at the heart of civil-military relations within the U.S. command structure. As secretary of war, Davis became responsible for the defense of a nation that had extended its boundaries to the Pacific Ocean. Communication across the vast expanse of the continent was slow and uncertain, yet the United States would need to be able to coordinate its defense in the event of a crisis. Seeing the importance of this challenge, Davis initiated surveys of the western territories with a view to identifying the best route for a transcontinental railroad. Although specific proposals failed because of the deepening sectional divisions in Congress, Davis' efforts generated much important information. Another, much-publicized experiment with camels as a means of transportation in the dry southwest was a reasonable measure, even if it seemed outlandish to some. Although a long, undignified, and contentious argu-

Jefferson Davis. In Congress he defended states' rights aggressively before the war, but as President he used the war-related powers of the Confederate Constitution to build a powerful central government. (Courtesy of Library of Congress)

ment with General John Wool filled too much of Davis' official correspondence, on the whole he was an energetic and responsible cabinet officer whose entire record reflected his keen interest in military affairs.[10]

As secretary of war, Davis also experienced firsthand a fundamental ambiguity or weakness in the American command structure. The Constitution clearly made the president commander in chief of the nation's armed forces. In this respect, civilian control over the military was unquestionable. But the powers and role of the secretary of war, relative to the commanding general, had long been uncertain and a locus of disagreement. Experience had shown that an active and energetic president, such as James K. Polk during the Mexican War, could exercise direct and effective control over the armed forces. But most presidents lacked the time or inclination to be as involved as Polk had been, and therefore there was a need to rely on the secretary of war to maintain the supremacy of civilian officials. General in chief Winfield Scott, however, denied that the secretary of war had the constitutional power to issue orders to him. Claiming that the president alone was his commander, Scott resisted the efforts of civilian secretaries to curb his powers. His contests with Jefferson Davis over this vital point were continuous and unpleasant enough that Scott decided to remove himself to New York City, where he could deal with the secretary of war through the mails. For his part, Davis never retreated from his assertion that the secretary of war had the power to issue orders to the military as the president's agent. Eventually Scott agreed to honor instructions if the secretary styled them as issued "by order of the President." The conflict over this principle surely sensitized Davis to the importance of establishing a clear line of command within the Confederacy.[11] It led him to act strongly and personally to effect civilian control.

In other direct ways Davis' history would incline him to be an active commander in chief. The allure of military fame continued to pull at Davis throughout his career as president of the Confederacy. His reputation for valor and military sagacity contributed to his selection as chief executive, and some hoped that he would assume command directly and lead the army into battle. The *Richmond Examiner* declared that "with him, the victory would be certain, and chance become certainty." Newspapers in Montgomery reported happily that Davis had asked a local gunsmith to sharpen the sword he had used in the Mexican War. His friend Leonidas Polk wrote that Davis would "take the field in person," and historian Steven Woodworth concluded that "faith in Davis' martial abilities and the expectation that he would personally lead the army to victory were factors behind the shift of the Confederacy's capital" to Richmond.[12]

Once at the scene of the major eastern engagements, the Confederate president frequently left his office and rode out to the front lines. He clearly wanted to be close to the action, and during battles Robert E. Lee and other officers sometimes begged him to retire to a safer location in the rear. On a few occasions, as in the first battle of Bull Run, he even issued impromptu orders to confused or panicked troops. Back in Richmond following that first Confederate victory, Davis thrilled the crowds with bold predictions of success. Mary Boykin Chesnut, whose *Diary from Dixie* is generally favorable to the South's president, wrote that on this occasion he "took all the credit to himself for the victory" and showed that he was "greedy for military fame." Thus, from the start there was no doubt that Jefferson

Davis, as president, would be involved intensely in the military affairs of the Confederacy. He probably longed to repeat his battlefield successes from the Mexican War, for his wife also testified that he had wanted a military command in preference to the post of chief executive.[13]

If white Southerners had high expectations for Davis as a military leader, their agenda for him in civilian affairs was even more demanding and complex. The active, vocal public expected success. Its members also desired tradition *and* change, particularly in the sense that they wanted to preserve and enjoy all good things from the heritage of the United States while amending that legacy to honor states' rights and safeguard slavery. Here lay the potential for enormous conflict. Exactly what kind of government was the Confederacy to have? What principles did its Constitution prescribe? How would war and military necessity impinge upon or modify these expectations?

Entangled with people's understanding of the Confederate Constitution was their conception of the purposes and nature of the Confederacy. Despite the fervor of secessionists, these matters were not clear. As events would prove, there was consensus on neither the constitution nor the fundamental goals of the new nation. The history of the sectional conflict had given Southerners some things on which they could agree, but important divisions remained. Most of these related to states' rights and the issue for which it was often a surrogate: slavery. The habit of vociferous dissent that politicians had acquired during the sectional crisis guaranteed that disagreements would not be subtle.

From Jefferson's conflicts with Hamilton and Adams in the 1790s through the sectional conflict of the 1850s, strict construction and states' rights were prominent issues in the South, but almost always they bore an intimate connection to the defense of slavery. Southern officeholders undoubtedly held sincere convictions about states rights as a matter of political theory, but political treatises seldom prompt human nature as forcefully as do matters of direct economic, social, or personal interest. During the War of 1812, Federalist New England had insisted on states' rights and threatened secession, but the economic distress that motivated these threats soon dissipated. For the South, by contrast, the growing extent of slavery and its incompatibility with dominant trends of thought in Western civilization guaranteed that states' rights would have a continuing function. The defense of states' rights ensured the defense of slavery, and few Southern politicians failed to make this vitally important connection.

In 1819, following a nationalistic period when Southern leaders, including even John C. Calhoun, sometimes looked beyond strict construction, Nathaniel Macon of North Carolina had recalled the core connection between slavery and states' rights. Macon, a former speaker of the House of Representatives and then a U.S. senator, opposed federal aid for internal improvements with a blunt, undisguised argument. "If Congress can make canals," he reasoned, "they can with more propriety emancipate."[14] A year later, in debates over the Missouri Compromise, several northerners criticized slavery, leading Southern politicians to respond with renewed sensitivity to the need to defend slavery. This time Macon insisted that "glad faces" and "hearty shaking of hands" typified a master's return to his plantation, and he voiced his fear that the "present excitement" could lead to unforeseen consequences.

> Why depart from the good old way, which has kept us in quiet, peace, and harmony—every one living under his own vine and fig tree, and no one to make him afraid? Why . . . take this new way, of which we have no experience? The way leads to universal emancipation. . . . A clause in the Declaration of Independence has been read, declaring "that all men are created equal;" follow that sentiment, and does it not lead to universal emancipation? If it will justify putting an end to slavery in Missouri, will it not justify it in the old States?[15]

Macon sternly warned anyone who might be tempted to meddle with slavery that "there is no power in the General Government to touch it in any way."[16] The protracted Southern battle to defend slavery had begun.

Macon soon had sympathetic and influential allies in South Carolina. During the 1820s events in that state brought the nationalistic phase of Calhoun's career to an end and focused his attention on the use of constitutional theory to defend slavery. Controversies over a federal protective tariff were the ostensible cause of South Carolina's conflict with the federal government, but the real issue was slavery, and the state's leading politicians knew it. Congressman George McDuffie warned publicly that any "measures which shall hasten the abolition of slavery . . . will bring upon the southern States the greatest political calamity with which they can be afflicted." He declared that he had "raise[d] my warning voice" because he saw "the irresistible tendency of this protecting system to precipitate us upon this great moral and political catastrophe." Calhoun revealed similar motives in a private letter:

> I consider the Tariff, but as the occasion, rather than the real cause of the present unhappy state of things. The truth can no longer be disguised, that the peculiar domestick institutions of the Southern States, and the consequent direction which that [sic] and her soil and climate have given to her industry, has [sic] placed them in regard to taxation and appropriation in opposite relation to the majority of the Union; against the danger of which, if there be no protective power in the reserved rights of the states, they must in the end be forced to rebel, or submit to have . . . their domestick institutions exhausted by Colonization and other schemes, and themselves & children reduced

to wretchedness. Thus situated, the denial of the right of the state to interfere constitutionally in the last resort, more alarms the thinking than all other causes.[17]

South Carolina's confrontation with Washington over the tariff was settled peaceably, but the 1830s brought new controversies over abolitionist mailings and petitions and the Gag Rule in Congress. Then an issue that would prove both contentious and durable—territorial expansion—intensified the sectional conflict. In 1846 Pennsylvania congressman David Wilmot offered his famous Proviso, proposing that slavery be barred from any and all territory that might be gained from the war with Mexico. Immediately this measure caused a revolution in Southern positions on the territories. Alexander H. Stephens, who one year before had declared, "I am no defender of slavery in the abstract," now argued tendentiously that slavery was grounded in the Bible and above moral criticism.[18] One week later, Calhoun introduced a fateful set of resolutions that applied his compact theory to the territories. Turning a blind eye to history and to the Missouri Compromise, he now argued that the territories belonged to all the states and that Congress could not deprive slaveholding states of their rights in the territories. Slaveholders had a constitutional right to take slaves into any of the lands owned by the United States.[19] Calhoun's bold new argument soon became *de rigeur* among Southern politicians. Nothing showed more clearly how Southern defensiveness on slavery became indistinguishable from an aggressive posture designed to promote the institution.

After Calhoun's death in 1850, Jefferson Davis became a leading spokesman for Southern interests throughout the rest of the decade, and he often complained bitterly and at tedious length about the tariff, internal improvements, or other measures of perceived injustice to the South. But the fundamental issue was always slavery. What he and other Southern leaders feared most was a loss of the South's ability to protect its peculiar institution from Northern threats. In a private letter to a friend, Davis commented that abolitionists had little to gain from the exclusion of slavery from the territories unless they also were planning "to disturb that institution in the States." Writing a public letter to Mississippians in 1857, he asserted that the North's desire to bar slavery from Kansas was part of a design to throw a cordon around the slaveholding states, cutting off their expansion and thus beginning slavery's destruction. He predicted that Kansas would be only the entering wedge; from that state abolitionism would spread to Missouri, Arkansas, New Mexico, and Texas. Although Davis hoped in 1860 to maintain the unity of the Democratic Party and thus avert disunion, he feared the Republican Party because he believed that "the vital element" of that organization was its hostility to slavery.[20]

Those who later claimed that secession was about constitutional rights and not about slavery and racism have to ignore the statements of the prominent men who represented five seceded states of the deep South—Mississippi, Alabama, South Carolina, Georgia, and Louisiana—on official visits to neighboring states in the winter of 1860–61. These men traveled to nearby state capitals in order to urge these states to leave the Union as well. As Charles Dew has shown, the message of these "apostles of disunion" focused unapologetically on slavery and race. Over and over again they emphasized that slavery was threatened and that the dangers of racial equality loomed. They insisted that the founders had established "a government for the white man" and had rejected "the negro, as an ignorant, inferior, barbarian race" not entitled "to be associated with the white man upon terms of civil, political, or social equality." Lincoln's "Black Republicans," they warned, sought "the abolition of slavery upon this continent and the elevation of our own slaves to an equality with ourselves and our children." Such developments would subject "our women" to "horrors . . . we cannot contemplate in imagination."[21] The protection of slavery and white supremacy dominated the emotions of Southern leaders.

But the decades of protest against Northern policies had already created a myth of Southern constitutionalism. Southern politicians believed that they honored and followed the constitution whereas Northerners had ignored it and trampled on its provisions in order to create a domineering and powerful central government backed by the military. With predictable frequency Southerners had seized upon every opportunity to claim that they, alone, respected and honored constitutional limits. In a typical Southern speech delivered shortly before he left the U.S. Senate, Jefferson Davis denounced the North's "studied tendency to convert the Government into a military despotism." A "Government of the Army and Navy," he protested, "was not the Government instituted by our fathers," by patriots such as "the great man, Washington." To emphasize the South's unbroken loyalty to the constitutional beliefs of the Founding Fathers, Georgia's Thomas R. R. Cobb urged the Montgomery convention to adopt "The Republic of Washington" as the name for their new nation. Similarly, South Carolina's Robert Barnwell Rhett, in a report submitted to the Confederacy's Provisional Congress in April 1861, denounced the "consolidated government" of the United States and its "despotic tendencies." "Nearly all the political contests in the United States," he declared, "have originated from violations of the Constitution." Thus, he argued, to resist oppression and preserve the constitutional rights that they alone continued to respect, Southerners had to secede.[22]

Seeing themselves as the aggrieved party, loyal to the letter and spirit of a constitution that the North was habitually violating, Southern leaders presented their new government to the world as one devoted to constitutional forms and principles. The Confederacy was born, in their eyes, as the exemplar of constitutionalism. It would respect the rights of the states and the people. Violations of the constitution were now a thing of the past, a relic of the U.S. government's corrupt nature. The new government claimed an already venerable tradition of respect for constitutional rights, and in the first year of his presidency Jefferson Davis would stress this continuity with the founders' constitutionalism as a central theme. Consequently, the nature of the Confederate Constitution and its relation to vital Southern interests became very important.

What did the Confederate Constitutions do to limit central power, restrain the military, and protect slavery and its position in the Confederacy? How much did the constitution of the new government differ from that of the old?

Both the Provisional and the Permanent Constitutions of the Confederacy were based on the U.S. Constitution and very similar to it. Given that Southerners were not dissatisfied with that constitution but "held it dear," this was not surprising.[23] Even the fierce state rights advocate R.B. Rhett felt that the changes needed were "more a matter of restoration, than of innovation," and journalist J.D.B. De Bow asserted, "We are upholding the true doctrines of the Federal Constitution. We are conservative."[24] But as delegates to Montgomery swiftly drew up their Provisional Constitution, they did not forget to make some changes that favored states' rights and slavery. The preamble omitted any reference to "we, the people," and instead referred to "the Deputies of the Sovereign and Independent States" that were coming together to form a confederation. Words such as "delegated" and "expressly granted" also emphasized that the central government derived its power from the states. Tariffs were permissible only for revenue, not for protection of infant industries. In regard to the slave trade, Rhett and James Chesnut of South Carolina objected to a constitutional prohibition on the importation "of African [N]egroes from any foreign country other than the slave holding States of the United States," but they were overruled. Most delegates placed priority on encouraging the other slaveholding states to join the Confederacy, and they knew that opposition to the international slave trade was firm in the upper South.[25]

The Permanent Constitution incorporated similar changes. Although the preamble began, "We, the people of the Confederate states," it continued with the qualifying words: "each State acting in its sovereign and independent character, in order to form a permanent federal government." Likewise, the Permanent Constitution prohibited protective tariffs and put restrictions on internal improvements. A bicameral congress was created, but this legislature did not receive power to provide for the "general welfare." A stronger fugitive slave clause became part of the constitution, and the duty of Congress to protect slavery in Confederate territories was made explicit. The states also gained greater power to initiate and guide constitutional amendments than had been the case in the Union. But an attempt to require that any new states be slaveholding failed, and efforts by South

Carolina to allow Congress to legislate on the status of the international slave trade again were unsuccessful.[26]

Moreover, such changes were less significant than the fact that the Confederate constitutions followed the federal example in many important respects. Both documents gave Congress the power "to make all Laws which shall be necessary and proper for carrying into execution" its enumerated powers as well as "all other powers vested by this Constitution in the Government of the Confederate States, or in any department or officer thereof." This "necessary and proper" clause, of course, had been the crux of disagreement between Jefferson and Hamilton in 1791 when they debated the creation of the Bank of the United States. It expanded Congress' authority significantly. In addition, both documents affirmed the supremacy of Confederate laws by declaring that the constitution and the laws and treaties made under it were "the supreme law of the land; and the judges in every State shall be bound thereby, anything in the Constitution or laws of any State to the contrary notwithstanding." The powers granted to Congress were almost as extensive as those within the United States. In light of subsequent controversies, it is important to note, for example, that Congress had the power "to raise and support armies" as well as the separate power to call forth the militia and to govern any part of it used in the service of the Confederate states. The president was designated "commander-in-chief of the army and navy of the Confederate States, and of the militia of the several States, when called into the actual service"—language that was identical to wording in the U.S. Constitution.[27]

Although some new language addressed old sectional controversies, the Confederacy had established a federal government whose powers were similar in breadth and depth to that of the United States. The president's role was not diminished; although he was limited to one six-year term, he gained the ability to veto specific parts of appropriation bills, and only he could initiate an appropriation measure.[28] Clearly, he could be a powerful executive, especially in time of war, when executive efficiency became vitally important. The Confederate judiciary derived its powers from language that was very similar to that in the U.S. Constitution. In practice, the chief difference turned out to be that Congress never established the Supreme Court that was authorized. Nevertheless, state and Confederate district courts played an important role and ultimately contributed to the substantial power of the central government.

But as the new government began, many did not see this reality. To R. B. Rhett state sovereignty was the hallmark of the new government. His *Charleston Mercury* argued that for decades the U.S. government had "usurped powers not granted—progressively trenched upon State Rights." By contrast he argued that the new constitution "leaves the States untouched in their Sovereignty, and commits to the Confederate Government only a few simple objects, and a few simple powers to enforce them." This was a stunningly oversimplified description of the new governmental system. It described the Articles of Confederation of 1778 rather than the Confederate Constitution. Clearly Rhett did not expect or want the Confederate government to be very powerful, and he was not a lonely exception. Other political leaders held exalted ideas of the power of the states. To cite just one example, Governor Joseph E. Brown of Georgia knew when his state seceded that it would quickly join the Confederacy, yet during that short period of independence he dispatched a diplomatic representative to Europe to seek recognition from Queen Victoria, Napoleon III, and the king of Belgium.[29] Apparently he believed that the state of Georgia deserved the respect of the world, apart from its role in the Confederacy.

Such extreme ideas foreshadowed difficulties for Jefferson Davis and controversy in the Confederacy. What would happen if a strong military effort interfered with accustomed ways of doing things? What would be the reaction if military needs required the central government to take strong steps under the constitution and to interfere with civilian life or with slavery?

The record indicates that Davis began his presidency promoting, and perhaps expecting, unity. He seemed to assume that years of sectional crisis had unified the white South and that secession had removed the causes of the states' complaints. On the day of his arrival in Montgomery as president-elect, he opened a speech with the words, "Fellow Citizens and Brethren of the Confederate States of America—for now we are brethren, not in name, merely, but in fact—men of one flesh, one bone, one interest, one purpose, and of identity of domestic institutions." By leaving the United States, the South had left internal conflict behind. Though he granted that there might be difficulties ahead, he expected unity in a slave society removed from antislavery agitation. "Thus we shall have nothing to fear at home, because at home we shall have homogeneity."[30] Such expectations left no room for disaffection or disloyalty.

Despite these optimistic words, Davis was thinking in directions different from Rhett's because he had a realistic understanding of what lay ahead militarily. Davis avoided unrealistic projections of easy victory, for he knew that armed conflict with the United States was likely to be terribly destructive. In January 1861 he predicted a war "the like of which men have not seen" with "masses of men sacrificed" and "destruction upon both sides."[31] As a former professional soldier, he understood the necessity of marshalling the South's resources and carrying on a coordinated—rather than a weak and disunited—defense. And as an ambitious political leader, he was not afraid to use the powers that clearly and constitutionally belonged to his office. A vigorous Confederate president, commanding the military and acting in time of war, could have immense influence in shap-

ing a government that some thought possessed only "a few simple powers." Unpredictable events also would affect the new government and demand unforeseen measures.

Thus, the Confederacy began its national existence under the influence
of deeply respected traditions but without an agreed upon or definite path.
Confederates valued military virtues and sought military glory, but they
often condemned military despotism. They wanted their president's powers to be limited carefully, yet sometimes longed for him to be a military
savior. Confederate leaders often talked about a weak central government
formed by a loose alliance of sovereign states, yet their constitution gave
the government in Richmond most of the powers of the U.S. government.
Where would they strike the balance among these factors in a war of unprecedented scale? How would war affect the central government's role and
the status of opponents and dissenters? In designing their government, Confederates showed that slavery was to be protected, but few could deny that
slavery would be affected deeply by a long war. What was its fate to be?

The Civil War forced unexpected answers to these questions. Confederates were to find that their conservative goals were utterly incompatible
with the enormous conflict in which they soon found themselves. In choosing secession as the means to avoid change, Southerners unleashed forces
that would bring radical change to most of their society. Military needs and
realities had an unprecedented impact on civilian life and values. As civil-
military relations unfolded amid an enormous war, the Confederacy developed in ways that few could have foreseen.

2

Policy-making Produces
Innovation and Controversy

Proud of their much-vaunted devotion to constitutionalism, Confederate leaders entered the Civil War confident that their actions would preserve their society and vindicate American traditions. Among these sacred traditions was the control of military forces by civilian authorities. The beliefs and practices that had developed through the history of the United States came close to establishing what modern scholars regard as "democratic civil control." To satisfy this definition, a number of conditions must be accepted and customary. Those heading the government must be civilians who represent and are accountable to the majority, and this condition—for both the Confederacy and the United States in 1860—applied to white males, though not to women or blacks. In addition it is necessary that those heading the armed services be under constitutional and effective control by the heads of government, that the military departments are managed by civilians in the government, that elected representatives make the key decisions on funding and war and exercise control over policy, and that courts can hold the military accountable for protection of people's basic democratic rights.[1]

Thus, all three branches of government—the executive, the Congress, and the courts—play a role in civil control of the military. In most respects the Confederacy conformed to these requirements and to familiar American patterns during the Civil War. Civilians clearly were in control of the Confederate war machine; at least the situation for the Confederacy was fully comparable to that in the United States.[2] But two things proved interesting in the Southern case: the role and relative influence of the different branches of government and the scope of measures undertaken to support the war effort. Within the government, the pattern of influence in the Confederacy diverged from that existing in the North, and, in addition, another category of government institutions—the states—often interfered or tried to obstruct policy through the actions of their governors. To support the war effort itself, the Confederacy took measures that were startling and controversial because they were so strong and so comprehensive.

The Confederacy had an active, vocal Congress that regularly discussed and argued about military affairs. Indeed, some of the most ambitious and assertive members of Congress made military affairs their area of special interest. Yet, for all its vigorous debates, the Confederate Congress was curiously ineffective in designing and controlling the South's war measures. Jefferson Davis seized the initiative in policy-making and held it throughout the war. He and his executive departments shaped and gave direction to the Confederate war machine. Like its Northern counterpart, the Confederate Congress generated considerable heat as its members raised questions and made charges of incompetence or mismanagement, but a comparison of the two legislatures falls apart on measures of effectiveness. In the North the Joint Committee on the Conduct of the War had unusually broad scope, and "there is abundant evidence that it meant to dictate the purposes of the war and manage its campaigns." In fact, some scholars believe that the aggressive actions of this committee helped to establish the supremacy of Congress over the executive that prevailed in the United States for a third of a century after Reconstruction.[3] The Confederate Congress had no such influence. Why did it remain so subordinate to the guiding influence of the president, and how was Jefferson Davis able to exert so much control over the South's war effort?

The Confederate war effort that Davis directed was remarkable for the scope and startling innovations of its methods. Strong measures never before contemplated in U.S. history became law under the Confederacy. In the land of states' rights and limited government, a national draft and seizure of goods from civilians became the means to raise and support the army. Bold steps to harness the South's economy and direct it to the support of the war established new directions that surprised many Southerners. In the view of some later scholars, the Confederacy pursued an economic policy of "state socialism" to keep its bid for independence alive.[4] Even measures that were tied narrowly to military necessity produced wide disruption of normal social routines and changed the basic ground rules of Southern life. Under the Confederate government ambitious, innovative, and controversial policies marked the civilian administration's prosecution of the war and gave new meaning to civilian control of military affairs.

Although Jefferson Davis dominated the Congress, he encountered greater resistance from certain states. Thus the role of the states—particularly certain governors—merits special attention in the Confederacy. The personalities and political strategies of men such as Joseph E. Brown of Georgia contributed to the controversies that embroiled Davis with the states. But differing conceptions of the Confederate Constitution and polity also came into play. These differing views of the nature of the Confederate system had to be settled, not in an atmosphere of theoretical deliberation but under the exigencies and uncertainties of war. As governors reacted to the surprising innovations of the Confederate government, they challenged the legitimacy of these policies and the government's right to make them.

The role of the courts was also anomalous in the Southern war effort for two very different reasons. During the brief life of the Confederacy, the court system of its central government remained incomplete. Although the Confederate Constitution authorized a Supreme Court, many congressmen feared that a supreme judicial body would undercut state rights and increase central power. For these reasons, Congress never passed legislation to bring this tribunal into being. Thus, although there were inferior Confederate courts and judges, they lacked the ability to render a single, final judgment on constitutional and other questions. State supreme courts, if they would agree, could command greater respect for their decisions. Another anomaly was rooted in the differing use that southerners made of their traditions. Although all white southerners professed a belief in states' rights, for lawyers the fundamental legal doctrine of *stare decisis* proved very influential. Courts and judges worked with that body of law—U.S. law and precedents—that was most familiar and most useful to them, and they followed and built upon it. In this way the Confederacy's courts proved more supportive of federal doctrines than most would have expected—another of many surprising results.

The Confederate Congress seemingly had the opportunity to exert strong control over the armed forces and military policy of the Confederacy. The South's national legislature was active throughout the war and involved with major issues. Among its members were many ambitious and outspoken individuals who craved the spotlight and sought to make an impression. Indeed, many congressmen acted as if their first thought was to establish themselves as important figures on history's stage. They were extremely self-conscious and well aware of the impact of their speeches on colleagues, newspapers, and later students of history. The South's political culture also predisposed them to be assertive. Given the history of the sectional crisis, Southern politicians felt it was desirable to dissent, to take a stand on principle, and to go against the majority or fight against long odds. Many members of Congress were seeking glory, and they did not expect to gain this by being timid.

Assembling first in Montgomery and then in Richmond, the legislators met frequently. The Provisional Congress had five called sessions (although only four actually were held) in slightly more than a year of existence, which ended on February 17, 1862. Not counting absences during intersessions, its members sat and deliberated for a total of 260 days. Under the

Permanent Constitution, the Confederacy elected two congresses. The First Congress promptly began work on the very next day after the Provisional Congress went out of existence. This First Congress had four sessions before the newly elected members of the Second Congress assembled on February 18, 1864. Two sessions of that Second Congress were held. Excluding the days of intersessions, the First and Second Congresses together sat for a total of 655 days.[5] By nineteenth-century standards the Confederate Congress was an industrious legislature that met frequently to do its nation's business.

In the first year of the war, the Provisional Congress carried out an experiment that was unique in American legislative history. Cabinet members were allowed, under the Provisional Constitution, to hold a seat in Congress while they served in the executive branch, and four individuals assumed these dual responsibilities. Robert M. T. Hunter, Christopher G. Memminger, John Reagan, and Robert Toombs all represented their states in Congress while also heading cabinet departments. (Toombs and Hunter were the first two secretaries of state, while Memminger was secretary of the treasury, and Reagan served as postmaster general.) The drafters of the Provisional Constitution thought that this arrangement, borrowed from parliamentary systems of government, would allow greater coordination between lawmakers and the departments charged with carrying out policy. The Permanent Constitution allowed Congress to grant a seat on the floor of either house to cabinet members, and some legislators proposed doing so. But the majority apparently felt uncomfortable about the way this practice undermined the separation of powers, and proposals to continue it failed.[6]

Even if the heads of executive departments were not available on the floor of Congress, however, Confederate lawmakers had ample opportunity to formulate, monitor, and influence policy. One means to exercise control over the military was the system of standing committees. Both houses of Congress established committees on military affairs and on naval affairs. These were recognized as two of the most important assignments available, and some of the most ambitious and energetic congressmen secured seats on these committees.[7] In the Senate, the Committee on Military Affairs included both supporters of Jefferson Davis, such as G. A. Henry of Tennessee (a friend from early school days) and Robert W. Barnwell from South Carolina, and foes such as Edward Sparrow of Louisiana and Louis Wigfall of Texas. Sparrow, the richest man in the Confederate Congress, had a nationalist outlook on policy, but he had objected to Davis' removal of P.G.T. Beauregard from command of the Army of the West after Shiloh. When Sparrow and his colleague, Senator T. J. Semmes, met with Davis to petition for Beauregard's return, Davis insulted them by reading their petition aloud and interspersing caustic comments.[8] The ambitious Wigfall was one of the strongest critics of Davis in Congress. He broke openly with the president in 1862, conspiring thereafter with disaffected commanders to attack the president's decisions while his wife, a native of Charleston who had called Varina Davis a "coarse western woman," became a social rival of the first lady.[9] In the House, the Committee on Naval Affairs included South Carolina's W. W. Boyce, who quickly became part of a "coalition against Jeff Davis." Mary Boykin Chesnut considered him one of the leaders of the anti–Davis party. The Committee on Military Affairs contained some strong Davis supporters, but men such as its chairman, William Porcher Miles of South Carolina, and J. L. Pugh of Alabama showed that they could be very critical of the government when they believed its policies were mistaken. Moreover, the most active member in House debates was Henry S. Foote of Tennessee, who nursed a bitter personal and political grudge against Jefferson Davis from his days as an officeholder in Mississippi.[10] There was no shortage of potential critics in the Congress.

Nor was there a lack of means to challenge the administration. The resolution of inquiry was a tool used often by the legislature. For example, on February 19, 1862, Congressman Foote "offered a resolution, that a committee be appointed to inquire into the cause of the recent disasters which have befallen our arms in the States of Virginia, North Carolina, Tennessee and Kentucky." The next day Foote proposed another resolution to declare that the "defensive policy" of the government "must be abandoned henceforth and forever." Such resolutions were common, and "for the first half of the war," according to historian Buck Yearns, "Congress tried to investigate all major defeats." Other aspects of the administration's conduct of the war came under close scrutiny. In 1863, for example, Henry Foote presented another resolution, this time to investigate the Quartermaster and Commissary bureaus, because he "said he knew the most enormous frauds to exist in these departments." When dissatisfaction and war-weariness reached threatening proportions in North Carolina, dissident congressman James T. Leach framed a resolution to require the president to report how many men had enlisted, been conscripted, and died or deserted from the various states.[11]

In similar fashion Congress made many requests of the president and the executive departments. At the beginning of 1863 Senator Simms of Kentucky put forward a resolution, which was speedily adopted, "That the President be respectfully requested, if compatible with the public interests, to communicate" about impressments that were reported to be taking place in Virginia.[12] Congress made inquiries of this sort on a broad spectrum of issues, and the administration usually responded with reasonable promptness. The request for information from the executive was an important legislative tool that could be used to gather information, monitor performance, and lay the groundwork for future legislative action.

Some congressmen and generals went far beyond normal procedures to get their way. Shortly after the victory at First Manassas, the vain Louisiana

P.G.T. Beauregard. Vain and always attracted to impractical, grand strategies, General Beauregard also challenged the supremacy of civilian officials in foreign affairs. (Courtesy of Library of Congress)

general P.G.T. Beauregard convinced himself that he could have taken Washington and won the war for the South, except for Jefferson Davis' caution and failure to provide logistical support. Pursuing his own glory, Beauregard wrote to two influential members of the Provisional Congress— William P. Miles and James Chesnut—both of whom had been volunteer aides to him. He argued to them that the administration's failures had held the army back from an historic victory. "We ought at this moment to be in or about Washington," Beauregard arrogantly claimed, and his unqualified assertion led to considerable controversy. After James Chesnut read Beauregard's complaints on the floor of Congress, the legislators immediately launched an investigation. Soon thereafter, Beauregard wrote to Miles, proposing that his own commissary should replace commissary general Lucius B. Northrop, and his chief of staff began circulating a rumor that Davis wanted to ruin Beauregard, even at the expense of the nation. In October, still nourishing dreams of his own greatness, Beauregard filed his official report on the battle of Manassas. It opened with a description of Beauregard's plan to rout the federal army and seize Washington, and it contained passages that again assailed Davis and the army staff. Portions of the text appeared in the *Richmond Dispatch*. This controversy continued into January 1862, when "a long and sharp secret debate" occurred in the Congress, all over claims that had more to do with oversized egos than practical possibilities.[13]

Collaboration between foes of the administration and unhappy generals was only beginning, for Louis Wigfall formed an alliance with General Joseph Johnston after he invited the general, wounded at Seven Pines, to convalesce in his home in Richmond. As Johnston recovered, he allowed himself to be drawn deeply into discussions among Davis' congressional opponents. In November 1862 he attended a breakfast given for two of the president's most hostile critics, Henry Foote and Alabama's senator William Lowndes Yancey. Thereafter Johnston remained in frequent communication with Senator Wigfall. By the summer of 1863 Wigfall assumed that he could count on Johnston's collaboration against the president. "Send me copies [of your official papers]," Wigfall wrote to the general, "to be used when & as I see fit." Clearly Wigfall intended to use this back channel to assail or embarrass the administration whenever he wished and to advance his interests or those of General Johnston. After the fall of Vicksburg, he sought to publish Johnston's report on the defeat, but the administration countered by leaking General Pemberton's report, which criticized Johnston's inaction and failure to take the initiative. From the spring of 1864 through the end of the war, Wigfall wrote frequently to Johnston, lambasting the president and making plans to advance the general's interests.[14]

A variety of generals interested in devising a strategy for the western or trans-Appalachian theatre also used their contacts with prominent congressmen to advance their military and personal aims. As Thomas Connelly and Archer Jones have demonstrated, there was a loose association of generals—including Joe Johnston, Wade Hampton, John B. Floyd, William Preston, John C. Breckinridge, P.G.T. Beauregard, Leonidas Polk, Braxton Bragg, and James Longstreet—who for various reasons lobbied for changes in western strategy. This "western concentration bloc" communicated with various politicians, particularly Wigfall and William Porcher Miles, to try to advance their ideas on strategy.[15] Such ties between generals active in

the field and leaders in Congress added to the legislature's potential to play
a leading role in decision-making.

When behind-the-scenes maneuvering did not avail, congressmen also
could approach the president directly to bring their influence to bear, and
this technique was not neglected. Delegations from various states either
called upon Davis personally or sent to him requests that he solve specific
problems. At one time or another (often on multiple occasions) every Confederate state felt that it faced unusual dangers and deserved special consideration. When Vicksburg was under siege, the delegates from Davis' own
state called on him to send 30,000 troops to relieve the city, and "Congressmen from the lower Mississippi River area demanded improved river
defenses and often presented detailed defense plans." Arkansas' congressional delegation likewise argued to the chief executive that certain steps
were essential to save that state.[16] Thus, Congress could use many methods to enlarge its influence on policy.

Nevertheless, Jefferson Davis dominated military policy, and Congress'
influence in this vital area was slight. Wilfred Buck Yearns concluded that
Congress "seldom asserted itself in military affairs, and even on those few
occasions when it did act it did so cautiously and almost apologetically."
J. B. Jones, the well-known clerk and diarist in the War Department, judged
the legislature to be "a body of subservient men, registering the decrees of
the Executive," and he reported that "even Mr. Miles . . . before introducing a bill, sends it to this department for approval or rejection." Most investigations of military reverses or "disasters" concluded without fixing
blame on any particular individual. This was true, for example, after the
losses of Forts Henry and Donelson in Tennessee and the North's occupation of Nashville and New Orleans. An investigation of Secretary of the
Navy Stephen Mallory by the House took a year and a half but ended in
praise for him and the accomplishments of his department. By 1864 the
House refused to investigate defeats in Virginia, claiming that other matters were more pressing. Even the Quartermaster and Commissary Bureaus,
which in the opinion of most scholars discharged their enormous responsibilities rather poorly, were cleared of charges of fraud or inefficiency by
congressional reports in 1862 and 1863. In broader areas of policy, the legislature also followed Jefferson Davis' lead. Even a faithful administration
supporter, Senator Herschel Johnson of Georgia, confessed, "I am amazed
at the lightness with which State sovereignty & constitutional obligation
are treated by influential members of Congress—those too, who in former
days were Sticklers upon those points."[17] Despite its roar, Congress proved
to be a paper tiger. Why was this so, and why was Congress' role so modest?

Part of the explanation lies in the fact that appearances can be deceiv-
ing. For the Confederate Congress, style diverged from substance. Observers who followed the speeches of men such as Louis Wigfall, William

Lowndes Yancey, Henry Foote, W. W. Boyce, and others might well have concluded that Southern legislators all were energetic and tenacious bulldogs who would insist on controlling policy. But these individuals were merely the primary exemplars of what had become a Southern political style. Through the years of sectional conflict, in which Southern officeholders fought aggressively to counteract their minority status, politicians practiced skills of confrontation and dramatization. They were accustomed to making charges, taking stands, decrying misdeeds, and demanding that changes be made. The competitive male world of politics also encouraged them to be outspoken. But part of their bluster was simply show.

Beneath the surface of events, two more powerful forces were at work. One of these was a realization that the South truly was attempting a revolution and that its prospects were fraught with peril. Once the heady days of secession had passed, legislators could not help but acknowledge that their new country faced a long and difficult struggle. With the fate of the new nation hanging in the balance, no one wanted to be identified as an obstacle to victory or a traitor to the cause. Thinking of America's revolutionary forefathers, southern legislators vied with each other in assertions that no sacrifice was too great and that they would give everything cheerfully for the cause. This led not only to submission in unpleasant measures and unwelcome policies but also to patriotic posturing that nourished expansive egos while it concealed much discontent.

For example, on February 26, 1862, the Senate adopted a resolution "to encourage the burning of cotton, tobacco" and other crops that were threatened by the enemy. Such a policy was never popular with planters, even though they were to be indemnified against their losses, but on that same day Senator William E. Simms of Kentucky went further. To show the extent of his patriotism, Simms offered another resolution pledging "*the last man and the last dollar* within the limits of the Confederacy" to win independence. His prolix proposal asserted, in the kind of phraseology that was often heard on the floor of Congress, that "a brave and manly people can neither be appalled by danger nor intimidated by defeat" and "will submit to any sacrifice, and endure any trial, however severe" to win their freedom. Three years later, as defeat neared, the Senate adopted a stronger version of the bill on crops—one allowing a general to destroy the threatened commodities or order them removed, *without* compensation. Although a few senators objected to policies that "strip our people of everything necessary for their subsistence," the leaders of the Committee on Military Affairs stood firm and trumpeted their patriotism. Senator Sparrow decried the fact that Lincoln had benefited from the capture of a large store of cotton in Savannah and that Sherman's troops had fed themselves well on Georgia's hogs. "What Senator had not rather see [food] destroyed than fall into the hands of the enemy?" Sparrow asked. Louis Wigfall went further, speaking of "the horrours [*sic*] of subjugation" and declaring that Confederates must be "filled with the spirit that inspired the Dutch when they inundated and destroyed their country to prevent its subjugation." To emphasize his devotion to independence, Wigfall added that "he would rather to-day that Savannah were a smouldering [sic] heap of ruins than that thirty thousand bales of cotton should have been saved for Abraham Lincoln. . . . It was no time now to talk of the rights of man, while war was being made upon us like beasts."[18] Such statements from administration foes revealed both political showmanship and a felt imperative to support the cause, even as conditions grew more desperate.

More significantly, the structure of the Southern political system inhibited opposition. Confederates conducted their politics absent the traditional dynamics of the American two-party system, and the consequences of this deficiency were far-reaching. There was no opposition party in the Confederacy. This was true, in part, because the events of the 1850s had led to the collapse of the Whigs, leaving only the Democratic Party as a viable and robust organization in the South. But old loyalties died hard, and the material for two-party competition existed. Many Confederates who had been Whigs still viewed themselves as a group distinct from their old foes, the Democrats. Moreover, many of the problems that plagued the Whig Party had been national, not regional, in character, and the division between early secessionists and Unionists also was strong.[19] Within the Confederacy's political culture, there existed a fairly substantial basis for division that could have supported the return of two-party competition. Something more fundamental was holding back the rise of an organized opposition.

That force was the unspoken but powerful assumption that in a new nation an opposition party was illegitimate because it would violate the loyalty to the cause that was so necessary. Two-party competition bore a stigma that would need to dissipate over time as the stability of the nation increased. To support the new nation and its government, on the other hand, was patriotic by definition. To criticize its policies was acceptable, but to participate in an organized, declared opposition remained unconscionable. In the 1790s, when the United States was a new nation, the Founding Fathers also had believed that formal and avowed division implied weakness or a deficiency of patriotism.[20] Thus, Confederate congressmen could object to administration policies and criticize the president or his cabinet officers, but opponents always stopped short of uniting in a party that was frankly designed to oppose, obstruct, or replace the government. For this reason, the ranks of those who voted against key administration initiatives were not stable. There was much opposition, but instead of an opposition party the Confederacy experienced frequently shifting coalitions of dissenters.[21]

Unity of this type was no advantage to the Confederacy. As historian David Potter first pointed out, the absence of a two-party system weakened

the South because it inhibited the development of public support for difficult decisions or controversial policies.[22] Battles over such issues were not
fought out fully, with alternatives clearly presented to the electorate by rival
parties. Because voters were not responsible in this way for making the difficult choices, Confederate society could not derive full benefit from the
electoral process. Decisions taken at the polls confer legitimacy and en-
gender acceptance. Without such choices, dissent and criticism are only partially addressed and can prove to be more corrosive of unity than an issue
fought and settled. The absence of an opposition party "denied re-
spectability, standing, and effectiveness to minority opposition."[23] Had
there been an organized opposition party in the Confederate Congress, political competition would have produced different results or generated a
higher level of support for unpleasant decisions.

As it was, Congress debated and divided in other ways, with two patterns growing progressively stronger beneath the surface of continuing approval for administration proposals. Voting in the Confederate Congress
reflected a steady increase in war-weariness and disaffection within Southern society. Many Southerners became less and less willing to sacrifice further for the cause as it began to seem hopeless or because it demanded too
much of them. Individual citizens withdrew their cooperation from the government or obstructed its policies in their neighborhoods. In Congress such
disaffection revealed itself in declining levels of support for necessary but
unpalatable war measures. The decline was especially pronounced in the
eastern seaboard states, including the Carolinas, Georgia, Florida, and
parts of Virginia. Some of these states had been among the first to secede,
but they also contained many who disliked key Confederate policies, and
all of them were contributing heavily to the war effort. Because these states
or areas remained under Confederate control for almost all of the war, the
government continually called on them for men, money, crops, and other
useful supplies. Thus, they carried more than their share of the burdens of
war, just as some had complained from an early date. For example, North
Carolina, with one-ninth of the Confederacy's white population, furnished
almost one-sixth of its soldiers, one-fourth of its conscripts, and one-fourth
of its battle deaths.[24] Staggering under these burdens as defeat drew nearer,
many citizens became disaffected, and their representatives voted accordingly, even if they orated about undying patriotism and determination.

A second pattern revealed the surprising and atypical source of much of
Jefferson Davis' support. From the first year of the war, much of the administration's support in Congress came from areas that scarcely contributed to the war effort, and this pattern increased enormously as the war
continued. "One of the most far-reaching and fateful decisions of the Confederate Congress," observed Kenneth Martis, "was the admission of Missouri and Kentucky in late 1861." These two states held nineteen of 106
seats in the House of Representatives, and although their territory and re-

sources had already been substantially lost to the South at the time of admission, each enjoyed two of the twenty-six seats in the Senate. Together they accounted for 17.9 percent of the House and 15.4 percent of the Senate. Events soon added two more states—Arkansas and Tennessee—to their category, for early in the war these states fell under Union control. When their legislators are added to those of Missouri and Kentucky, these occupied states held 32.1 percent of the votes in the House and 30.8 percent of the decision-making power in the Senate.[25]

Legislators from these states, or from other congressional districts that had fallen under the control of the United States, came under a unique set of influences. As Confederates they hoped for a dramatic reversal in the war's fortunes, but as occupied areas they could make little or no direct contribution to the war effort. They had nothing to lose and everything to gain from strong measures that might require painful sacrifice from others. Thus, they were dependable votes for the administration as it sought to prosecute an ever more demanding war. Moreover, Union advances on the battlefield placed a steadily growing number of congressional districts into this category. Parts of Louisiana, northern Virginia, Mississippi, and ultimately Georgia and the Carolinas also fell under Union control. According to the calculations of Martis, who examined districts that were either occupied or disrupted by federal military operations, only 63.2 percent of the Confederacy's congressional districts remained under the government's control by October 1862. This percentage had fallen to 52.8 percent by February 1864. Thirteen months later, as the war and the Second Congress came to an end, the Confederacy controlled only 33.9 percent of its congressional districts.[26] This reality, of course, worked strongly in Jefferson Davis' favor. Though he would have wished for different circumstances, these secured for his proposals a growing body of dependable supporters.

Thus, the initiative and direction for military policies lay with President Davis, and with little hesitation Davis struck out in new directions that surprised many Southerners. He acted boldly to build a strong army and a war effort that was national in scope. Davis' vigorous leadership brought innovation to military policy and unexpected change to the South. Without these measures the Confederacy could not have fought the North on essentially even terms for almost four bloody years, but their innovative nature and far-reaching effect also generated controversy.

Conscription was one of the war's most fundamental innovations in military policy. Throughout their colonial and national history, American governments had raised armies in time of war through calls upon the states and by means of volunteering. The regular army was customarily very small, and when conflict required a larger force the central government asked the states for troops. Those governments, in turn, usually met the calls by receiving volunteers. All this changed swiftly in the Confederacy;

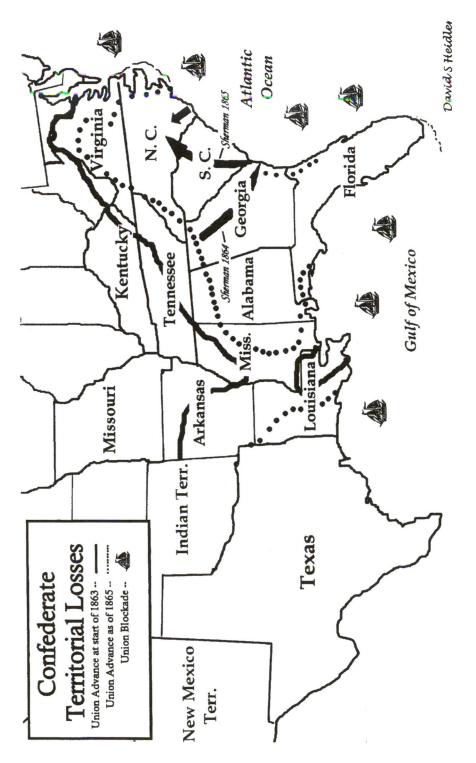

Confederate Territorial Losses. (David Heidler)

before the war was one year old Jefferson Davis asked Congress for a comprehensive conscription law.

What drove this striking innovation was necessity. Most Southerners who had volunteered for military duty at the beginning of the war had enlisted for one year of service. As the spring of 1862 neared and major campaigns began to get underway, the Confederacy faced the dissolution of its armies. Unless most of the troops in uniform reenlisted, the Southern nation would be defenseless. Accordingly, the War Department tried a variety of means to induce men to stay in the armies. Davis' second secretary of war, Judah Benjamin, offered a liberal bounty plus a furlough to all those soldiers who would reenlist. When that had little effect, he called on the state governors to raise volunteers, but the results were so disappointing that four states—Georgia, Texas, North Carolina, and South Carolina— quickly instituted or threatened a draft. The problem was fundamental. As an official report nine months later by Secretary of War James Seddon admitted, "the spirit of volunteering had died out." Or, as the *Richmond Enquirer* abstractly observed, stronger measures had become "extremely advantageous, if not indispensable, to the public interests."[27]

Supplying those measures, Jefferson Davis asked Congress on March 28, 1862, for authority to draft into military service all men between the ages of 18 and 35. His proposal had been shaped by Secretary of War Randolph with the advice and support of General Lee. By April 16 the conscription act became law. Its scope went beyond filling the ranks of the army with men, who were obliged to serve for three years (or less, if the war ended sooner), for an accompanying act established a system of exemptions that would develop into a mechanism for organizing the society's human resources to meet the needs of war. Initially, Congress exempted selected categories of men whose contributions were economically or militarily vital, such as railroad workers, river pilots, telegraph operators, iron miners, foundrymen, workers in wool and cotton factories, and officers of state and Confederate governments. In the first of many changes, Congress soon added an exemption for overseers of slaves, a measure that would provoke enormous controversy. But through legal coercion, the Confederacy gained a new means to raise armies, and it did so a full year before the United States turned to a similar measure. Conscription put some men directly into the army and induced a much larger number to volunteer before they were drafted.[28]

Over time Davis pressed for changes in the law. Later in 1862 the age limit was raised to 45, and in 1864 the limits of eligibility expanded again, at the administration's request, to 17 and 50. Congress' original law had allowed those who were drafted to furnish substitutes, individuals not eligible for conscription who would serve in their place. Not only did this provision favor the wealthy and arouse resentment, but it also brought into the army many men who were poor soldiers and unreliable; some made a

racket of substitution, collecting hefty fees to be a substitute and pr
deserting in order to bargain with another conscript. At the end o
the War Department and the president urged the end of substitution, and
Congress soon complied. More important, Davis pressed to reduce the
number of exemptions and replace the system of exemptions with specific
work assignments or "details," as a means of managing the South's labor
supply to support the war. Davis wanted to draft men into the army but
be able to assign them back to work at a factory or farm, if their skills
were more useful there. In this way the War Department could allocate
labor where it was most needed and bolster the South's production for war.
In the 1864 law Davis gained the authority he sought, but at that late date
results were not dramatic, for the South's manpower was considerably de-
pleted and resistance to the government was on the rise.[29]

Another military policy that had a deep impact on the South's economy
and society was impressment. From the first days of the war, Southern
armies in the field often took what they needed from citizens whose farms
and homes were nearby. Food, wagons, horses, slaves, or anything required
by the army and not available through regular supply channels could dis-
appear at the army's behest. Commanders left the distraught owner with a
certificate estimating the value of the goods taken and promising repay-
ment by the government. This was "a harsh, unequal, and odious means
of supply," as Secretary of War Seddon admitted. President Davis described
impressment as "so unequal in its operation, vexatious to the producer, injurious to the industrial interests, and productive of such discontent among
the people as only to be justified by the existence of an absolute necessity."
Yet that necessity persisted throughout the life of the Confederacy. The
army's supply system often failed. In addition, inflation encouraged many
farmers to delay selling their goods, and speculators raised prices to un-
reasonable levels. As a result, the army depended very heavily on impressments—almost totally at times, according to the secretary of war. When
Congress passed a law in 1863 to regulate impressments, it was merely
sanctioning a long-established policy and setting up a method to try to de-
termine fair prices for goods seized.[30]

Another sign of the strong policies promoted by the Davis administration was the suspension of the writ of *habeas corpus* and the use of martial law. Early in 1862 the president asked Congress for power to suspend
the writ and declare martial law in areas that were threatened by enemy
attack, and Congress responded with a grant of broad, blanket authority.
Although Congress soon limited this power to cases "involving violation
of Confederate law," military considerations had infringed deeply on the
respect for individual rights about which Southerners boasted. This suspension lasted a year, and a second was authorized from February 15, 1864,
to July 31, 1864. As will be discussed in greater detail in chapter 4, army

commanders took strong action when these powers were in force, and denials of individuals' civil rights also occurred at many times when the law had expired. It may be true that "the only major executive proposal that Congress flatly rejected during [the Provisional and the First Congresses] was that of a third suspension of the writ of *habeas corpus*," which Davis requested near the end of the war. But this does not mean that Confederates scrupulously protected individual rights. Military commanders and a government acting on perceived military necessity curtailed these rights far more extensively than has been recognized previously.[31]

The restructuring of civilian life to serve military needs took many other forms. To strengthen the Confederacy's ability to wage war, Davis sought and obtained from Congress a wide array of powers over the economy. Eventually, these involved so many aspects of commerce and production that scholars dubbed them "state socialism." Commanders in the field gained the authority, as mentioned above, to destroy valuable crops that were in danger of falling into enemy hands. Transportation, a crucial challenge for the less developed, less industrialized South, fell under government supervision, as Congress gave the government power to run the railroads. These powers were so extensive that the Davis administration, feeling that it needed the cooperation and expertise of railroad managers and perhaps fearing criticism, refrained from using them fully. Nevertheless, government freight—whether commodities or soldiers—claimed priority in rail shipments and maintenance of the roads answered to government priorities. Nor was shipping neglected. In 1863 the government required owners of vessels to reserve one-third to one-half of their cargoes for the Confederacy. After Congress allowed the president to regulate exports of cotton and other valuable items, the government claimed one-half of the cargo space on all outgoing ships, except those owned wholly by the states. Meanwhile, on land the government was pursuing a constellation of policies to encourage, reward, and regulate manufacturing. Government contracts brought some factories into being or funded their expansion, government laws guaranteed and limited profits, and the Conscription Bureau saw that industries had and kept the laborers that they needed. To an unprecedented degree the South rearranged its civilian economy to serve the needs of the military, and this innovation came about through direct government control to a much greater extent than was the case in the North.[32]

Manufacturing and heavy transportation had not been at the center of the Southern economy, it is true, but the government's supervision of economic life did not ignore agriculture. The widespread reduction in cotton acreage, undertaken in support of mistaken assumptions that a "King Cotton" diplomatic strategy would succeed, was actually only encouraged, not mandated, by the central government. But other controls over agriculture had the force of law behind them. Using the conscription and exemption statutes, the government detailed some farmers with explicit agreements stating what they were to grow and in what quantities. Those who did not fight in the army would be required to produce food for those who did. The impressments of slaves, which went far beyond anything that planters had ever expected, took much of the nation's labor power from the farms and put it at the disposal of the army, to serve military needs. Then, in April 1863 the government instituted a tax-in-kind. This was a direct levy on one-tenth of the production of most agricultural commodities. "Wheat, corn, oats, rye, 'buckwheat or rice,' sweet and Irish potatoes, hay and fodder, sugar, molasses, cotton, wool, tobacco, peas, beans, and ground peas" all came under the government's tax. Farmers had to deliver the taxable portion of their crops to government storehouses, under the supervision of appraisers and collection agents whose numbers quickly exceeded 3,400.[33]

In all these matters related to support of the military, Davis achieved his goals with Congress, and his success extended to areas that affected the armies directly. These sometimes proved harder to control, because Davis and his administration needed the cooperation of commanders. For example, an idea that Davis strongly favored was the forming of regiments into brigades by states. The Confederate president realized that his policies challenged many state rights shibboleths, and therefore he tried, whenever possible, to show respect for state loyalties or sympathies. He himself had been upset when he noticed that "Mississippi troops were scattered, as if the State was unknown." Moreover, Davis believed that soldiers would feel more identification with the army if they served side by side with men from their home state, and thus the policy would benefit morale in the army as well as at home. Many brigades were organized by state, but the practice was not universal, and generals were not always cooperative. Early in the war the president pressed General Joseph Johnston hard on this issue, but Johnston firmly resisted. Later General Robert E. Lee also opposed the idea, saying "I would rather command a brigade composed of regts from different states." Not wanting to interfere too minutely in the operations of field commanders, Davis let this cherished notion drop.[34]

Generals were not, however, Davis' most vigorous opponents. In clashes with state governors, he discovered that, instead of "homogeneity" and unity, there was fundamental disagreement in the South about the Confederacy's nature. Nothing exposed the gulf between state rights thinking and Confederate nationalism more starkly than Davis' efforts to build a national army. This chasm appeared very early in the war and reached its greatest extent over the issue of conscription. Though the Confederate president never gave ground to his opponents, their heated protests damaged morale and vitiated enthusiasm for his leadership.

When Jefferson Davis arrived in Montgomery, Alabama, to take up the duties of his office, he found that all things military—forts, navy yards, guns, ammunition, and soldiers—were in the hands of the states. The creation of a military establishment for the new nation had not yet begun. Promptly Davis reported to Congress that "efficiency requires the exclusive control" of the central government. Although some states quickly complied, others did not cooperate fully. Thus, when Virginia transferred many supplies and troops to the Confederacy but held on to some arms-making machinery that it had seized at Harpers Ferry, Davis persistently reminded Governor John Letcher of the need to transfer these resources to the nation. With impatience he monitored the progress of other states in turning their weapons over to the government. Some, such as Georgia, wanted to retain ownership of state-owned rifles, by actually disarming their state's volunteers when the men crossed over the state border in service to the Confederacy.[35]

Congress' first law to raise armies relied on the states to furnish troops, but for Davis it established the principle that all units became part of the Confederate army once they entered national service. Later in the spring of 1861 legislation authorized the central government to accept volunteers directly into Confederate service, and the Davis administration quickly began its own recruitment efforts. In small clashes with the governors of Virginia, Missouri, and Texas, Davis let these state executives know that he would not allow state recruiting to interfere with the Confederacy's efforts. Similarly, he made plain his determination that the national government would have full control of all troops in the army.[36]

Davis' West Point training had convinced him that the army needed effective, central direction, and he never doubted that the Confederate Constitution gave him and Congress the power that was needed to build a national army. He set to work to shape strategy that would serve the Confederacy as a whole, rather than any particular locality. Thinking in terms of one army, Davis planned to move its parts about and employ them in ways that advanced the nation's interest. Observers soon noticed the direction of Davis' thought. J. B. Jones, the famous clerk and diarist in the War Department, noted in 1862 that a proposal from North Carolina to organize a force of 10,000 men for state defense was sure to put the secretary of war in a difficult position. "He must know," Jones wrote, "that the President frowns on all military organizations not under his own control. . . . Beware Mr. Seddon! . . . Forget your old State-Rights doctrine, or off goes your head."[37]

States' rights doctrines as well as practical considerations frequently motivated the governors to work at cross-purposes with Davis. Every Southern state worried about its security and defense. Given human nature, the threats to any one state always seemed more urgent and frightening to its residents than dangers that may have been developing elsewhere. The realities of electoral politics meant that public officials, such as governors, would fight to address the concerns of their constituents and thus retain their support. When the authority of states' rights doctrines was added to these facts, collisions with state leaders were certain, and they arose often. To cite only a few examples, North Carolinians felt panic after the fall of Roanoke Island, and the state appealed to Richmond to send some North Carolina troops back to defend their borders. Davis's reply was diplomatic and attempted to be reassuring, but he also was clear on the central point: Soldiers from all the southern states would be used "for the common defense as its necessities require." He turned down similar appeals from Virginia in September 1861 and from both Carolinas in the winter of 1862–63. When the Arkansas congressional delegation pleaded for the return of troops in 1863, Davis put down in writing his convictions on this vital issue:

> The idea of retaining in each State its own troops for its own defense [was a] fatal error. . . . Our safety—our very existence—depends on the complete blending of the military strength of all the states into one united body, to be used anywhere and everywhere as the exigencies of the contest may require for the good of the *whole*.[38]

Davis was in earnest. On another occasion, when governors of four states were clamoring for the return of arms that originally had been purchased by them, the president remarked in disgust, "if such was to be the course of the States . . . we had better make terms [with the U.S.] as soon as we could."[39]

Another conflict with governors was rooted in a less justifiable motive: their desire to cultivate political advantage back home. The power of appointment gave a state leader many opportunities to please powerful or influential constituents, and Governor Joseph E. Brown of Georgia sought to take maximum advantage of these opportunities in organizing army regiments. Under Confederate law, he could appoint subordinate officers up through the level of colonel in regiments that his state raised for national service. Repeatedly Brown offered to forward to the central government Georgia regiments that contained a full complement of officers but very few privates. These "skeleton" regiments helped Brown politically, but they would be of little use to the army. Unabashed, Brown simply argued that future enlistments could fill in the gaps.[40]

Davis' greatest confrontation with Brown, however, was over vital constitutional questions. When Congress passed the conscription law, Brown objected almost immediately and in nearly apocalyptic terms. Conscription, he claimed, was unnecessary since Georgia would meet any requisitions made on it for troops. Charging that this law encompassed a power to "destroy the civil government of each State," Brown demanded that a long list of state officials and other Georgians be exempted from enrollment, and he ordered his state's enrollment officers to refuse to cooperate with the Confederacy. A few weeks later he declared that conscription was "subversive of [Georgia's] sovereignty, and at war with all the principles for the support of which Georgia entered into this revolution." Turning to legalistic arguments, he asserted that the Confederacy had no right to draft "the whole militia of all the States." By defining militia as "the whole arms-bearing population of the State who are not enlisted in the regular armies of the Confederacy," Brown in effect denied that most men in the South were subject to conscription.[41]

Davis answered with strong but well-considered constitutional arguments. After noting that a primary reason for forming confederations was to create a central authority responsible for foreign affairs and defense, the president listed the broad war powers granted by the Confederate Consti-

Joseph E. Brown. Governor Brown of Georgia denounced conscription, opposed the suspension of *habeas corpus*, and plotted with Linton and Alexander Stephens to weaken the President. (Courtesy of Hargrett Rare Book & Manuscript Library/University of Georgia Libraries)

tution. Conscription was based on the power to raise armies, not the additional power to call out the militia. Also, he argued, conscription did not disband the state militias; the Confederate army could induct men liable to service, but the states could enroll the remainder of the military population for militia duty. Then Davis confronted a major issue of interpretation. Although Brown had claimed that conscription was unnecessary, Davis declined to refute that assertion with specific facts. Rather, he wrote: "I hold that when a specific power is granted by the Constitution . . . Congress is the judge whether the law passed for the purpose of executing that power is 'necessary and proper.' " It was fallacious, Davis continued, to argue that conscription was unnecessary because armies could be raised in other ways, because such an argument could be used against every method of raising armies, as long as there was some alternative. "The true and only test is to inquire whether the law is intended and calculated to carry out the object, whether it devises and creates an instrumentality for executing the specific power granted; and if the answer be in the affirmative, the law is constitutional."[42]

Brown recognized that he and Davis were reenacting the original confrontation between Jefferson and Hamilton over the powers of the federal government. Like Davis, Hamilton had insisted that the test of constitutionality must be "the *relation* between the *measure* and the *end*," while Brown was arguing, like Jefferson, that only measures explicitly mentioned in the constitution or *absolutely* necessary should be allowable. Sardonically Brown wrote that Davis had argued a position "first proclaimed . . . *almost as strongly* by Mr. Hamilton," and he attacked Davis' broad constitutional construction. Conscription and the president's position amounted to "a bold and dangerous usurpation by Congress of the reserved rights of the States, and a rapid stride towards military despotism." A few months later, when Congress extended the ages in which men were liable to conscription, Brown declared that this action "strikes down" the state's "sovereignty at a single blow." "No act of the government of the United States prior to the secession of Georgia," he thundered, "struck a blow at constitutional liberty, so fell, as has been stricken by the conscription acts."[43]

This determined challenge by the governor of a key state presented Davis with both political and constitutional problems. In the first instance he decided to respond in a quiet way to Brown's angry charges. Noting that the courts were available to examine and test controversial statutes, Davis tried to defuse his confrontation with Brown, but he did not alter any of his positions. After others joined Brown in protests, he had to do more. The *Charleston Mercury*, a member of the South Carolina Supreme Court, and Linton Stephens of Georgia all attacked conscription, and at one point the governor and executive council of South Carolina threatened to issue a "countervailing order" against a Confederate conscription officer. South

Carolina was insisting that any men exempted by state law from military service had to be exempted also by the central government. To this Davis answered, "If a State may free her citizens at her own discretion from the burden of military duty, she may do the same in regard to the burden of taxation, or any other lawful duty." Such a denial of Congress' powers "would render a Confederacy an impracticable form of Government."[44] Given this kind of opposition, the Davis administration took these matters to court.

Here the state courts of the South had their significant hour in defining the nature of the new Southern government. Because Congress never established a Confederate Supreme Court, the state courts would rule on some fundamental questions. Was the Confederacy merely an alliance of sovereign states? Were the states so powerful that their laws and wishes trumped anything the central government wanted to do—notwithstanding broad powers listed in the constitution and the "necessary and proper" and supremacy clauses? Jefferson Davis expressed "full confidence" that the conscription law would be upheld, and he was right. The Supreme Court of Georgia reached a unanimous decision in favor of the central government, and courts in South Carolina, Virginia, Alabama, Texas, Florida, and Mississippi also supported conscription.[45]

It was surprising to some that the victory of the central government was so complete. Certainly there were influential leaders in the South who believed that they had seceded to establish a state-dominated nation, a government that was far more akin to the Articles of Confederation than to the federal government of the United States. But these figures overlooked the fact that the constitution of the Confederacy had been closely modeled on the U.S. Constitution, and thus there was a great deal of specific language in the document that gave powerful support to Jefferson Davis' views. In time of war the powers of the central government naturally became more visible. Moreover, the personnel of the courts had been trained in U.S. law and were familiar with the disputes that had been adjudicated under the U.S. Constitution. As lawyers they had learned to respect precedents and follow the doctrine of *stare decisis*. When the same issues and most of the same language presented themselves again, and in a similar constitutional context, judges could hardly reach a decision differing from those reached in earlier years.

Thus, the way was cleared for central direction of the war effort by the Richmond administration, and Jefferson Davis never wavered in his determination to direct a unified national army. He and his administration had to invest a great deal of energy in this effort, and he had to persist in the face of repeated challenges, but eventually he prevailed. Thus, it is not correct to conclude, as some have done, that the Davis administration struggled against a "state-dominated political system" that led to "a central government with limited authority to make wartime decisions."[46] In the end it was the Richmond administration that dominated the states. Even though the victory was not free—for it entailed substantial controversy that was damaging to unity and public morale—Davis overpowered the extreme state rightists.

Thus, the Confederate administration, led by a determined president, put bold and innovative measures into effect to give the South its greatest possible chance of marshalling inferior resources to achieve independence against a materially stronger foe. Ultimately, results on the battlefield would be decisive. To achieve independence, civilian and military commanders had to find the right strategy and work together effectively to provide direction for Southern armies. These challenges were part of the politics of command.

3

The Politics of Command

A key measure of the central government's success in mounting a strong war effort was the sheer size of the Confederate armies. Close to 900,000 white men served in the armies of the Confederacy at some time during the Civil War. Although tens of thousands of slaves performed essential labor under impressments, they were not considered as possible recruits until the last days of the war, and thus the eleven states that first seceded were only able to offer "just over 1 million young men of fighting age for service." To the potential military population of the Confederacy some analysts would add older men and young boys as well as the white males of the border states of Missouri, Kentucky, Maryland, and Delaware. But these four states contributed only about 90,000 soldiers to the Confederacy while more than twice that number of border-state whites fought for the Union. Moreover, approximately 100,000 white men from Arkansas, Tennessee, North Carolina, and Virginia fought for the Union before the war was over. Thus, it is plain that the Confederate government mobilized a high portion of the military manpower that was, in a practical rather than theoretical sense, available to it.[1]

The North, which brought 2.1 million men into its armies during the war, had three or four times as many men available for armed duty, and in addition it benefited from the military service of more than 93,000 African Americans from the seceded states. The Confederacy's efforts at raising an army, then, succeeded in reducing the Union's advantage in population, as the Southern government drew more heavily on its manpower. Conscription brought approximately 90,000 soldiers into the Confederate army directly, but indirectly a far larger number of men chose alternatives to being drafted, such as accepting the bonuses offered by state governments to volunteer. Even after allowing for a substantial number of unreliable substitutes, the levels of service were high. In some states that remained essentially under Confederate control, such as North Carolina, the number of men who served at *some* time during the war equaled or exceeded the voting population.[2]

How effectively the Confederacy used this force depended on the personality and judgment of leaders and on the efficiency of the organizations that they built. In other words, human factors were critically important. Vital decisions on strategy, means, and resource allocation had to be considered, debated, and made. Proud and ambitious individuals had to work together to achieve results. Inevitably, differing personalities and clashing egos played a large role in determining the outcome, for much in military history depends upon the politics of command. How did the civilian and military leadership of the Confederacy resolve crucial questions of power, organization, personnel, and strategy? Which leaders worked together well and whose conflicts damaged the cause? How should we evaluate the performance of Davis, Lee, Johnston, Beauregard, and the other civilian and military officials who were part of the Confederate high command and key players in the politics of command?

On the vital point of civilian direction of the military effort, the Confederacy avoided certain ambiguities and conflicts that had often dogged the United States, and this was primarily due to the fact that none doubted that Jefferson Davis was going to pay active, close attention to the conduct of the war. Under the U.S. government the secretary of war naturally saw himself as the agent of the president and entitled to give orders to all the generals. But from 1836 onward the wording of Army Regulations suggested that the commanding general was independent of the secretary of war and answered directly to the president. This situation had plagued various secretaries, including Davis himself in the 1850s, and it led to constant power struggles and confused the lines of command.[3] But throughout the life of the Confederacy it was clear that Jefferson Davis, as president, would be the commander in chief, directing both generals and his appointees at the head of the War Department.

Davis had five secretaries of war, although one of these men, James Seddon of Virginia, served loyally for more than two of the Confederacy's four years of existence. At the beginning of the war, Davis appointed Leroy Pope Walker of Alabama to this key post. Davis' reasons for choosing Walker probably had as much to do with attaining geographical balance in his cabinet as with anything else. Walker was a well-respected lawyer and politician with solid secessionist credentials, and many of the leading men of Alabama recommended him for a high government post. Once appointed, he faced a huge and difficult task—to raise and organize very quickly a large army where none had existed before. Struggling with this task and

Judah Benjamin. As the holder of various Cabinet posts, Benjamin was a loyal and effective member of Jefferson Davis' administration, although anti-Semitism in the Congress promoted hostile criticism of him. (Courtesy of Library of Congress)

working against the initial opposition of many governors, Walker could claim some success before he became ill and his deficiencies as an office manager became apparent. He left his post in September 1861, and there never had been doubt that President Davis made the key policy decisions while Walker attended to the myriad organizational details.[4]

In the next fourteen months, Davis had two secretaries of war. Judah Benjamin, who was talented and always supportive of the chief executive but unpopular with many in Congress, served for six months before Davis moved him to another cabinet position. The president then appointed

George Wythe Randolph of Virginia, a lawyer and grandson of Thomas Jefferson. Randolph was intelligent and well connected, and he played an important role in designing conscription and putting it into practice. He also brought some men with technical expertise into the War Department and gave considerable attention to the organization of military affairs in the trans-Appalachian west, but his tenure was brief, probably because of his dissatisfaction when Davis made it clear that he wanted his secretary of war to be an agent who would not act too independently. John C. Breckinridge served for the final two months of the war, after James Seddon resigned because leaders of his own state, Virginia, had called for reorganization of the cabinet.[5]

Thus, Seddon held the position of secretary of war for most of the conflict. Socially prominent in Virginia, Seddon in prewar days had been a lawyer, planter, and a strongly prosouthern Democratic congressman. He was a hard-working and intelligent man, and he had an able assistant secretary, the former U.S. Supreme Court Justice, John A. Campbell, whose comments appear on many important departmental documents. Seddon was not a cipher—he formed and advanced well-reasoned views on strategy, organization, and the talents of individual commanders—and his department was not a rubber stamp for any idea that President Davis expressed. But Seddon was not an egotistical person, and he understood that he had to accept the decisions of his more egotistical superior and work closely with him. He contributed much hard work and intelligent advice, including ideas on the western theatre and criticism of General Braxton Bragg that would have benefited the Confederacy had they been taken more seriously.[6] But it was clear that Jefferson Davis made the major decisions on strategy, policy, and appointments, after listening to Seddon and to his generals.

There is some evidence that Davis had to find his proper, executive role and learn to be comfortable with it during the early days of the war. As a hero from the Mexican War, Davis longed for a return to command and an opportunity to win fame on the battlefield. On July 21, 1861, as he arrived late at the battle of Manassas, the president called to stragglers and urged them to follow him back into combat. Discovering that a victory had been won, Davis took direct control of the army that night and met with Generals Joseph Johnston and P.G.T. Beauregard to organize a pursuit of the federal forces. Davis was eager to follow up the victory and actually started to dictate orders to particular units, but his generals felt more cautious and held back. As a result no decisive steps were taken. This was probably the right outcome, for Confederate troops were exhausted, inexperienced, and hampered by a steady rain. In less than a week General Beauregard decided that a great opportunity had been missed and, misrepresenting himself to congressional allies as eager to advance and seize Washington, blamed Richmond for inadequate logistical support. Beauregard's actions did nothing to help unity and morale, yet the key point here is that Davis had shown a desire to take active command on the field of battle. Again, during the Seven Days' battles, Davis was present each day and occasionally issued some orders to troops. But by this time he was learning to restrain himself and leave field command to his generals.[7]

Davis channeled part of his eagerness into efforts to send reinforcements to the commanders who needed them most. Taking a direct, personal interest in the arrangements, Davis acted in a timely way to speed troops to the battlefield at First Manassas. Thereafter he continued to show great interest in troop movements, and in the fall of 1862 he helped execute a complex plan to send reinforcements to Chattanooga, Tennessee. Using six existing railroad lines, which made a circuitous route possible, the government improvised a pipeline of troops moving from Tupelo, Mississippi, through Atlanta to Tennessee. As they traveled, troops would be available, if needed, to help defend the points through which they passed, and at the end of the pipeline needed reinforcements would arrive in Tennessee. Davis also could be depended upon, when every major battle approached, to telegraph the governors of nearby states, urging them to forward all available forces to the scene of conflict.[8]

Davis was involved deeply in the formation of overall strategy and in the advance planning for major battles or operations, and he has often been criticized for being too closely engaged with military affairs. In one sense the Confederacy's president was guilty of micromanagement. His correspondence and his hand-written notations on many War Department documents show that he devoted too much of his valuable time to minor administrative details that an official with his heavy responsibilities should have left to others. But Davis did not *micromanage* his commanders' decisions any more than Abraham Lincoln did on the Union side. Both chief executives accepted their roles as commanders in chief—both in its breadth and in its practical limitations. They did not hesitate to exercise authority on overall strategy or to advise their generals about campaign strategy, aims, and the kinds of tactics to emphasize, but neither wanted to interfere with decision-making on the battlefield. At one point in 1862 members of the cabinet urged Davis to warn General Joseph Johnston about the risks he had taken in positioning his troops in Virginia, but Davis replied that such advice was inappropriate with operations underway. "When we entrusted a command to a general," Davis argued, "we must expect him, with all the facts before him, to know what is best to be done; . . . it would not be safe to undertake to control military operations by advice from the capital."[9] Throughout the war Davis gave advice but did not attempt to control operations in this way, even when he (like Lincoln) was deeply frustrated by the inaction of commanders.[10]

In relationships with his generals Davis sought to work within the structure of a departmental system. The War Department defined geographical regions of the Confederacy as different military departments, and it redefined them often as the fortunes of war brought change. Before the war was over "at least forty-six named departments and independent districts had been created," but usually there were four or five major departments in existence at any given time. Each department was under the command of a general, who bore the responsibility for military operations in his command and was entitled to control the armies or forces under him. To these generals Davis gave considerable discretion over decisions within their departments.[11] More important, he usually relied on them to take a broad conception of the war and to cooperate with or reinforce other departments when such actions were needed. Although Richmond sent requests and strong suggestions to the departmental commanders, Davis looked to "co-intelligence . . . to secure such co-operation" as was necessary for the common defense.[12]

A number of considerations made the departmental system logical, at least in concept. The size of the Confederacy and the tenuous nature of communications and transportation facilities argued against an effort to exercise detailed control from Richmond. For practical efficiency generals in the field needed to be in charge of administrative details in the large areas for which they were responsible. Resources and supplies also could be organized, and protected, more effectively within these departments than through a thoroughly centralized effort in Richmond. Moreover, the delineation of departments sent a message to the citizens of the Confederacy that their government was defending its territory and concerned about all regions of the nation. At the same time the existence of these departments reinforced the South's case to the world that it was fighting a defensive war and wished only to be left alone.[13]

A danger of the departmental system was that it could promote a static and inflexible, or cordon, defense. But this did not happen in the first two years of fighting because Jefferson Davis revised and adapted his departments intelligently to adjust to changing realities and bolster military effectiveness. The major departmental assignments became: northern Virginia (which eventually encompassed the areas of southern Virginia and North Carolina as well); South Carolina, Georgia, and Florida; the trans-Mississippi region; a central western department that went under various names but typically included Tennessee and Alabama; and a department of Mississippi and eastern Louisiana that later included Alabama. As he reorganized the departmental structure, Davis arranged for strategic reinforcements and identified troops that could be conceived of as reserves available for use at key moments. He also came to think of Lee's command as setting the priorities for the entire Atlantic slope. Thus, before the defeats at Gettysburg and Vicksburg, Davis had "made significant strides in securing unity of control over the Confederate war effort, while at the same time retaining a large measure of autonomy for department commanders."[14]

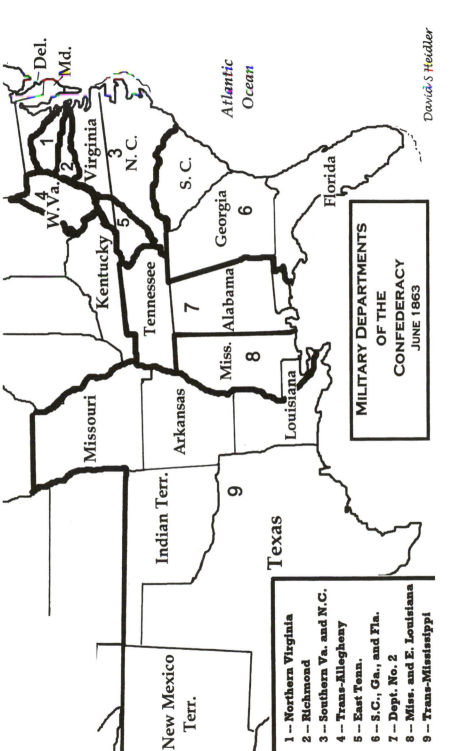

Confederate Military Departments, June 1863. (David Heidler)

However, from that point on, events outran Davis' schemes of organization. As the Confederacy lost strategic points and large blocks of territory, departmental reorganizations did not keep pace with reality, a fact that has led some scholars to conclude that his decisions in the last half of the war "divided the Confederacy into a departmental structure which made victory more difficult."[15] The evidence for this judgment lies primarily in the fact that Bragg's western department was strategically critical, yet too small to garner all the support and resources that it needed, and that as General Johnston conducted operations to defend the approaches to Atlanta he actually moved into territory in Georgia that lay outside his area of departmental control. Davis has also been criticized for giving the commanders of large theatres unclear directions about the scope of their authority or for intervening with their subordinates after giving assurances that the theatre commander had complete control. What seems more salient and serious, however, is that the departmental commanders—threatened and outnumbered as they usually were—always had difficulty seeing the importance of operations outside their command. Thus, they were habitually reluctant to send some of their forces to another region. Only rarely did Davis succeed in obtaining cooperation between departments, as he briefly did when Lee allowed General James Longstreet's forces to leave Virginia and join the western army before the battle of Chickamauga in Georgia. Stronger guidance from Richmond, in the form of orders to detach units or conduct operations in support of other armies, might have helped the beleaguered Confederacy in the latter stages of the war. By then, of course, its difficulties were multiplying.

The details of the War Department's operations were always vast and challenging. To run the war machine, this cabinet department eventually employed several bureaus—Quartermaster, Commissary, Engineer, Ordnance, Niter and Mining, Medical, Indian Affairs, the Signal Corps, Conscription, and the coordinating Bureau of War. Together these made up the bulk of the large Confederate bureaucracy. Of the Confederacy's more than 70,000 civilian employees—a greater number in relation to population than the North's civilian bureaucracy—57,124 worked for the War Department. As many as 17,000 people worked in the Engineer Bureau and in Nitre and Mining.[16] The Bureau of Conscription sent out 2,443 agents to execute the conscription law and forward men to the armies. To collect the tax-in-kind, which became a major source for food for the Confederacy's troops, the War Department dispatched 2,965 men throughout the South.[17] By 1863 Josiah Gorgas' Ordnance Bureau, which met the South's increasing demands for arms and powder and was clearly the most successful of all branches of the War Department, operated "seventeen arsenals, armories, foundries, depots, and powder mills."[18] Gorgas' great achievement was to supply the South with all the guns and powder it needed before the war ended.

If Gorgas was the most outstanding of many able heads of bureaus, Colonel Lucius B. Northrop, the commissary general, was the most deficient. Although his bureau had an immensely challenging job in obtaining and forwarding food to the armies, most scholars have concluded that Northrop was incompetent and that only Jefferson Davis' personal friendship with him kept him in office until near the end of the war. Northrop had had an undistinguished career in the U.S. Army and had been dropped from the rolls at one point due to persistent ill health. When the war started Davis offered him a post in the Commissary Bureau and may have named him commissary general because no one else was interested in taking that demanding post. Difficult as its challenges were, Northrop made them worse by trying to centralize food production and procurement in a way that exceeded the capabilities of the Confederacy's infrastructure. Northrop wanted to purchase raw materials where they were cheapest (rather than in the neighborhood where they were needed) and then transport them to central processing facilities, from which the finished products would be sent to the hungry armies. Although this was a logical idea, "currency shortages, wartime inflation, [and] transportation difficulties" soon led to the spoilage of perishable foods that piled up in railroad depots. Such waste in turn forced greater reliance on impressments, which were highly unpopular and increasingly resisted. Not until Robert E. Lee added his voice to a loud chorus of complaints was Davis willing to replace Northrop in February 1865.[19]

Another area in which the president's personnel decisions were often controversial was the selection of generals, but this was due as much to the personalities and egos of officers as to Davis' deficiencies in judgment. One charge frequently made against the president was that he favored the professional soldier and was prejudiced against military talent that sprang from a nonmilitary background. Robert Toombs of Georgia, who held an exalted opinion of his own abilities in any field, secured a commission as a general but soon resigned it in frustration over his lack of progress in responsibility. Angered at his treatment, he declared that the epitaph of the Confederacy would read, "Died of West Point." But Toombs, who had little military skill to contribute, cannot be taken as an objective observer, and it does not appear that Davis overlooked nonprofessional military talent. Of the Southern army's 425 generals, 146 were graduates of West Point. Another 10 had attended the U.S. Military Academy without graduating, and 20 more had attended some other military school. Thus, the remaining 226 "were presumably more or less rank amateurs."[20]

Like Lincoln, Davis felt obligated to make some appointments of "political generals"—individuals who had so much political clout that they and others expected a high rank for them despite their lack of military experience. Twenty-four of the Confederacy's generals were politicians prominent before secession. Although it was true that their appointments could "increase the public's support of the war," some of these men were less than competent and only created problems for the army.[21] At Fort Donelson, political generals John B. Floyd and Gideon Pillow failed to take advantage of a golden opportunity to break out of General Grant's encirclement. Then, worried that their status as prominent secessionists might subject them to reprisals, they shrank from the risks of surrendering in person. Instead they passed command to General Simon Buckner, a West Point graduate, escaped from the fort, and made Buckner surrender "in the famous opera bouffe episode derided by subsequent generations."[22]

Other nonprofessional soldiers, however, proved to have military talent, and a number of them began service to the Confederacy at the rank of colonel or lower and rose to be generals on the basis of demonstrated ability and success. Among the most prominent of these were Richard Taylor, Patrick Cleburne, John B. Gordon, and Nathan Bedford Forrest. Taylor fought well in the trans-Mississippi region despite being greatly outnumbered and in 1864 was given command of the Department of Alabama, Mississippi, and eastern Louisiana. Cleburne and Gordon fought with distinction in the Army of Tennessee and in Virginia, respectively, and Forrest was probably the most successful Southern general who learned on the job. A military historian who analyzed their careers and promotions noted that they received substantial responsibilities as their experience increased and that they went through a learning process as they served the army. He concluded that, overall, they probably were advanced as rapidly as their abilities and knowledge permitted.[23]

In a few cases the Confederate president should have demoted or ceased to rely on commanders whom he continued to support. Davis' personality was extremely sensitive to criticism, and he had to suffer a great deal of it during the war, so perhaps it was not surprising that he valued loyal support and gave it unstintingly to his friends. One of these, unfortunately, was General Leonidas Polk, who had been at West Point with Davis and graduated one year ahead of the president. Although Polk almost immediately resigned his commission in order to enter the ministry, Davis appointed him a major general when the war began and put him in command of western Tennessee and eastern Arkansas. There Polk made a catastrophic mistake. Kentuckians were struggling to stay neutral, and Polk alienated them by sending troops to occupy the town of Columbus, whose military value was slight. This action put most of Kentucky on the side of the Union for the rest of the war. Later, as a corps commander in the Army of Tennessee, Polk carried on a vendetta against his commander, Braxton Bragg, and refused at times to obey his orders. When Bragg finally forced the issue by removing Polk from command, Jefferson Davis still did not act against Polk but put him in command of the Department of Alabama, Mississippi, and East Louisiana. Historian Richard McMurray has concluded that Polk's error in Kentucky was "a geopolitical mistake of the first magnitude" and that he "weakened the Army of Tennessee." Nevertheless, Polk never lost the favor of President Davis, who mourned the general's death in action in 1864.[24]

The case of John Pemberton, another West Point graduate, attracted much attention but was not so egregious. Born in Philadelphia, Pemberton had married a Southern woman, and after secession occurred, he agonized for weeks before declaring his allegiance to the South. He thereafter did his best to serve the Confederate cause, but his background and his initial lack of enthusiasm for secession caused South Carolinians to be suspicious of him in 1862, when he commanded the Department of South Carolina and Georgia. Pemberton took up this command with little public support, but he made the situation worse when he remarked that he would give up territory rather than lose his army. Robert E. Lee had recently acted on the same thought, when he pulled in Confederate defenses along the rivers of the Carolinas, sacrificing the coast. But in response to complaints from angry South Carolinians, Lee instructed Pemberton that he must defend his area at all costs. Later, in 1863, when Pemberton was placed in charge of the defense of Vicksburg, he stayed in or close to the city, remembering his past experience and Lee's admonition. In addition, President Davis had told him not to give up the city "for a single day." After Vicksburg fell, General Joseph Johnston placed the blame on Pemberton, who had failed at one point to lead out his army in order to make a junction with Johnston's forces. Much of this blame stuck, although there was ample reason for Johnston to share responsibility for the loss of Vicksburg. The criticism of Pemberton never subsided, but his negative impact on the cause was not as dire as was Polk's, and Davis' defense of Pemberton was more justified.[25]

Davis' difficulties with commanders began early in the war in connection with the initial appointment of generals. In March 1861 Congress had passed a law promising officers who left the U.S. Army to join the Confederacy that they would retain the same rank that they had enjoyed in the federal service. Later that spring another law allowed for the appointment of generals, and Davis proceeded after some delay to make appointments in conformity to these laws. The details of the first act, however, would prove to be highly significant. One section of the law provided that, for purposes of command, one's rank would be identical to the rank held in the old army in that arm of the service—staff or line—in which one was serving. Thus, a promotion gained in a staff (or supporting) position would not carry over to one's rank when functioning in a line (or field command) position. It is likely that Davis delayed making appointments not merely because of the press of business but also because he wanted to be certain that Albert Sidney Johnston, a soldier whom he respected greatly, would arrive from California to serve the Confederacy. Once that was clear, Davis proceeded in a logical fashion.[26]

Adjutant and Inspector General Samuel Cooper had been a staff colonel in the U.S. Army for a considerable period, and since he was serving the Confederacy in a staff position, he became the first and thus most senior general appointed. Albert Sidney Johnston, a line colonel who was going to command in the field, came next. Robert E. Lee, who had been a colonel of the line but junior to Albert Sidney Johnston, received the third appointment. Fourth in order came Joseph E. Johnston, who had been a lieutenant colonel in the line. Before he joined the Confederacy, however, Joe Johnston had become quartermaster general, with the staff rank of brigadier general, and this fact—plus Johnston's ego—would lead to misunderstanding and conflict.[27]

Rank and seniority were matters of great importance to Joseph Johnston. When he was merely a cadet at West Point his pompous demeanor earned him a nickname, "the colonel." After he graduated from the U.S. Military Academy and entered active service, he repeatedly manifested an overriding concern about his rank and advancement. Eight years after graduation he resigned his commission in frustration, because he was not being promoted rapidly enough. But when he found that civilian life was not enticing and an opportunity arose to join a newly created corps of topographical engineers, Johnston jumped at the chance. Before signing up, however, he sought and obtained assurances that he would receive the same rank and seniority that he would have enjoyed if he had not left the army. When the Mexican War came, he obtained a commission as lieutenant colonel in a regiment organized just for that war, and when it was disbanded Johnston was upset to return to his earlier, lower rank. For eight years he carried on an argument with the War Department (and, for part of that time, with Secretary of War Jefferson Davis), trying to have his higher rank restored. Finally, when a new cavalry regiment was formed, he obtained the rank of lieutenant colonel but soon was plying his influence to become a brigadier in the office of quartermaster general. Thus, it was not surprising that Johnston wanted the full benefits of his ascent in the old army.[28]

When he learned that his coveted rank of general in the Confederate army was only fourth in line of seniority, Johnston grew livid. He believed that an injustice had been done, one that must be corrected. Johnston asserted that he was "the ranking General of the Confederate Army" and branded as "illegal" orders that had come to him from General Lee. President Davis tried to respond to Johnston in a mild and patient manner, making reference to the complexities of the law, but it did no good. In a long and angry letter, Johnston staked out an uncompromising position: "I now and here declare my claim that, notwithstanding these nominations made by the President, and their confirmation by Congress, I rightfully hold the rank of first general in the armies of the Southern Confederacy." The president's appointments, he declared, were "a studied indignity" and "a blow aimed at me only." Again Davis tried to respond temperately and even ordered that Johnston's diatribe should not be placed in the official files.[29] For a time this disagreement quieted down, but it marked the start of an increasingly troubled relationship between the two men.

Jefferson Davis would encounter serious conflicts with more than one of his most prominent generals during the war, and most of these difficulties sprang from personality issues and unrestrained egos.[30] The Confederate president was a proud and sensitive man who tended to be defensive, but by no means was he the only cause of the problems. His two most troubled relationships were with Johnston and P.G.T. Beauregard, and their egotism and capacity for self-absorption probably exceeded those of Davis. In fact, a thorough examination of Davis' papers reveals that he controlled his emotions quite thoroughly throughout the war and often showed considerable restraint when dealing with difficult commanders.

Davis' prior record had been different. In the decade of the 1850s his pride and haughty sense of honor embroiled him in many bitter and protracted exchanges that accomplished nothing. As secretary of war he had engaged in interminable and prideful written arguments with General John Wool that reflected poorly on both men. But the war years revealed a changed pattern of action, if not a changed personality. Jefferson Davis brought to the presidency an acute sense of his role and his responsibilities as leader of the Confederate nation. From the outset he resolved to give his all for Confederate independence and for the good of that cause. He was determined that history would demonstrate that he had done all that was possible to help the South achieve success. To serve that purpose he restrained himself repeatedly when the Confederacy could gain nothing from the expression of emotions that he previously had indulged. Though Davis was not a humble man, he usually succeeded during the war years in rising above his most contentious impulses because he was following an internal code that compelled him to work for the cause. Repeatedly he put the good of the war effort above himself and his emotions.

In Beauregard's case, scholars have found a personality that was "bombastic," "haughty and imperious," and convinced of his own brilliance. Certainly Beauregard promoted himself relentlessly and was enamored of grand strategies that made more sense on paper than in practice. These characteristics received full expression during the war. Although he spoke of the heavy burdens of military command, these duties never prevented him from carrying on an energetic and self-serving correspondence with sympathizers, editors, and allies in Congress. Before summer had fully arrived in 1861, Beauregard in front of his staff and his friends was condemning Jefferson Davis as "a stupid fool."[31] By mid-1862 he had in his own mind dismissed President Davis as "either demented or a traitor to his high trust."[32] Yet Beauregard himself was seduced by grand, Napoleonic visions, "a man of pipe dreams," given to "wildly unrealistic schemes" and plans "so optimistic as to be little short of fantasy." One of the most stubbornly persistent facts of Civil War military operations was the inability of large armies to maneuver quickly and execute crisply, but Beauregard repeatedly generated exceedingly ambitious plans that would have required swift movement and close coordination from multiple commands.[33] If his overly ambitious and impractical ideas were not accepted, Beauregard concluded that his genius had been overlooked.

The hauteur and pride of this Louisiana Creole, who grew up speaking only French in his early years, was often on display and never far below the surface. A pointed exchange with Secretary of War Judah Benjamin in the fall of 1861 illustrated this aspect of Beauregard's personality. Following the battle of Manassas, Beauregard sought to be recognized as in command of an army, rather than holding major responsibility under General Joseph Johnston and within Johnston's army. If he was not the commander of his division, Beauregard declared, he would like to be relieved. Secretary Benjamin, a skilled attorney, gave a legalistic and somewhat condescending explanation that this was impossible under existing legislation, noting that Beauregard was second in command of a whole army, not first in command of half of the army. To this Beauregard replied tartly and imperiously that his "motives must not be called into question." If he had been mistaken, Beauregard declared, when "errors are pointed out, it must be done in a proper tone and style."[34]

Unlike Jefferson Davis, who succeeded often during the war years in subordinating his pride to the higher goal of furthering the Confederate cause, Beauregard put his ego needs first. He lacked "a heart for the cause," concluded one historian, and "really had his heart only in his own reputation." When Beauregard wrote to the *Richmond Whig*, promoting his role at Manassas and criticizing the president, he vaingloriously headed his letter with the words, "Centreville, Va., Within hearing of the Enemy's Guns." His "outsized ego" fed "a nasty propensity for meddling in politics when he was not getting his way from his superiors."[35] And meddle he did. To Beauregard belongs the dubious distinction of succeeding, through his political allies and machinations, in having fifty-nine congressmen sign a petition urging the administration to give him a high command. Yet Davis tried to use Beauregard's military talents. He sent him first from Virginia to the west, to be second in command to Albert Sidney Johnston. After the battle of Shiloh, in which Johnston was killed, Beauregard took charge of the army in the west. However, Beauregard displeased the administration by retreating all the way to Tupelo, Mississippi, and then decided to leave his command, on his own initiative and without permission, to rest and improve his health. An angry Jefferson Davis learned of these plans and relieved Beauregard from duty. But Davis later put him in charge of defenses in Charleston and in 1864 gave him responsibility for guarding the Southern approaches to Richmond, where he worked under Lee until the end of the conflict.[36] Despite Beauregard's ego and self-promotion, Davis made substantial use of his talents.

It probably galled Jefferson Davis even more to place Joseph Johnston in highly responsible positions, yet he did so repeatedly during the war—and was always disappointed. Like Beauregard, Johnston was obsessively concerned about his reputation. A fine marksman, he often went hunting with friends, the historian William C. Davis tells us, only to return without having shot at a single bird. Although Johnston cited various complicating factors, the real reason that he did not shoot was that he feared missing and spoiling his fine reputation. A similar caution seemed to govern his actions when facing the enemy. Johnston had "a consistent instinct to fall back without a fight," and Steven Woodworth concluded that "Johnston could hardly be induced to fight even on the defensive and apparently would sooner accept certain Confederate defeat than risk his own reputation." The general had displayed his tendency to fall back before he was wounded at the Battle of Seven Pines, but his powerful friends in Congress, his good reputation, and the lack of other, more successful generals led Davis to give him important new responsibilities when he had recuperated.[37]

As Grant began to mount his campaign against Vicksburg, Davis put Johnston in overall command of all forces in the Department of the West and urged him to take action to relieve and defend the citadel. But at this point the president encountered another troubling characteristic of the general. Johnston was a person who often complained "that he could not take responsibility for something," and he had taken up his new assignment with the complaint that the department was too big for one general to command. Now, with Vicksburg in the balance, he repeatedly raised questions about the scope of his authority.

> For the next eight months Johnston engaged in a correspondence with Davis that must be unique in Civil War annals for its apparent obtuseness. No matter how often and explicitly Davis explained to the general the full range of his authority and prerogatives, Johnston just wrote back yet again asking the same question. He refused to understand that he had full responsibility because he was terrified of full responsibility.[38]

To avoid that burden, Johnston demonstrated considerable ingenuity.

After a number of futile exchanges and a conversation with the general's friend, Senator Wigfall, Secretary of War Seddon tried to confront the problem on February 5, 1863. "You seem," he wrote to Johnston, "to consider the several armies within your department too far separated by distance, and too distinct in the aims of their operations, to be wielded as a whole," and he noted that Johnston also expressed deep concerns about the propriety of interfering with generals in the field who were supposed to be serving under him. In response to these issues, Seddon employed both flattery and directness to clarify Johnston's role. The West needed as its supreme commander a man of exceptional attainments and abilities, a man who enjoyed the confidence of the nation, someone who would guide those distant armies as Jefferson Davis and Seddon did the forces in nearby Virginia. The president wanted Johnston to direct those armies in support of each other, order transfers from one army to another, and "assume directly the supreme command" of any army at a crucial moment. Counseling the general not to be so respectful of the feelings of his subordinates, Seddon urged Johnston at least to take command of Braxton Bragg's army and stated directly that he was "disappointed" that Johnston had not done so earlier.[39]

Jefferson Davis tried to mollify Johnston in a similar way. Because Davis had asked his opinion of Bragg's performance and of the conflicts within Bragg's command, Johnston insisted that his position was delicate; it would be impossible for him, with honor, to replace Bragg. In response Davis assured the general that there could be no question about his honor and reputation. Johnston had, in fact, defended Bragg staunchly. Davis made the case that Johnston had acted only as the "commanding general of all the forces of the department" should, providing advice and information upon request. And Davis, too, stressed that he wanted Johnston to assume direct, hands-on command. "When you went to Tullahoma, I considered your arrival placed you for as long a period as you should remain there in the immediate command of that army. . . ."[40]

But persuasion was futile, for the problem lay deeper. Seddon's conversation with Senator Wigfall had exposed the crux of the matter. Johnston feared that his control of the armies in such a large department would be nominal, not real, and that he would "stand responsible for the failures, without receiving the credit of the successes of each." Moreover, Johnston was very pessimistic about the prospects of the West. When Richmond attempted to send a Florida brigade out of his command, he immediately objected. "The force in this department is now quite inadequate," Johnston insisted, "not more than sufficient to deal with internal enemies." To withdraw even that one brigade, he claimed, "might produce disaster." Johnston did not want a disaster to be on his record, and to avoid that he repeatedly avoided direct command.[41]

On March 3, 1863, Seddon again stressed that the nation and the president wanted Johnston to take charge of the entire situation in the Department of the West. He "entreat[ed]" him "at once to assume the command." Perhaps sensing, however, that these efforts were accomplishing nothing, Seddon issued a direct order six days later: "Order General

Bragg to report to the War Department here for conference. Assume your-self direct charge of the army in Middle Tennessee." This direct order only stimulated Johnston's ingenuity. Three days later he replied that he was in Mobile, Alabama, and on his way to see General Pemberton at Vicksburg. Consequently, "I shall obey the order as soon as I can." Then, while stress-ing the need for major reinforcements, he asked that Seddon himself send the order to Bragg, which Seddon did on March 16. Next, on March 19, Johnston wrote that he had reached Tullahoma only to find that General Bragg's wife was ill. "On account of Mrs. Bragg's critical condition, I shall not now give the order for which I came. The country is becoming practi-cable [for military operations]. Should the enemy advance, General Bragg will be indispensable here." Finally, on April 10, Johnston informed Jef-ferson Davis that he himself was sick and "not now able to serve in the field," so Bragg had to remain in command.[42]

Only Bragg's physical departure could have put Johnston, by default, in command of an army, because he was determined not to accept responsi-bility. Ignoring his power to take direct control of any force within his de-partment, Johnston did not act. What modest steps he took as Grant raided through Mississippi and closed in on Vicksburg were ineffective, and the Confederacy suffered a serious defeat. Then, after the citadel was lost, Johnston displayed much greater energy in waging "a behind-the-scenes war against the president, first in the press with critical accounts of Pem-berton . . . and then in Congress, when friends started to call for copies of Davis' correspondence and reports in the case, seeking to embarrass the president."[43]

With these events as background, Davis was exceedingly reluctant to put Johnston in charge of the defense against Sherman's army, which began its advance on Atlanta in 1864. But many people still believed in Johnston, and there seemed no better alternative. The events that unfolded fit a fa-miliar pattern: Johnston steadily withdrew, pulling back before the federal advance. In justice to him, it is clear that he conducted his operations skill-fully. Selecting strong defensive positions, Johnston forced Sherman's army to pay a price for every mile that it moved forward. From a purely mili-tary point of view, these were skillfully executed delaying tactics. But John-ston was in steady retreat, and there was no reason to think that his tactics could lead to victory. An even greater problem was the fact that Johnston was out of touch with his president and at odds with Davis' entire strat-egy for 1864.

Johnston would not keep Davis informed. He "had no plans," writes William Davis, and, "He would not communicate with Davis." Even when Davis sent an aide to sound out Johnston, he learned nothing. The gen-eral's refusal to communicate was partly a matter of personality and partly a distrust of civilians' discretion, for Johnston had been upset in 1862 by well-informed gossip about his defense of Richmond.[44] But Davis, as commander in chief, needed to know what Johnston was planning, and such information was especially critical in 1864.

With the presidential election approaching in the North, and with a strong peace movement developing in the Democratic Party, Jefferson Davis hoped to wear down northern resolve. It was critically important that the southern armies put up a stubborn and successful defense until after northern voters had spoken, for a different U.S. president might allow Confederate independence. This was the best and probably the only remaining chance to gain southern independence. Thus, Atlanta—a prize of great logistical and symbolic importance—could not be lost, and many Southerners knew it. Mary Boykin Chesnut, for example, wrote in her diary that, "Our all depends on that Army at Atlanta. If that fails us, the game is up." But Joseph Johnston did not see it that way. In the words of two prominent military historians, "he never stopped withdrawing until he reached the environs of Atlanta," and "it became apparent that [he] was going to abandon Atlanta without a fight."[45]

Jefferson Davis communicated frequently with Johnston as the campaign approached this critical juncture. On July 7, 1864, after Johnston had fallen back to the Chattahoochee River, Davis informed him that all possible troops had been sent to his army and now "[we] are dependent on your success." Nevertheless, Johnston continued to ask for reinforcements, asserting on July 8 that 4,000 cavalry, if taken from Alabama and Mississippi, could sever the Union army's supply lines, "thus compelling Sherman to withdraw." Davis then explained twice that no reinforcements were available and urged Johnston to use the cavalry that had been sent to him. Although Davis' words on this point were clear and strong, others were even more emphatic. Georgia's Senator B. H. Hill sent this terse message to Johnston on July 14: "You must do the work with your present force. For God's sake do it." Finally, on July 16 Davis asked his general for information so that he could "anticipate events." Johnston replied that since he was outnumbered, "we must be on the defensive. My plan of operations must, therefore, depend upon that of the enemy."[46]

Johnston's admission that he would continue his mode of operations forced Davis to act. On July 17, 1864, orders came from Richmond that

> as you have failed to arrest the advance of the enemy to the vicinity of Atlanta, far in the interior of Georgia, and express no confidence that you can defeat or repel him, you are hereby relieved from the command of the Army and Department of Tennessee, which you will immediately turn over to General Hood.

Davis, focusing on the great political and strategic issues at stake, decided that changing commanders was the only alternative to "continuing in a pol-

Joseph E. Johnston. Like McClellan, Johnston was an overly cautious, defensive-minded general. Though very ambitious and well-connected politically, he showed no interest in becoming the dictator that Senator Louis Wigfall wanted him to be. (Courtesy of Library of Congress)

icy which had proved so disastrous." But Johnston, ignoring the necessity of holding Atlanta, looked to the defense of his reputation and claimed victory in retreat. In response to the War Department, he argued that his performance was superior to Lee's.

> I assert that Sherman's army is much stronger compared with that of Tennessee than Grant's compared with that of Northern Virginia. Yet the enemy has been compelled to advance much more slowly to the vicinity of Atlanta than to that of Richmond and Petersburg and has penetrated much deeper into Virginia than into Georgia.

The facts did not support these assertions in any way—in fact they were wrong in every particular—but they accurately reflected Johnston's concern for his reputation. "Confident language by a military commander," Johnston argued in closing, "is not usually regarded as evidence of competency."[47] It was left to Davis to face harsh criticism when Johnston's replacement, John Bell Hood, fought and failed. But given what was at stake in 1864, Davis had no choice.

Joseph Johnston demonstrated during the Civil War that he could be a skillful tactician on the defense and that he was a talented political infighter. But he gave no sign that he was a fighting general. When the Confederacy needed him to act boldly, he always felt the risks were too great. In a withering judgment, William Davis wrote that "One does not study Johnston for long before coming to the conclusion that he would not have fought for anything, even a woman."[48] It also is difficult to avoid the conclusion that Johnston was mostly to blame for his unsatisfactory relationship with Jefferson Davis. Though Davis was not an easy man to get along with, he often restrained his feelings and gave Johnston numerous second chances. He also communicated his wishes and instructions clearly enough. But the general refused to respond to direct requests, much less take Davis into his confidence. The inability of these two individuals to work together successfully had serious consequences for the Confederacy.

In the case of General Braxton Bragg, there was no deficit of mutual regard. Instead, President Davis probably gave Bragg more support than he deserved or should have received. A West Point graduate, Bragg served well in the first two years of the war. Initially assigned to Florida, he did a good job there of organizing undisciplined volunteers and turning them into effective soldiers. Then he served under Albert Sidney Johnston and acquitted himself honorably at the Battle of Shiloh. When Beauregard abandoned his post, Davis assigned Bragg to command the Department of the West. In the fall of 1862 he led an invasion of Kentucky, which along with Lee's invasion of Maryland was part of the Confederacy's two-pronged offensive. Although this was not a success, Bragg performed far better than some of his subordinates, such as Polk, who disobeyed an order that might have

Braxton Bragg. Though respected by Jefferson Davis, General Bragg lost the support of all of his subordinate generals in the Army of Tennessee and was ineffective as a field commander. (Courtesy of Library of Congress)

produced a successful concentration against the federal forces. But during the first six months of 1863, the situation in Bragg's command deteriorated steadily. While he took no decisive action, quarrelling and backbiting escalated among his generals. After the Battle of Chickamauga in September, which was a Confederate victory without strategic benefit, divisions within Bragg's officer corps became so serious that Davis had to intervene.[49]

Traveling from Richmond to the army near Chattanooga, Davis met with Bragg and all of his generals. Despite the fact that Bragg had sacked some complaining commanders and replaced them with others, dissension was rife and mutual recriminations had poisoned the atmosphere. The way Davis handled this situation, however, surely constituted one of the president's greatest failures in managing personnel. In Bragg's presence, Davis required each subordinate general to state his opinion of whether the army needed a new commanding general. Each of Bragg's subordinates chose to risk an open declaration that their commander should be replaced. Astonishingly, in the face of this unanimous vote of no confidence, Davis' response was to affirm Bragg and keep him in command.[50] Cooperation and success were certainly unlikely to develop after an episode such as this, and Davis should have known it. After the federal army dislodged Confederate forces from Lookout Mountain and Missionary Ridge, Bragg brought an end to the impossible situation by asking to be relieved from command.

Only in his relationship with Robert E. Lee did Jefferson Davis avoid conflicts that took a toll on military effectiveness. This relationship, however, was as outstanding as the others were troubled. Steven Woodworth has judged their collaboration "one of the more successful civilian-military partnerships in the history of warfare," and he added:

> Rarely has the chief executive of a republic at war worked as closely and effectively with his top general as Davis did with Lee. Rarely has a commanding general shown the wisdom and tact in dealing with his civilian superiors that Lee did with Davis. And rarely has such a team had the successes that Davis and Lee enjoyed.

The two men forged this relationship rapidly in the months after Lee assumed command in Virginia in the spring of 1862. In addition to signs of personal consideration for each other (such as Davis offering his horse to Lee), their relationship was characterized by profound respect and, certainly in Davis' case, by deep confidence in Lee's military judgment. Before long Davis accorded Lee "an almost instinctive deferential respect" that was unshaken by the defeat at Gettysburg and endured until the end of the war.[51]

The key to the growth of this successful partnership was Lee's tact and perceptiveness in dealing with his chief. Certainly a necessary condition of success was Davis' willingness to put the good of the cause above his own ego or personal aggrandizement, and Davis should receive credit for that. But on the whole, the Confederate president disciplined himself throughout the war and displayed this willingness toward *all* his generals. What was missing in his relationship with other Confederate commanders was the personality of Lee. The Virginian was always willing to show his respect for Davis' authority, and, more important, he understood and honored Davis' need for information. Never did Lee try to promote himself with politicians or the public, either for his own benefit or at the president's expense. Instead, he was willing to work in concert with his superior and able to understand what Davis needed and wanted to know. As Lee demonstrated his cooperative and consistent character, Davis quickly came to rely on it, and the two worked together with great harmony, even though their strategic visions were different.[52]

Lee's influence on the Confederate war effort came primarily through his role as a field commander, but he also functioned as general in chief and adviser to the president for most of the war. On the whole he did not choose to make this position as influential on overall war plans as Ulysses S. Grant did in the United States. Nevertheless, the position was an important one in the Confederacy's military establishment. Lee had advised Davis in Richmond in the summer of 1861, before he was sent first to western Virginia and then to South Carolina, to coordinate plans for defense in both places. In March 1862 Davis brought Lee back to Richmond, for his plan was to make Lee "Commanding General of the Armies of the Confederate States," a post similar to the one Winfield Scott had held. To effect this, Davis had his supporters in Congress introduce a bill that would establish such a position. As often happens with legislation, however, the bill that emerged from the legislature was different from what Davis had wanted. The president had enemies in Congress, and they discerned in this bill an opportunity to diminish the president's influence on military operations. As a result, the bill that passed would have permitted the commanding general to take direct charge of any army in the field, without consulting or being authorized by the president.

Davis quickly decided that he would—indeed, had to—veto this legislation. In his veto message he pointed out that "The officer so appointed is authorized to take the field at his own discretion and command any army or armies he may choose, not only without the direction but even against the will of the President, who could not consistently with this act prevent such conduct of the general otherwise than by abolishing his office." Not only was this provision unpalatable to any chief executive, but it also violated the principle of civilian control of the military. The constitution made the president commander in chief of the armed forces, and he could not be in charge if the commanding general was independent and free to operate on his own judgment. Davis rightly recognized and quashed an attempt (which would not be the last) to vitiate this constitutional principle.[53]

The problem remained, however, of finding a way to use Lee in the manner Davis desired. Davis found a simple solution, either alone or with the help of others. The secretary of war issued an order through the adjutant and inspector general's office declaring that "General Robert E. Lee is assigned to duty at the seat of government; and, under the direction of the President, is charged with the conduct of military operation in the armies of the Confederacy." As Steven Woodworth has observed, this resolved the matter neatly: "No new office was created, no act of Congress was needed, and no threat was posed to the constitution or Davis' authority."[54]

In accord with this action, Lee took up his duties, and he continued for months to hold this responsibility after he assumed active command of the army in Virginia. In February 1864 Davis brought Braxton Bragg to Richmond to act as his military adviser, and Bragg did a good job advising the president and improving the efficiency of various military bureaus. After eight months, however, Bragg returned to command in the field, and Davis relied ever more heavily on Lee's advice.[55] As final disaster neared, the Congress passed a law in February 1865 making Lee commander of all the Confederate armies. Although Davis signed this law, the circumstances of its drafting and passage again involved issues of civilian control, which will be treated in chapter 6.

Robert E. Lee was always willing upon request to give Davis his advice on military affairs throughout the Confederacy, but he did not see his primary role as proposing strategic concepts for all of the Confederacy's territory. Unlike Beauregard, who loved to devise grand and impractical schemes, Lee never was the initiator of sweeping proposals for action in the West or across the Mississippi. In fact, he seemed not to take a profound interest in strategic issues outside Virginia. Perhaps he centered his gaze on Virginia because of his oft-mentioned love for his home state, or perhaps he believed that the major battles would be fought between Richmond and Washington and the contest settled primarily by those armies. Whatever the reason, he chose to be an adviser whom Davis could consult about matters involving other armies rather than someone intent on shaping national strategy beyond the theatre in which he operated.

Events in August 1863 furnish a good example of Lee's behavior. Davis was worried about the west, and therefore he scheduled a series of conferences with Lee to try to formulate some plans about Tennessee. These discussions ended with the president asking his best general to go to the west and take command there personally. Lee was not interested. Without refusing outright to do whatever he might be ordered, he convinced a reluctant Davis to leave him in Virginia. Typically Lee resisted proposals to detach some of his troops in order to strengthen a position elsewhere, but in this case he allowed General Longstreet and his corps to depart for the west in support of Bragg. Soon, however, "Lee's correspondence . . . [read] like an ongoing lament for the decision that was made," and by the spring of 1864 Longstreet was back in Virginia.[56]

Since Lee was the Confederacy's most important general and the president's most trusted adviser, however, he did have a major influence on the Confederacy's overall strategy.[57] Lee and Davis conferred at length during the war and together addressed virtually every major strategic decision facing the Confederacy. They acted in concert and with mutual agreement, yet their basic convictions about strategy differed. To understand the strategy of the Confederacy, one must understand the perspectives of these two men. Although volumes have been devoted to this subject, one can penetrate to the heart of the matter by focusing on these two leaders at the top of the Confederate command structure.

The key decisions turned on questions of physical and psychological resources. How could the southern nation most effectively use its limited resources? What would give the Confederacy its best chance of achieving independence? How would a prolonged contest affect the people of the South and the electorate of the United States? These questions had profound implications for the choice of an offensive or a defensive strategy, and the alternatives could not be analyzed without considering the impact of military choices on morale and political support. Because they began from differing basic assumptions, Lee and Davis often reached differing conclusions. Because they worked together so closely and respected each other so well, their decisions were often a blend of their two perspectives.

Both Davis and Lee were acutely aware that the South would have to overcome a vast inferiority in resources, for by every measure the North had greater industrial might and more abundant materials for war, both human and material. President Davis, understandably enough for a career politician, viewed and interpreted this fact through a lens that was primarily political. He was more aware than Lee of the South's historical and diplomatic position and more sensitive to the concerns of his constituents and the issues used by his critics. He also was more confident of the South's will and determination. Perhaps because he was so completely dedicated to attaining independence, he gave little thought to the idea that his compatriots would not be with him. In the U.S. Congress Davis had carried on the long battle of his region against what were seen as Northern aggressions, and when he became president of the Confederacy he committed himself totally to the goal of independence. As soon as he arrived in Montgomery, Alabama, to assume the duties of his office, Davis declared that, "The time for compromise" had passed. "NO COMPROMISE: NO RECONSTRUCTION CAN NOW BE ENTERTAINED."[58]

Davis knew that Confederates, just as the American colonists of the previous century, could win through persistence—could gain their independence in the end by avoiding defeat. This was one of many parallels that he drew between the South's cause and that of the Founding Fathers, who also had rebelled to gain their independence. The Confederacy, he often argued, was perpetuating, not destroying, the American system, for Southerners alone had remained loyal to the true principles of the Founding Fathers. Even the Confederate Constitution, he maintained, differed from the founders' only "in so far as it is explanatory of their well-known intent."[59] Like the American colonists, Confederates had a smaller army and inferior resources, but like their forebears they possessed a vast territory that the enemy would have to subdue, and the capture of no one city or state would spell victory. As long as Southerners carried on a resistance, the North could not force reunion.

A strategy that was basically defensive and looked to a victory through persistence also was consistent with the Confederacy's declared aims and its diplomatic posture before the world. The new Southern nation was not trying to conquer territory or subdue another people. It wanted only to be left alone. Southerners "ardently desire" peace, Davis insisted, and "But

for the interference of the Government of the United States in this legitimate exercise of the right of a people to self-government, peace, happiness,
and prosperity would now smile on our land."[60]

More important, a defensive strategy answered fundamental political
needs of an administration seeking to establish the new nation on a firm
footing. Southerners in every state expected to be defended by their government, and no state was willing to be sacrificed. The martial spirit of the
Confederacy sprang, in large part, from people's readiness to defend their
homes, and state leaders constantly clamored for more effective defense
from the Richmond government. Thus any radical plan that might involve
abandoning large sections of the nation would have been demoralizing and
politically suicidal.[61] On the other hand, if the administration nurtured the
people's martial spirit and wisely used the logistical advantages that interior lines would provide, a defensive strategy could lead to victory.

Davis rejected a static, perimeter defense. Many times he rejected pleas
from the states that their borders needed a stronger defense. For example,
when Roanoke Island fell and North Carolinians urged Davis to send some
of their troops back to the state, he politely refused and explained that the
nation's resources had to be used "for the common defense as its necessities require." Even more clearly, he responded to a protest from the
Arkansas congressional delegation in 1863 by insisting that "the idea of
retaining in each State its own troops for its own defense" was a "fatal
error."[62] Not only was the defense of every inch of territory beyond the
Confederacy's resources, but the idea of striking a powerful blow against
the enemy and gaining independence through victories always attracted
him. This interest in the offense is certainly one reason that he supported
so many of Lee's initiatives. Davis' overall strategy was the "offensive-de-
fensive," which meant that he wanted the Confederacy, within a generally
defensive posture, to seize opportunities to attack and to go on the offensive when chances of success were strong.[63] But it was Davis' responsibility to maintain the nation, and he felt constrained not to take excessive
risks. Early in 1862 Davis wrote, "I have felt and feel that time brings many
advantages to the enemy, and wish we could strike him in his present condition; but it has seemed to me involved in too much probability of failure
to render the movement proper with our present means."[64] Whenever offensive actions were proposed, Davis felt obligated to weigh their advantages against the risks of disaster.

Robert E. Lee was by nature much more aggressive. Although his personality appeared quiet and reserved as the result of a tight control that he
exercised over his emotions, Lee became very aggressive in battle. His instinct was to attack whenever "his blood was up." In the Mexican War he
had seen General Winfield Scott win repeatedly with smaller forces through
aggressive actions involving attack and maneuver. As one of Scott's engineers, Lee had often helped to identify the paths for maneuver that led to

attack and victory. Undoubtedly this experience taught Lee an influential lesson. But clearly his aggressiveness as a commander also was part of his character. A Southerner who had served on Lee's staff, Joseph C. Ives, observed that Lee was "head & shoulders far above every other [man] in either army in audacity. . . . Lee is audacity personified. His name is audacity."[65] Thus, Lee saw the goal of military operations as the destruction of his opponent's forces. When Lee took over the defense of Richmond in the spring of 1862, most Southerners hoped that he would simply defend the city. But, as Emory Thomas has written, "Lee's goal was much more ambitious: he planned to obliterate his enemy."[66]

Alone among Southern generals, Lee seemed to possess the military genius to achieve this goal. From the spring of 1862 to the summer of 1863 he won battle after battle, displaying abilities—and a willingness to take risks—that were unmatched by other commanders. Such proof of Lee's abilities made it difficult for Davis to resist his requests, and through the spring of 1863 Lee repeatedly urged that troops be moved from other regions to increase the power of his army. He sought to win the war by staking the outcome to one big Napoleonic battle. When he marched north toward what would prove to be the battle of Gettysburg, Lee was aiming to win a decisive victory that could set the North reeling and bring about Confederate independence. Whereas Davis, according to Steven Woodworth, was unwilling to gamble if defeat could mean "national ruin," Lee sought "a series of crushing battlefield victories that destroyed the will of the North to continue prosecuting the war. No matter how long the odds of achieving such victories might be, they would be desirable odds if time did not favor the South."[67]

And Lee believed that time was on the side of the North. The problem was not simply the superior physical resources of the North or its access to greater numbers of soldiers. Lee worried, according to Woodworth, about "a would-be nation of people whose loyalties were divided and consciences uneasy—people who felt as Lee had before committing himself." Such a populace "would need resounding victories and an early peace, or its morale was bound to crumble." Thus, whereas Davis felt that "the war could be won simply by not losing," Lee assumed that "it could be lost simply by not winning." Lee believed—and feared—that "southern bravery must triumph before southern fortitude failed."[68] His confidence in the staying power of Confederates was less than Davis', and more accurate as events proved.

The closest Lee came to testing his theory was in his invasion of Pennsylvania. He had not succeeded in convincing Jefferson Davis to move additional troops into Virginia, but Davis had resisted the panic of many and ignored calls to detach soldiers from Lee's army before he could begin his march. Thus Lee fought his great battle at Gettysburg. Deprived of the intelligence that his cavalry should have been providing, Lee's army encoun-

tered the federals unexpectedly near the little town, and as night fell after
the first day's fighting, federal troops seized the high ground. Although
urged to find more favorable terrain for the battle, Lee determined that he
would stand and fight. He joined the battle and sent General George Pickett on his impossible charge on the third day. This was his desperate attempt to win the war, but it was, in Woodworth's phrase, "audacity run
amok." James Longstreet's plea that "no 15,000 men ever arrayed for battle" could take that position was proven correct, and Lee was defeated.[69]

By 1864 the South's capacity to wage an offensive campaign was essentially gone, and necessity forced Lee to adjust his efforts to conform to Jefferson Davis' strategy of persistence. Consequently, Lee fought defensively
and effectively during that year, with great cost to Grant's army. Lee had
his men break out their shovels again, as they had done in West Virginia
in 1861 (when Lee was derided by newspapers as the King of Spades), and
his army used extensive entrenchments to slow the federal advance and ex-
tract disproportionate losses from the enemy. But the chance for this strategy to work had passed, at least after Johnston's failure to protect Atlanta
brought rejoicing to the North, utter dejection to the South, and electoral
victory to Abraham Lincoln. As desertions increased alarmingly, the eventual surrender of the Southern armies became unavoidable.

Did Lee and Davis fail to fashion a coherent strategy? Steven Woodworth concludes that they did, and he lays the fault at the feet of President
Davis. To Woodworth the Confederate president did not compel Lee to follow the defensive strategy and likewise did not adjust his own thinking to
embrace the aggressive strategy in a way that would have given Lee maximum resources to risk everything in "an all-out bid for victory." Davis
"supported Lee's ventures to an extent that was all but reckless within his
defensive framework, but he clung to the notion of taking no risk that
would preclude the Confederacy's ability to go on enduring should the gamble fail." This meant, Woodworth believes, that "neither [strategy] got a
fair chance."[70]

Perhaps this is correct, but the choice that Davis had to make was certainly an agonizing one. And surely Woodworth erred when he observed
that had Davis risked everything on a Napoleonic victory by Lee in 1863
and lost, "few military pundits" would have faulted him for taking such a
huge chance.[71] More to the contemporary point, citizens of the Confederacy would have faulted their president had he pulled large numbers of
troops from coastal and western defenses in order to concentrate on a grand
offensive in Virginia. The Confederacy's forces were thin from the start,
and its capacity to endure loss and dismemberment was limited. The government's first responsibility was to protect its citizens. Fearing change, the
South's revolutionaries had created a government that they expected would
defend their states and people, not abandon them. Even the nationally focused war effort was controversial because it neglected many counties and

cities. Yet, it could be made politically acceptable as long as Southerners understood that the Confederacy was trying to defend all regions of the country, if not every inch of its perimeter. The big gamble that attracted Lee was another matter. It would have required the Richmond administration to leave large portions of the country practically defenseless while Lee rolled the dice, and no state would have accepted this level of risk. The public outcry would have been immediate, the opposition from state officials and Confederate congressmen would have been deafening, and the central government's ability to command the support and enjoy the confidence of its citizens would have been destroyed. To hold a fragile new nation together, Jefferson Davis had to demonstrate his concern for the whole Confederacy. He was not at liberty to stake everything on a Napoleonic offensive in the East.

There also was no assurance that such an offensive—even if successful—would win the war or gain for the Confederacy its independence. Suppose that Lee's army had routed the Army of the Potomac, inflicting heavy losses and sending U.S. forces reeling back toward Washington. What would have followed? The Confederacy was in no position, in terms of logistics, men, and resources, to hold and occupy northern territory, and Lincoln's government was not the kind of administration that would have surrendered, even if it had to abandon the capital. Although it seems clear that panic and recriminations might have flourished in the immediate aftermath of a major defeat, the North could have drawn on its abundant resources to throw up a new defense in the east. Meanwhile, in the west and other parts of the Confederacy, U.S. armies, numerous and still in place, would have had a golden opportunity to go on the offensive. The South's grand offensive in the east would have been for the North a great opportunity in the west. In any event, a bold gamble in Virginia would not have been successful unless it brought the war to a speedy conclusion, and that result was far from certain.

The strategic choices that the Confederacy faced were stark, yet the offensive defensive, stretched to accommodate General Lee, came surprisingly close to success. Battling staunchly against internal complaints and dissension, Davis held the Confederacy together and kept up the contest. Well into 1864 Southern armies continued to give the Union a vigorous fight, and during the summer of that year war weariness became palpable in the North. The peace-oriented activists in the Democratic Party gained strength, while Lincoln came to despair of his chances of reelection. It was late in August 1864 that Lincoln concluded, "it seems exceedingly probable that this Administration will not be re-elected."[72] If General Johnston had held Sherman back from Atlanta until after the North's presidential election, the war's outcome might have been different.

As it was, the Confederacy fought with a strategy that was primarily defensive, with a leading general who seized almost every opportunity that

Robert E. Lee. His military prestige enabled him to play a major policy role as the advocate of employing slaves as soldiers. (Courtesy of Library of Congress)

came his way to be aggressive, and with considerable dissension between the president and other key commanders. One can question whether the Confederacy, in the end, made the best use of its military resources. Yet to some extent these problems may have been unavoidable because the war was fought by human beings. Certainly Abraham Lincoln encountered similar difficulties with some of his generals and had no better luck in finding a large number of commanders who were effective and reliable. Waging war in the Civil War era was costly, difficult, and frustrating for both commanders in chief.

In the South these problems were no more serious, in the end, than the internal social and political issues that eroded the army's strength as the war continued. Jefferson Davis faced a growing challenge to keep men in the army's ranks, for class resentments and disaffection grew rapidly even from the first year of the war. Ironically, these issues arose in large measure from laws that were intended to support and strengthen the army. But the Confederacy's war effort had a deep impact on Southern society. It affected and changed it in ways that were very painful and controversial then and in certain ways that had been unrecognized until very recently.

4

Toward a Militarized Society

The Civil War had an enormous impact on the United States. Northern society reorganized itself in many ways to fight the war and preserve the Union. Government control of banking and transportation increased significantly, and federal support of key manufacturing and business interests helped shape the economy. Over 364,000 Northerners died, a total almost as large as all of this nation's deaths in World War II. Government spending soared to twenty times its prewar level, as the Lincoln administration expended five times as much money fighting the war as all previous administrations had spent for all purposes since 1789. By 1865 the federal government's expenditures accounted for 26 percent of the gross national product, and annual interest on the national debt rose to almost $3 billion. More than fifteen years after Appomattox, interest on the debt still claimed 40 percent of the federal budget, and soldiers' pensions absorbed another 20 percent.

In the South the war's impact was not merely similar; it was proportionally greater. With a smaller population and fewer resources, the Confederacy had to make a greater effort in order to contend with its powerful adversary. A significantly higher proportion of men served in the military, and an estimated 258,000 Confederate soldiers lost their lives. Because the government raised less revenue through taxes, government borrowing and debt were excessive and led to rampant inflation that soared beyond 7,000 percent. The size of the Confederate government increased enormously as the administration took progressively bolder steps to organize the war effort. The war rapidly changed the economy, as the Davis administration required and rewarded manufacturing and commercial ventures that were essential to the support of the military. The economy, the political system, and social life all were affected, and historian Emory Thomas has rightly labeled the Confederacy's war years a "revolutionary experience."[1]

Nevertheless, few have appreciated fully the dimensions of this transformation. The impact of war was not simply greater in degree in the South than in the North; its scope was so extensive that it became a difference in kind as well. The war effort affected virtually everything in the South, and little remained unchanged. Moreover, the war was actually fought within the South, increasing its effects dramatically both in areas close to the battlefield and in regions that had to support the troops. At no time in U.S. history was civil society as deeply affected by war as was the Confederate South. Even during the United States' vast industrial mobilization during World War II, change on the home front was less radical and more consistent with existing trends.

The relationship between military affairs and civilian life in the Confederacy was unusually close. Although we normally think of these two spheres as separate and distinct, extensive interpenetration became the rule as war engulfed daily life. In an unprecedented manner, military events and military needs became salient in the civilian sector, and the civil realm recast itself in service to the military effort. Society changed radically as the war came to dominate its activities. In some ways the war had a destructive impact, breaking down customary arrangements or rendering them unworkable amid changed conditions. In other ways the war and the varied efforts to further it transformed what had been, introducing new elements into the economy or society and nourishing their growth.

The South's revolutionary experience was filled with irony. Conservatives had launched the revolution, as the planter elite led the South into war to avoid perceived threats from the next, incoming Republican administration. This elite traded the possibility of change for what became the certainty of vast alterations under the Confederacy. External pressures and internal decisions flowed together to form a tidal wave of change that remade Confederate society. The war revised reality and required new measures, and the Davis administration and Congress made choices that "all but destroyed the political philosophy which underlay the founding of the Southern republic."[2] And yet the unexpected was also, in virtually every instance, constitutional.

Moreover, these events constituted a kind of test case for our nation, an extreme example of how much the normal pattern of civil-military relations could alter in time of war. As barriers between the military and civil domains broke down, a self-consciously conservative region of the United States, one that had praised tradition and denounced change, experienced destruction and re-creation. The South's society transformed itself in the face of war, and as Confederates discovered how much they could change, their actions revealed what really mattered to them. Their story suggests that the impact of war can be immeasurably greater than we expect and that the core values of our political system can be both more flexible and more brittle than we know. When the security of society and the existence of the state are threatened, cherished principles can be ignored or discarded in favor of new imperatives more relevant to the crisis.

As chapter 2 demonstrated, the Davis administration was responsible for bold and far-reaching measures that harnessed the South's resources in unprecedented ways in order to fight the war. The war itself brought other unexpected alterations in daily life, as armies marched over the southern landscape and drew on all of the region's resources to sustain themselves. The collective impact of laws and battles, of actions planned and unpredictable, was breathtaking. The Confederate South rewrote the normal balance of civil and military affairs, sending a huge portion of its men into the military and redirecting its economy. As a result it experienced the sudden impoverishment of a large portion of its population; rapid and unprecedented urbanization; a dramatic stimulus to its industries and factory production; and a new degree of control and coercion over the civilian population, including very significant infringements of individual liberty.

The causes of widespread poverty in the South were multiple, but almost all related in some manner to the war effort. The most fundamental problem was the loss of labor on tens of thousands of family farms spread throughout the thinly settled South. In the antebellum South's predominantly agricultural economy, large plantations that constituted only a small proportion of the region's farms had produced almost all of the region's export crops, such as short-staple cotton, long-staple cotton, sugar, and rice. The great majority of Southern farmers, by contrast, operated small farms that were subsistence or semisubsistence in nature. Three-quarters of the white families in the South did not own slaves, and most of these Southerners farmed on a small scale. Although production for the market was beginning to spread among nonslaveholders, in 1860 most nonslaveholders still grew their own food or raised crops primarily for their own use, trading with others in the neighborhood to gain some commodities that they did not or could not produce for themselves. Their farms were family operations in which the father did most of the outdoor work in the fields, assisted by his sons and possibly by his wife or daughters at certain key times, such as harvest. Neighbors might "swap" work or help each other on occasion, but food production for most white Southern families depended on the male members of farm families.[3]

Soon after the war began, signs of trouble in the rural economy began to appear as men joined the armies. A wave of enthusiasm for the war in the spring of 1861 brought extensive enlistments. By July Secretary of War Leroy Walker reported that "200,000 additional volunteers" could have been added to the ranks of the army if additional arms had been available, and in August he said that only the shortage of arms and munitions was preventing the Confederacy from "bring[ing] into the field and maintain[ing] there with ease 500,000 men." With so many volunteers at hand, the War Department eventually stopped accepting one-year enlistments and asked instead for a commitment of three years or the duration of the war.[4] Though helpful for the military, this outpouring of patriotic enthusiasm had unexpected consequences for civil society. From one sparsely settled neighborhood after another, letters began to arrive at the War Department. "Our Section of Country," read a petition from Alabama, has been "left entirely Destitute of any man that is able to keep in order any kind of Farming Tules." A group of citizens from Patrick County, Virginia, argued that their blacksmith could "render more good Service as a Smith at home than he would in the Confederate army." Similar appeals, from all over the South, asked the War Department to discharge a tanner, a miller, a wheelwright, or some other artisan whose absence in the army seriously inconvenienced a rural district that had no one left to supply his services.[5] The growth of the army led to unexpected difficulties in the sparsely settled and only semideveloped rural economy.

Raising troops for the war affected many family farms directly and quickly. Every farm that lacked adequate male labor, after a soldier joined the ranks, soon faced small harvests or the prospect of diminished yields. Early in 1862 dire warnings began to be heard. From South Carolina, the first state to secede, came an alarm in the *Edgefield Advertiser* that, "The duties of war have called away from home the sole supports of many, many families. . . . Help must be given, or the poor will suffer." An experienced North Carolina officeholder lamented that "suffering among the poor . . . is dreadful to contemplate," and the brother of the state's treasurer said, "If more men are called to the field, . . . many *must* starve." In Georgia, the *Atlanta Daily Intelligencer* concluded in September 1862, that "want and starvation are staring thousands in the face. . . . Around fireless hearths many will be the cries of cold and hunger." An elderly Virginian explained, "If you dount send [my son] home I am bound to louse my crop and cum to suffer," and a desperate woman from the same state pleaded, "I ask in the name of humanity to discharge my husband."[6]

Continuing efforts to strengthen the armies only made this problem worse. North Carolina was a state with many small farms and relatively few districts of large plantations, so it was not surprising that Governor Zebulon Vance frequently pressured the Confederate government to delay or suspend the raising of troops in his state. In March 1863, for example, Vance warned Jefferson Davis that conscription had swept off "a large class whose labor was, I fear, absolutely necessary to the existence of the women and children left behind." At other times Vance urged the government to send men home from the army to plant or harvest their crops or to exempt a particular area from further calls for troops. The governor agreed with one of his constituents, a private in the army, who concluded, "By taking

Zebulon Vance. This popular Governor of North Carolina often sparred with the Richmond administration as he worked to protect his constituents from the heavy demands and power of the central government. (Courtesy of Library of Congress)

too many men from their homes, [government officials] have not left enough to cultivate the land, thus making a shortage of provisions." And the leaders of other states supported this analysis. The governor of South Carolina complained in 1864 that almost no men remained at home in his state's nonslaveholding districts, and he opposed requisitions for state troops, even to help with the defense of Charleston. His reason was compelling: he feared "possible starvation."[7]

Military operations frequently aggravated these basic problems. Impressments were astonishingly heavy, so heavy that in Georgia their value was three times greater than Confederate taxes, almost nine times greater than the tax-in-kind, and three times greater than the combined total of state and local taxes. These impressments "took more than half of all the material resources demanded of Georgians by their national, state, and local governments during the Civil War," and they hurt the poor even more than the rich.[8] Sometimes impressments deprived families of food or equipment that they desperately needed, and citizens protested that no "orders from [a] Gen'l" could justify the "rob[b]ing and plundering" that they had suffered. Although Congress had authorized impressments, no law could hide the fact that these were fundamentally seizures by military force, a striking measure of how deeply the military had intervened in normal civilian life. Governor Joseph E. Brown of Georgia branded as "ruinous" impressments in 1863 in the northeastern part of his state, where he judged that 80 percent of the families "may not have half enough" of the food they needed. On another occasion he reacted to seizures of food by warning, "If this continues the rebellion in that section will grow, and soldiers in service will desert to go to the relief of their suffering families."[9]

Without the formality of impressments, soldiers often ruined crops, slaughtered animals, or dismantled fences and outbuildings to obtain firewood. In August 1862 the *Daily Richmond Enquirer* observed, "We often hear persons say, 'The *Yankees cannot do us any more harm than our own soldiers have done.*" The worst offender, in many people's eyes, was the cavalry. Governor Vance charged that Confederate cavalry units were poorly disciplined and unconcerned about the citizens whom they injured by taking or destroying property. In frustration he once complained to the War Department that if the God of the Hebrews had needed "another plague worse than all others which he intended to have let loose on the Egyptians in case Pharoah still hardened his heart, I am sure it must have been a regiment or so of half-armed, half-disciplined Confederate cavalry." In the face of such marauders, the ruler of Egypt "never would have followed the children of Israel to the Red Sea! No sir; not an inch!"[10]

In addition, there were other unavoidable problems that led to suffering. Drought, untimely rains, or diseases that damaged crops affected various parts of the Confederacy and caused diminished yields that became harder to deal with due to the circumstances of the war. For all these reasons, suffering spread widely. Long before the end of the war, it reached dimensions that were alarming and unprecedented. Hunger was a serious problem in all parts of the Confederacy, but we have quantitative measures of it for only a few states. The governor of Alabama declared at the end of the war that more than a quarter of the white citizens of his state were on relief, and a study of conditions in several North Carolina counties has found that one-fifth to two-fifths of the families appear to have depended on the government for food.[11] There is every reason to believe that the extent of suffering was comparable in all areas that remained under Confederate control.

This development was unexpected and its consequences profound. Since the founding of the Republic, the South had not faced a problem such as this. Established means for ensuring social welfare or providing relief for the poor were rudimentary, and as a result state governments in the Confederacy scrambled to respond to a wholly new situation. Improvising solutions, some states expanded the efforts of their county governments to buy and distribute basic foodstuffs. New officials were appointed and charged with the responsibility of finding and purchasing corn or pork for future distribution. Some governors, such as Georgia's Joe Brown, took on new powers and seized important, scarce commodities such as salt. Since salt was essential in the preservation of meat, Brown refused to allow its distribution to be determined solely by the market and by the wealth of individuals. To make sure that soldiers' families had access to some salt at a reasonable price, he took control of all supplies and supervised their distribution. State legislatures passed a series of ever increasing appropriations in hopes that their funds could purchase enough food to feed the hungry. As the burden on state budgets grew, spending on other programs—such as public education—had to be curtailed or eliminated. The structure of state appropriations changed dramatically while the size of state budgets mushroomed.[12]

In and of themselves, these were remarkable changes. Due to the war, local governments expanded greatly in a region that trumpeted its belief in limited government. Governors who criticized Jefferson Davis for expanding his role suddenly assumed powers that they had not exercised before and may not have possessed legally. Priorities of the state governments underwent radical revision, all because the war and the needs of the military had transformed life on the home front. But in regard to hunger and poverty, this was only part of the story.

All the efforts of Southern governments to alleviate suffering proved inadequate to solve this critical social problem. Huge appropriations that were authorized by states and counties in the latter stages of the war never materialized. Local officials who sought to buy foodstuffs often ran short of funds or could not find adequate supplies. When purchasing agents traveled farther and farther from their home counties to buy food, they discovered that the central government was competing with them wherever supplies could be purchased. The South's relief efforts proved inadequate materially, but—even more fundamentally—they were inadequate psychologically, for the provision of relief could not remove the essential objection of suddenly impoverished Southerners to their situation. The nonslaveholders and yeomen farmers of the South had prized their economic and social independence. Their ability to take care of themselves gave them standing in society and allowed them to feel that they were the equals of anyone else. Loss of that independence destroyed the status they prized and corroded their self-respect. This was an open wound that fueled the spread of powerful class resentments within Confederate society.

A North Carolina private neatly summed up the disillusionment and anger that growing numbers of small farmers felt toward the wartime society that had impoverished them. Writing to Governor Vance at the beginning of 1863, this man noted that he had left a wife and four children "to fight for his country . . . thinking that the Govt. would protect his family, and keep them from starvation." Instead, his loved ones faced "a scarcity of provisions" that caused him to fear that "there will be much suffering and probably many deaths from starvation." He asked how soldiers like himself could "support our families at $11 per month" in soldiers' pay. "How can the poor live?"[13]

Moreover, this man's letter pointed clearly in two additional and significant directions. First, it revealed that unequal and misguided policies of the Confederate and state governments had added class resentment to the soldiers' economic alarm. "The Govt. has made a distinction between the rich man (who had something to fight for) and the poor man who fights for that he never will have. The exemption of the owners of 20 [N]egroes & the allowing of substitutes clearly proves it." Such exemptions aggravated the painful effects of rampant inflation and profiteering, whose impact on soldiers' families was harder to bear because many single men occupied minor but exempted positions with the railroads and with state government. "Our soldiers cant understand why so many young magistrates are permitted to remain at home and especially so many militia officers."[14] Given economic and social realities in the South, these young magistrates often came from families of wealth or power, and unequal sacrifice stoked class resentment among those who were not privileged.

Second, this soldier predicted that serious consequences for the Confederacy would flow from poverty and class resentment. "A man's first duty is to provide for his own household," he declared. "The majority of our soldiers are poor men with families who say they are tired of the rich mans war & poor mans fight, they wish to get to their families. . . . There is great dissatisfaction in the army . . . the soldiers wont be imposed upon much longer."[15] Suffering on the home front would stimulate desertion. In tacitly making this observation, the North Carolina private was only echoing stronger statements made by wives and mothers. Mary Boykin Chesnut recorded a graphic scene in her diary. As conscription officers took a deserter into custody and sent him off to the army, a woman in a "cracker bonnet" squalled after him, "You desert again, quick as you kin. Come back to your wife and children. Desert, Jake! Desert agin, Jake!" Confederate and state officials, and commanders such as Robert E. Lee, recognized that despairing letters from home led to many desertions. One Southerner noted that "many deserters are passing the various roads daily . . . they just pat their guns and defiantly say, 'This is my furlough.' "[16] Thus, poverty on the farms frequently led to desertion from the armies and to a cluster of serious problems that were difficult for military force to resolve.

At the same time, other actions by the government were bringing change to society, introducing new and unfamiliar elements to the social order. One of the most unexpected developments was rapid urbanization in what had always been a rural society—an agricultural region whose elite celebrated a plantation ethos. At the time of the Civil War, the South remained sparsely populated compared to all but the newest frontier regions of the United States. Texas contained only 2.3 persons per square mile, Louisiana had 15.6 persons per square mile, and the figure for Georgia, one of the original thirteen colonies, was only 18.0. By contrast, population density in the nonslaveholding states east of the Mississippi River averaged 43 persons per square mile, almost three times higher than the South as a whole. The Northeast had 65.4 persons per square mile, and for Massachusetts the figure was 153.1.[17] But in the rural South, major urban areas were few. New Orleans was the South's largest city by far, with 169,000 residents, but Charleston had only 41,000 people and Mobile only 29,000. Richmond, the capital of the Confederacy, had a population of 38,000 in 1860.[18]

Suddenly, cities began to grow under the Confederacy. Primarily this urban growth was the direct result of actions by the Richmond government. The Confederacy needed to build and supply a war machine, and that meant new bureaus, new employees, new contracts, and new factories. Augusta, Georgia, became the site of a major arsenal and a key producer of gunpowder, and as a result it experienced a surge of growth and prosperity. Charlotte, North Carolina, became the inland location for the Marine Engineering Works, needed to help bring a navy into existence. Selma, Alabama, gained 3,000 workers in an arsenal and more than 10,000 employees of other war industries. Petersburg, Virginia, and Columbia, South Carolina, each began manufacturing more than 20,000 pounds of powder per month. When the fall of Nashville to Union forces became imminent, citizens in Atlanta asked that the Ordnance and Arsenal works be relocated to their town, and their success initiated Atlanta's rise to economic prominence.[19]

Entrepreneurs responded to the government-generated demand and brought new companies into towns and cities to manufacture war materiel.

One example was Charles Rigdon, who first participated in the establishment of a sword factory but soon began manufacturing revolvers for the Confederacy. His concern developed a product of good quality, made over 12,000 revolvers in Augusta, and became known as the government's "ace revolver manufacturer." Established factories, such as the shoe shops and textile mills in Columbus, Georgia, expanded their production in response to large government contracts and guaranteed profits (75 percent at first, a figure later reduced to 33 percent). Historian Mary DeCredico notes that "Men and women from the surrounding countryside flocked to the town to obtain employment in government and private shops." In 1863 the *Columbus Daily Sun* wrote, "There is perhaps no city in the Confederacy that has felt less the deprivations and inconveniences of war than Columbus," and a visitor was amazed that the growing town "shows so little of the traces of the war . . . a delightful contrast to the war-worn, poverty-stricken, dried up towns I had lately visited." The military often improved drainage and carried out other public works in cities where it had substantial projects, leaving some permanent improvements.[20]

The dislocations and defeats of war also caused cities to grow. Wives moved to towns to be close to their husbands' military unit. Training camps and recreation centers were located there. Hospitals to care for the sick and wounded also came into being in cities, where it was possible to locate the supplies and workers needed to run them. Illicit trade sprang up in cities that were close to the boundary between Northern and Southern forces. "Refugeeing" also became a way of life for literally thousands of Confederates, especially those of the upper class who had the financial resources to cushion the shocks of war. When coastal areas fell to Union forces, many Confederates moved inland to cities and rented accommodations or shared space with relatives. In the way of urban economies, it also was true that as the population of a city expanded, businesses appeared to serve the needs of new residents, thus producing scores of additional enterprises, both legitimate and illegal. Stores and restaurants, hotels, bars, and brothels all thrived together.[21]

For all these reasons the cities boomed. Exact figures on population are sketchy, but Mobile, Alabama, grew from 29,000 residents to 41,000. New Orleans "grew tremendously" between 1860 and its capture in 1862. Richmond's population multiplied dramatically, although estimates that quantify its growth vary from two and one half times to six times the prewar population. Although statistics are imprecise, the pattern is indisputable. The Confederate period brought about the most dramatic urban growth that the South had ever seen, and even if hard times in the postwar economy erased many of these changes, they were nonetheless real—and unprecedented—for Confederates.[22]

Thus, in material and immaterial ways the military effort transformed Southern society in four short years of war. The existing resources of the

South were redirected to the war effort, and new resources were developed to sustain the war. The government took men from their farms and sent them to the army. It spent unprecedented sums to expand factories, build new ones, and staff new military-related bureaus. It taxed incomes and crops and authorized army officers to seize from civilians huge quantities of private property that were needed in military operations. As rural areas became depopulated of adult males, towns and cities experienced booming growth. Such changes caused dislocations, suffering, and hunger, and as these problems deepened, they led to serious resistance. It was with the development of widespread opposition that a new aspect of the militarization of the South appeared.

Military force soon became a means to enforce change and suppress internal resistance, so that the many innovations of the war effort could go forward. When dissent became resistance or threatened key policies, a government that was reshaping its society for military purposes turned to military power to enforce its programs and suppress opposition. Thus the South militarized its society directly as well as indirectly. Force usually came into play to give immediate support to the war effort. The impressment of supplies brought thousands of ordinary citizens into unpleasant contact with the military power of the state. Opposition to the draft soon spurred new military interventions into civil society. But as desertion and disaffection grew, these problems reached such dimensions in many localities that they threatened to undermine the entire structure of authority and legitimacy in Confederate society. Force then became necessary to preserve law and maintain social order.[23]

Officials could not ignore the swelling numbers of deserters, but legal sanctions often made the problem worse. As the North Carolina private who believed his "first duty" was to aid his family commented, "if we go [home] without authority we are arrested & punished. . . ."[24] Many men who shared his belief about their first duty and who resented the unequal treatment and unequal sacrifice that characterized the war effort were not content to suffer the penalties of the law. To help their families while demanding justice they chose to resist arrest. Banding together, they hid and camped out in wooded or mountainous areas. To assist their loved ones, they stole from the barns of wealthier families and from local officials who had "remained at home ever since the war commenced."[25] Often, in this process, they exacted retribution from a more privileged class that was enforcing the law against them. Organizing themselves as necessary, these deserters began to threaten or supplant the existing organs of civil authority.

Throughout the southeast, in remote or inaccessible areas and especially along the ribs of the Appalachian mountain chain, deserters and draft resisters became a force to be reckoned with. Citizens began to speak of "deserters' country." Reports poured into Richmond and into state capitals of "Mobs of deserters and disloyal men and women . . . Rob[b]ing and plundering the good and Loyal citizens of their Guns and their Scanty stock of provisions." Judges refused to hold court for fear of attack, while others worried that the county seat would be burned to the ground. "Robbing houses and stealing and shooting down Cattle in the woods has become to be [sic] the order *of the day*," reported one prominent North Carolinian, and another admitted, "We bolt & bar our doors every night, not knowing what hour they [the deserters and "Bushwackers"] may make their appearance." People became unwilling to travel the roads in certain areas, and in the waning months of the war bands of 300 or 400 deserters were often "bold and defiant" enough to fight pitched battles with regular troops.[26] "In nearly every county" of northern and southeastern Alabama there were reports of frequent "depredation[s] by deserters and ruffians." It was estimated that northern Alabama sheltered 8,000 deserters as early as July 1863, and one scholar has judged the problem to be "larger than that of any other Confederate state." Well before the war was over, a North Carolina official acknowledged that resistance had "overawed" the authorities in many areas. In November 1863, Assistant Secretary of War John A. Campbell declared that "the condition of things in the mountain districts of North Carolina, South Carolina, Georgia, and Alabama menaces the existence of the Confederacy as fatally as either of the armies of the United States."[27]

To counter such alarming resistance, the Confederate government resorted to the internal use of force. Army commanders were eager to take measures to suppress desertion, and they often acted on their own initiative. Preferring to establish more conventional channels, the secretary of war tried to bolster the authority of the Bureau of Conscription by giving it a military arm. On September 8, 1863, he authorized the bureau to raise "a battalion of six companies of mounted men" in each of the states of Georgia, South Carolina, and North Carolina, where desertion was rife. These mounted troops would be used "for the purposes of conscription, the arrest of deserters, and for local defense." As they pursued deserters, they were to coordinate their work for the bureau with the efforts of the regular army. Where "commanding generals" had charged some of their officers "with the duty of arresting and returning deserters and absentees," the War Department directed such officers to report to "the commandant of conscripts" in the states to which they were sent.[28]

The internal use of military force seemed to have the potential of bringing good results. In states further west—Tennessee, Alabama, and Mississippi—army units placed under the control of General Gideon Pillow had already been rounding up conscripts and deserters with alacrity. General Pillow boasted of his "complete net-work of organization which is spread like a map all over those portions of the States in our possession." He predicted that his "active corps of officers with supporting forces of cavalry will soon sweep the country clean of deserters and conscripts, and must,

John A. Campbell. As Assistant Secretary of War, this former Justice of the U.S. Supreme Court participated in the Hampton Roads Conference and was intrigued by Lincoln's and Seward's statements. (Courtesy of Library of Congress)

to the exhaustion of the population, rapidly build up our armies." In a short time Pillow's forces had added "several thousand" men to the armies in Tennessee and Mississippi. One unit in Selma, Alabama, reported 1,344 men sent to duty, while a force in Tuscumbia, Alabama, rounded up 334 men in the month of August alone. Pillow recommended that the government extend "this organization . . . over the States east of the Mississippi."[29] He and other military men were impatient with the more constrained and bureaucratic methods of the Bureau of Conscription, which was less efficient but equally unpopular.

But the three battalions authorized for the bureau were hardly a competent force, even for the states of Georgia, South Carolina, and North Carolina, for the scope of desertion required stronger methods. Even General Pillow argued that his force was much too small. "Cast your eye over the extent of our territory," he urged Secretary of War Seddon, "and you will at once perceive how inadequate is the working force . . . to coerce the reluctant population of the country to enter the Army." At that point Pillow had twenty companies of troops "actively engaged" in Alabama and Mississippi, but they were "inadequate" to their task without "forces of cavalry detailed by the commanders of departments." Even with the assistance of regular cavalry forces, Pillow declared that he could not deal with the large numbers of deserters that were hiding out in the mountains of Alabama. But Pillow's rough methods were so unpopular that the central government was unwilling to turn his operations into a regular and constant feature of the effort to support the armies. Rather than expanding his authority, it tended to rein him in as the war went on.[30]

Without a large force for internal coercion, the Confederacy turned to the regular army at intervals, to suppress crises. When conditions became too threatening, the government sent regular troops into the countryside to battle deserters, thus militarizing law enforcement and imposing another layer of military control on society. Repeatedly the government detached troops from the armies of Generals Lee or Bragg or Johnston and ordered them into troubled areas to combat resistance and capture deserters. In North Carolina alone, Confederate units left their regular posts to round up deserters on three different occasions between the fall of 1862 and the fall of 1863.[31] With military efficiency or ruthlessness, army units used force against disaffection. The benefits of the internal use of the military were not unmixed, for every soldier taken from the front lines represented a weakening of the armies, while the application of military force behind the lines had only a temporary effect. Military suppression did not remove the root causes of desertion and resistance, and therefore these ills quickly reappeared as soon as the regular army's troops were withdrawn. In addition, if troops had to live off the land, they often aggravated the suffering of civilians and deepened discontent.[32] But all these actions were a dramatic departure from the accustomed patterns of civil society. They militarized society and shored up the army's strength without bringing unquestioned benefits.

On a few occasions military forces suppressed dissent in an unauthorized manner. Perhaps the worst example of this kind of intrusion into civil society occurred in North Carolina in the fall of 1863. W. W. Holden, editor of the *Raleigh Standard* and a prominent leader of the old Democratic Party, launched a campaign for negotiations and peace. Saying that "the great mass of our people desire . . . a cessation of hostilities, and negotiations," the *Standard* pressured the government to enter into negotiations. "We have lost Missouri, Maryland, Kentucky, Tennessee, the Mississippi Valley, Texas, Louisiana, Arkansas, and considerable portions of other states," Holden argued. "We cannot hope to add materially to our forces. . . . It is time to consult reason and common sense." These views struck a chord with many North Carolinians, who organized a hundred peace meetings within two months, but they were very unpopular with soldiers who were making painful sacrifices to carry on the war. On September 9, 1863, troops from a Georgia brigade that was passing through Raleigh attacked the *Standard*'s office, destroying the paper's type and trashing the premises. A timely personal intervention by the state's governor restrained the troops from doing further damage, but the incident left Holden shaken, and two days later the governor again had to restrain an Alabama regiment.[33]

Adding to the militarization of daily life were the actions of state governments, whose leaders also felt compelled to use force against deserters and disaffected elements. In fact, the state militias were often the first line of military defense against internal resistance, because governors generally preferred to use their own state troops to suppress opposition rather than call for Confederate units. As desertion and resistance grew, the state militias took on responsibilities for enforcing the law and restoring order, and their actions frequently were none too gentle. In North Carolina in 1864, the militia dealt so harshly with the families and relatives of deserters that Governor Vance asked a prominent judge and politician, Thomas Settle, to investigate. After visiting several of the state's central piedmont counties, Settle reported that one prominent deserter's wife had been physically abused by officers who were completely unrepentant. Moreover, Settle found that in three counties "some fifty women in each county . . . were rudely . . . dragged from their homes & put under close guard." Not only were such arrests without warrant and illegal, but "the consequence[s] in some instances have been shocking. Women have been frightened into abortions almost under the eyes of their terrifiers."[34] Settle began prosecutions to punish militia officers, but clearly the suppression of internal opposition was leading to bitter personal reprisals.

The Confederacy did not become a totalitarian police state—there was a great deal of protest, complaint, or dissent in the South. But the govern-

ment used military force to control behavior—to crush resistance from deserters, to combat lawlessness, and to guard against and discourage disloyal acts. In doing so, it injected the military into civil society and violated
supposedly sacred values of civil liberty in ways that long went unrecognized. The use of military power to police civil society enforced the overwhelming importance that the Confederate government assigned to the war.

Just as the internal use of military power illustrated the recasting of priorities within the South, so too did the restrictions on individual freedom.
When Jefferson Davis addressed the Confederate Congress at the beginning
of the war, he declared that Southerners wished only "to be let alone." The
Confederacy wanted to enjoy the "legitimate exercise of the right of a
people to self-government." Its purpose was to preserve and defend cherished rights and liberties established by America's Founding Fathers, and
Davis argued that his government, not Lincoln's, was the true embodiment
of American principles of liberty. Because the North, according to Davis,
had repeatedly encouraged a "consolidated" or centralized government and
trampled on Southerners' rights, Confederates were left as "the last best
hope of liberty."[35]

Thus, the Confederacy's restraints on liberty were both surprising and a
dramatic illustration of how far the South had traveled from its avowed
principles. In fact, the Confederacy's journey away from civil liberties for
the white population and toward extensive military control was much more
extensive than scholars had recognized. Until 1999 historians had taken
Jefferson Davis' boasts about the South's devotion to constitutional rights
pretty much at face value.[36] Then Mark Neely Jr. published *Southern
Rights: Political Prisoners and the Myth of Confederate Constitutionalism*,
a book whose research forces scholars to revise many previous conclusions.[37] With a sharp eye for the significant, Neely took note of individual
documents that were scattered throughout a huge collection of letters to
the Confederate secretary of war. These documents gave indisputable evidence of thousands of irregular arrests and detentions. These had occurred
persistently and on a large scale, but because the evidence was not gathered together in one place, it had remained invisible and its significance
overlooked. Neely's findings raise profound questions about what the Confederacy's core values were and how drastically principles could change
under the stress of war.

Prewar Southern politicians had been known for their assertive individ-
uality, their belligerence against those who would want to control them,
even their violence in interpersonal relations. Yet within a few short months
a governmental leviathan was coming into being, and Southerners, including Confederate politicians who served in Richmond, were submitting
meekly to constant and intrusive supervision of their freedom of movement.
A senator from Texas complained about the fact that he was "not allowed
to go from [Richmond] . . . to North Carolina without going to the Provost

Marshal's office and getting a pass like a free [N]egro." Another congressman, Senator John W. Lewis of Georgia, detailed the system:

> When Congress shall adjourn I wish to go home, but before I can be permitted to do so I must get someone who can identify me to go along with me to the Provost Marshal's Office to enable me to get a pass. At the Provost's I shall be met at the door by a soldier with a bayonet. After getting the pass, I shall be again met at the [railroad] cars by other armed men, and be obliged to obtain other passes and undergo other examinations.[38]

J. B. Jones, the diarist and War Department clerk who ran Richmond's passport office from August 1861 on, reported that "the origin" of the office "consisted merely in a verbal order from the first secretary of war" and admitted, "There was no law for it." Nevertheless he controlled all travel out of Richmond, and before long he was issuing up to 1,350 passes per day. Armed soldiers patrolled not only the trains and coaches around Richmond but rail lines and important roads in many parts of the Confederacy.[39]

The War Department began to require passports in the summer of 1861. The original intent was to control the immediate area of military operations, but "it proved impossible to confine the use of passports to the vicinity of the armies."[40] As military operations affected new parts of the Confederacy and as disaffection or threats of disloyalty grew, the army's supervision of movement spread. Historian Mark Neely concluded that passports were required "nearly everywhere by the summer of 1864." A British visitor who was traveling from Mississippi through Alabama to Tennessee in 1863 found that a sentry blocked the door of each railway car and examined everyone's papers "with great strictness"; after passengers boarded the train, an officer from the provost marshal's department repeated the inspection. Tennessee's outspoken politician, William G. Brownlow, described the situation with more ire: "Every little upstart of an officer in command of a village or crossroads would proclaim *martial law*, and require all going beyond, or coming within, his lines to show a pass, like some [N]egro slave." Similarly, a Virginian objected in 1863 that guards on the road between Franklin and Petersburg were stopping and searching all carts and wagons "on the *public highway*" and thus interfering with his "Constitutional Liberty."[41]

Although the passport system may have been the most ubiquitous instance of governmental interference in the lives of ordinary citizens it was not the most serious. The military frequently made illegal arrests, imprisoned people without trial, held them for indeterminate periods, and committed other violations of the normal, peacetime rights of citizens. In fact, from the beginning of the war until its end, Confederate commanders often acted on their own, whenever they judged that there was a necessity for military control. For example, Colonel Solon Borland was one of the first to take action, issuing his own declaration of martial law in Arkansas in November 1861. Although Borland's order was later overturned by the War Department, that did not deter other commanders worried about disloyalty. General John Magruder ordered the arrest of several civilians in Texas even though he admitted that martial law had not been declared and that he had no legal authority to do so. Magruder's action illustrated the thinking of many in command—he felt it was sufficient to explain that "military necessity" had compelled him to take action.[42]

The provost guard, the army's police force, was responsible for rounding up stragglers or deserters, maintaining discipline and order, and suppressing disloyalty, and its duties often led to deep intrusions into civil society. It had imposed the passport system mainly to combat desertion. To maintain order it closed saloons, broke up distilleries, and enforced curfews. Vigilance against disloyalty led to many arrests of civilians, and perhaps it was understandable that many provost officers took strong actions. The Confederate Articles of War, which guided the provost's action, contained some broadly worded clauses, such as the following:

> Article 56: Whoever shall relieve the enemy with money, victuals, or ammunition, or shall knowingly harbor or protect an enemy, shall suffer Death, or such other punishment as shall be ordered by . . . a court-martial. Article 57: Whoever shall be convicted of holding correspondence with or giving intelligence to the enemy . . . shall suffer death.[43]

On their face, these words seemed to apply to civilians as well as to soldiers, and in the emergency of war, provost guards often ignored distinctions between military law and civil procedures.

So many people suspected of Union sympathies were arrested and searched in 1861, following passage of "An Act respecting alien enemies," that two special commissions were appointed to investigate abuses. Governors, cabinet officials, and even the War Department inveighed against the numerous arrests of civilians, but none of these protests stopped actions that provost guards perceived as necessary. In an effort to minimize the detention of civilians, the provost guards were ordered to make prompt and detailed reports of their arrests. Some districts reported faithfully, but others were dilatory, unreliable, or simply ignored the order. The historian of the provost guard, Kenneth Radley, concluded that "in many instances [it] rode roughshod over the rights of citizens." One provost marshal arrested a man, seized his property, and then sold it at public auction. Collisions with the civilian judiciary were common, and not infrequently military officers defied the orders of judges.[44]

Suspension of the writ of *habeas corpus* and declarations of martial law gave legal authority for many of the infringements of civil rights that were occurring, but they did not make them less drastic. Faced with evidence of illegal arrests, Jefferson Davis recognized the need for congressional action and first requested power to suspend the writ of *habeas corpus* in the fall of 1862. The lawmakers promptly passed an appropriate statute that was renewed and extended until February 13, 1863. One year later Davis again requested suspension of the writ, and Congress gave new authorization from February 15 to July 31, 1864. Even before that law had expired, Davis saw the need for another renewal. In May he asked Congress to suspend the writ again and repeated his request in August. In this case, however, although bills to that effect passed in one house or the other, no measure gained the approval of both bodies of Congress to become law.[45]

Suspension of the writ swiftly led to martial law in many urban areas, and commanders such as General John H. Winder in Richmond imposed stringent military control. Typically they restricted or forbade the sale of liquor, seized corn from distillers or issued orders against distilling, sequestered firearms, took over much of local policing, and gathered information on all people moving in or out of the area. Often commanders used their military power to address other problems, such as shortages or rising prices, that plagued the citizenry. In Richmond, Mobile, and New Orleans, the military imposed price controls and seized goods from their owners. These steps, surprisingly, won as much praise as criticism. The *Atlanta Daily Intelligencer* decreed blessings on "the day when martial law shall relieve us from the intolerable oppression" of "monopoly and extortion," and many individuals wrote to the War Department in praise of strong actions that might alleviate suffering.[46] But there were infringements on speech and on individuals' rights and freedom as well. As the military guarded against those who might be disloyal, it scrutinized dissidents, critics of the administration, or suspected Unionists. Military commanders sometimes called on citizens to inform on others who might be security risks, and they imposed censorship in Richmond, Charleston, New Orleans, and Vicksburg. The orders of censorship went beyond concern for protecting the secrecy of troop movements. For example, General Earl Van Dorn ordered newspapers to publish nothing "calculated to impair confidence in any of the commanding officers."[47]

Most seriously, thousands of people were arrested and held, including an unknown number for short periods of time. Mark Neely's research identified over 4,000 individuals whose incarceration became lengthy enough to generate inquiries and records of their examination.[48] After early arrests by the military of people who seemed suspicious or possibly disloyal, detentions only became more common as the prospects of the Confederacy grew more desperate, and the Southern nation never established a satisfactory system for determining the guilt or innocence of suspects. In the summer of 1861 General Winder, who was then supervising military prisons in Richmond, noticed that detainees were becoming numerous, and he recommended to Secretary of War Leroy Pope Walker that steps be taken to examine and release those who did not pose a real threat. In response, Walker asked two Richmond lawyers to examine and "pass upon" cases of this type.[49] This was the origin of the system of *habeas corpus* commissioners that the Confederacy developed to deal with those arrested by the military.

At first the *habeas corpus* commissioners were a few individuals, rather informally appointed. Later Congress established their office by law and granted to them the powers of district court judges. But throughout the life of the Confederacy, these commissioners functioned in a casual, extrajudicial manner. Individual commissioners inquired more or less closely into the status of detained citizens and kept records of their investigations that were fairly complete or very sketchy—depending on the inclination of the commissioner. The commissioners reported only to the secretary of war, if they reported at all. As Mark Neely summarizes this system (which hardly deserves to be called a system):

> There were no penalties for failing to report, for inaccurate reports, or for lost or misfiled reports. The commissioner could recommend a prisoner be freed or turned over to civil authorities for trial, but no other powers were known or advertised. As a matter of fact, the commissioner had a very great power frequently exercised: he could simply *not* recommend their freedom and in effect sentence them to long confinement in military prison.[50]

A few lawyers and congressmen protested against the military's detention of citizens, but the Confederate government deflected these complaints and held to its course. In the fall of 1862 Adjutant General Samuel Cooper admitted that civilians should not be tried by military courts martial, but he argued that "the power to *arrest* offenders continues in the Provost Marshal. . . ." Army officers needed no encouragement to put perceived military needs above individuals' civil rights. The Confederate army continued to arrest people that it viewed as dangerous or suspected of disloyalty, including those who were simply too outspoken in their criticism of the government or were considered to be Union men. The fate of all these detainees then rested with the action or inaction of the *habeas corpus* commissioners. Clearly the existence of these officials provided no reliable safeguards for the rights of suspects, and by 1863, as Mark Neely has pointed out, Jefferson Davis ended his proud boasts that the Confederacy was scrupulously respecting civil liberties.[51]

Thus, the war effort had profoundly altered civil affairs in the Confederacy. To support the military, the South reorganized its economy and way of life, damaged the welfare of its ordinary citizens, and jettisoned its core

values of limited government and individual rights for white men.
were vast changes—truly a "revolutionary experience" in the words
scholar, or "state socialism" in the estimate of another, or "a degree of control over civil life unique in American history" as summarized by a third.[52]
They inject a new dimension into the customary discussion of civil-military
relations in U.S. history. Whereas one normally asks whether civil authorities maintained control over the military, here one must ask instead
whether things military took control of the civil realm, transforming it almost beyond recognition.

How did such radical changes come to be? Who made the decisions that
led to this state of affairs? Were the civil authorities really in control, if the
military could exert such a profound influence on long-standing traditions,
customs, and beliefs? Was the military accountable to civilian authorities
and to the political system's majority? Was there judicial control over military power? And since Confederates shared in the wider American culture,
what does Confederate history reveal about the civil-military relationship
in American society?

The answers to these questions lead beyond normal analysis of politics
and institutions, because the experience of Confederates was not normal.
Their society was in a profound crisis—indeed, during at least half of the
war it was in an accelerating process of disintegration. With surprising ra-
pidity, Confederates confronted the need for unprecedented change, but no
sooner had they argued over and debated radical measures than they found
that events were controlling them, forcing them to contemplate unpalatable
choices and compelling them to live in a world they did not own. In a deepening crisis, political elites acted in ways that revealed their true values, and
ordinary citizens made unaccustomed choices in order to survive. Both
groups abandoned, to a greater or lesser degree, their customary beliefs.
Because the events of war overwhelmed Confederates, the normal boundaries between civil and military realms crumbled and became permeable.

At first the Confederacy's political leaders demonstrated that they were
willing to adopt bold and unpopular measures in order to prosecute the
war. The executive branch, directed by Jefferson Davis, took the lead and
remained always in advance of Congress on such measures. It was Davis'
administration that called for a draft, advocated new economic directions,
sought suspension of the writ of *habeas corpus*, and pressed constantly for
men and materiel to strengthen the armies. Through April 1862, when conscription was adopted, it can be said that members of Congress were adapt-
ing and choosing to move in unfamiliar directions, although they were
alarmed by the pace of change. Thereafter, while the Davis administration
remained determined to do what was necessary to gain independence, it
steadily became more questionable how much the legislature supported new
measures of military necessity.

For two reasons, the will of Congress diverged from its official actions.

As shown in chapter 2, legislators from occupied regions increasingly held power in decision-making, and these lawmakers were men without responsibility, freed by circumstances from any consequences of the votes they cast. They did not have to face their constituents over stands that they took, and their districts paid none of the taxes and shared in none of the sacrifices mandated by their ballots. For representatives of the core areas remaining under Confederate control, the lack of a legitimate opposition party and the cultural imperatives of an aggressive, masculine patriotism inflated support for the administration. No congressman or senator was willing to appear unpatriotic in the crisis, and in fact legislators vied with each other during debates to present a façade of determination. These facts influenced many to vote, at least for awhile, in favor of measures they abhorred. But by 1864 most representatives from the Atlantic seaboard—the still beating heart of the injured new nation—were opposing the strong measures that sustained the war effort.[53] The elite within areas of Confederate control demonstrated that it was not willing to pay the high price that was demanded for independence.

Whether the majority of the Confederacy's citizens supported the militarization of their society also is questionable. On the one hand, ideological opposition to the unprecedented measures of the administration and the army came mainly from portions of the small planter elite. It was the wealthy slaveholders who fought the impressment of their slaves or the burning of their cotton, and the leading foes of Jefferson Davis and the vocal champions of states' rights were privileged politicians such as Robert B. Rhett and Joseph E. Brown. Among ordinary citizens, there is abundant evidence that many accepted intrusive government policies or even called for stronger measures because they saw that local authorities could not solve their problems. Rather than suffer further from rampant inflation, unequal burdens, and shortages of food, in desperation they called on the government to act and alleviate their pain. These people wanted a more powerful central government, or a larger state administration, if either one could be effective.[54] On the other hand, as conditions deteriorated and growing numbers of Southerners saw the Confederacy as a failed government "on her way up the spout," many people turned against Richmond's policies and withdrew their cooperation from the war effort.[55]

By 1863, opposition on the home front was spreading rapidly in the same way that desertion was growing in the army. While one prominent senator observed that "the disposition to avoid military service is . . . general," an obscure farmer railed at an impressment agent that "the sooner this damned Government fell to pieces the better it would be for us."[56] As the Confederacy demanded more from its citizens, it simultaneously lost the ability to protect them or maintain conditions necessary for their traditional way of life. In such circumstances, the government forfeited the support of a growing portion of its people. Ordinary Confederates rebelled quietly by withdrawing their support from the government and minimizing their cooperation with the war effort. As a result, the coercive power of the army became more and more predominant in keeping the war effort going. Voluntary support in the society and political system was diminishing, to be replaced by the military's resources of coercion. The government depended more and more upon the internal application of military force.

Thus, there is reason to question whether the military remained truly subordinate to popular authority. Jefferson Davis and his administration favored the military's efforts, and Congress acquiesced, but the government was becoming increasingly more dependent on the army—not just for its effectiveness but for its ability to function. Without military force the civil administration was weak, and the authority of its elected officials was slender and steadily decreasing.

It also is difficult to say that the military remained under effective control by the judiciary. Throughout U.S. history, a double and contradictory truth has persisted: Americans declare their belief in and commitment to the inalienable rights of the individual, rights that government cannot violate. Yet society allows infringements of these rights in time of collective danger. The greater the threat, the more extensively it seems that violations of civil liberties are tolerated, from the Alien and Sedition Acts through the internment of Japanese Americans to the nonjudicial incarceration of "enemy combatants." The principle of action seems to be that civil liberties are sacrosanct in normal times but merely desirable when the nation is in peril. Under Lincoln at least 15,000 civilians were arrested and held without trial or judged by military tribunals, and the Supreme Court remained quiet until after the war was won.[57] In the Confederacy fewer arrests may have occurred but the courts were no more effective in protecting sacred individual liberties.

On occasion a state court judge questioned the authority of the Confederate government, but only occasionally. In fact, the most significant protests against infringements of civil liberties came from a single jurist, Richmond M. Pearson of North Carolina. Pearson was the chief justice of his state's supreme court, and when the three-member court was not meeting in full session, each of its justices could hear cases and act for the court "in vacation." On several occasions Judge Pearson strongly challenged the suspension of the writ of *habeas corpus*, and he even invented new theories to limit suspension's scope and impact when there was no doubt that Congress had legally suspended the writ. Yet Pearson's actions were concerned only with releasing men (often rather privileged individuals) from military service. He did not act in defense of other civil rights, and he soon was outvoted and controlled by the court's other two justices, whose actions reflected the general posture of the Southern bench. Indeed, as Jefferson Davis pointed out, the state courts of the Confederacy, acting in the absence of a national supreme court, uniformly sustained the central government or declined to take up challenges to its authority. This outcome was surprising given the fact that for decades before the Civil War leaders of Southern society had thundered against Northern usurpations of their rights and had seemed obsessed with constitutional limitations on central power. During the war, though some prominent politicians denounced Jefferson Davis, they never mounted effective action to stop him, and the judicial system was remarkably quiet. Reflecting on these facts, Mark Neely concluded that Confederate society "was not obsessive about liberty. . . . Southern society, or large portions of it, desired order."[58]

Confederates themselves marveled at the extent of their submission to military necessities. Even the *Daily Richmond Enquirer*, a newspaper that was usually supportive of Jefferson Davis and his policies, reflected that, "We are not yet fully awake to the extent to which we have abdicated popular Government." Although Confederates had not, like the ancient Romans, "entrusted supreme and unlimited power to a Dictator . . . we have almost drifted into it."

> [W]e have . . . stripped ourselves, as a people, of one right after another, until power has passed almost without reserve, from the many to one, from the people to the ruler. . . . [T]he plea of military necessity has been presented in all its bearings, and its demands set forth in plain, candid words. The urgency of the plea has been acknowledged by us, and . . . we have willingly and cheerfully surrendered one privilege of freemen after another.[59]

For these developments the *Enquirer* did not blame Jefferson Davis, though other newspapers called him a tyrant. In fact, as the *Enquirer* noted, Davis had used "no cunning device, no base trick" to gain power. In their crisis Confederates had decided, time after time, that they "must have a strong central Government during the war." But even the *Enquirer* warned its readers that Southerners needed to be alert to reclaim their "national freedom and individual liberty."[60]

Thus, the history of civil-military relations in the Confederacy uncovers questions that go to the heart of Southern values and Confederate purpose, questions to which we will return. That history also demonstrates that military crisis can quickly transform society and that Americans have been willing to allow military needs to compromise prized political values very deeply. For in the Confederacy, society became militarized to a degree unmatched in U.S. history, and civil-military relations rapidly came to be defined by the drastic and multifarious efforts to support the war.

5

Military Power and Civil Debility

Although the Civil War transformed Jefferson Davis' Confederacy in remarkable ways, the high point of military influence over civil authority came not under Davis, but under one of his subordinates in a corner of the Confederacy far removed from Richmond. West of the Mississippi River, General E. Kirby Smith commanded the Trans-Mississippi Department, an assignment that was supposed to embrace the states of Missouri, Arkansas, Texas, and most of Louisiana, plus the Indian and Arizona Territories. Partially occupied, constantly threatened, poorly armed, and increasingly demoralized, this region experienced all the problems of the Confederacy in exaggerated degree. Some of the state governments of the trans-Mississippi region were essentially fictions, sovereignties led by homeless secessionists who claimed to represent territory occupied and controlled by Union forces. Throughout the department morale was low, and conditions on the home front were very discouraging. In the army things were no better, for Smith's command, though it generally had sufficient food, lacked arms, supplies, and in many cases both competent commanders and fighting spirit. Yet, ironically, Kirby Smith may well have exercised more unlimited, unsanctioned power in his crumbling fiefdom than any elected official of the Civil War era.

The region that contemporaries came to call "Kirby Smithdom" was certainly no easy command assignment. On paper its resources were impressive. It embraced about 2.8 million whites and blacks, plus upward of 60,000 Native Americans, most of whom belonged to the "Five Civilized Tribes"—the Cherokees, Creeks, Chickasaws, Choctaws, and Seminoles. Missouri had the largest population of almost a million souls, almost 90 percent of whom were white, whereas the four-fifths of Louisiana's land that lay west of the Mississippi River was home to 245,000 slaves and only

E. Kirby Smith. Faced with difficult and unprecedented circumstances, Smith assumed executive and civil powers that went well beyond his military role. (Courtesy of Library of Congress)

163,000 whites. Economically, Missouri had the largest number of factories and a varied agricultural output that included tobacco, wool, flax,
hemp, corn, wheat, pork, and other foodstuffs. Louisiana, in addition to
some rich sugar and rice plantations, produced large amounts of cotton,
and cotton also dominated in Texas and Arkansas. The population of the
region had been growing rapidly, and many parts of Texas and Arkansas
were still expanding frontier.[1]

In reality, however, the assets of the trans-Mississippi were fewer and
the challenges for Confederate commanders greater than one would think.
In many areas sentiment for secession had not been strong. Historians agree
that, "Much of Arkansas had been strongly Unionist" and that a "strong
minority," especially in the northwest part of the state, remained loyal to
the Union. Outside of its cotton counties there was never much enthusiasm
for the Southern cause, and enlistments consistently bore this out. In
Louisiana the overrepresentation of wealthy planters had helped them to
carry their state out of the Union. Secessionists were clearly the majority
in Texas, but pro-Union governor Sam Houston voiced the feelings of many
Texans in the northern and central portions of the state. As for Missouri,
its people assembled in a convention and rejected secession; thus, the "government" that seceded in the fall of 1861 was a rump legislature that met
in Neosho rather than in the state capital. In the next four years Missouri
would supply more than twice as many soldiers for the Union as it provided to the Confederacy. By the time Missouri "officially" seceded and entered the Confederacy, Union forces already controlled most of the state,
and its Confederate leaders were essentially on the run.[2]

Before long other trans-Mississippi politicians were sharing their fate.
By March 1862 Union forces seized the northern half of Arkansas, and
thereafter they pushed their power southward; by the end of 1863 the federal troops controlled almost all of the state. Also, "by September, 1862,"
writes historian Robert Kerby, "the Confederate Territory of Arizona was
nothing but a dim memory." Although most of Louisiana west of the Mississippi remained officially Confederate until the last phases of the war,
Union power and influence along the Mississippi River spread rapidly.
When Henry Allen was elected as the Confederate governor of Louisiana
in 1863 by a margin of more than 8 to 1, his smashing victory rested on
a total turnout of only slightly more than 8,000 voters. Meanwhile, in
Texas and elsewhere, dissatisfactions grew, trade with the enemy burgeoned, and large numbers of refugees poured into the area, straining its
social system, consuming its resources, and contributing little to the war
effort.[3]

This was the region that Jefferson Davis designated a separate military
department in May 1862 and of which Kirby Smith took command in January 1863. The region consisted of three military subdistricts: Arkansas,
which under Smith was commanded first by General Theophilus Holmes

and then by General John Magruder; Texas, which Magruder headed until General John Walker replaced him later in the war; and West Louisiana, for which General Richard Taylor had responsibility through most of the war. Except for the aggressive and fearless Richard Taylor, who had no West Point training but deserves most of the credit for turning back Nathaniel Banks' larger federal force during the 1864 Red River campaign, these generals were rather ineffective. All of them were hampered by shortages of weapons and a lack of enthusiasm among those left in the region after the early volunteers crossed the Mississippi to fight in the eastern armies. Kirby Smith himself proved to be a better administrator than fighter. Perhaps because he was keenly aware of the problems facing his command, he was cautious and generally defensive-minded in battle.[4]

These military leaders also faced an uphill struggle against the widespread demoralization of the civilian population. In 1862 Richard Taylor complained of the "notorious" fact that draft evasion was rampant in West Louisiana, and so many men fled to Texas that General Magruder urged that state's governor to call out his militia to hunt down the draft dodgers. By December 1, 1862, Governor Thomas Moore of Louisiana warned that his state might secede from the Confederacy unless Louisiana soldiers east of the Mississippi were allowed to return to their state. Meanwhile Texas authorities had to put down two armed rebellions, one among German American Unionists and another among Unionists on the northwest border. The next spring, when Kirby Smith relocated his headquarters from Alexandria, Louisiana, to Shreveport, he found that no one wanted to rent property to him. Their goal, he believed, was "to prevent headquarters being established here." By 1864 what few troops the department had were rebellious enough that they refused to cross the Mississippi River when ordered to serve in the eastern Confederacy.[5]

Yet ironically, in this unpromising theatre General Kirby Smith gathered into his hands more power than any American military commander has ever exercised on U.S. soil. Smith took over many powers that belonged to the Richmond government. Before long he was exercising authority that belonged not only to the executive departments of the government but also to the Congress, and his officers did not hesitate to face down the Confederate judiciary. Moreover, he gained remarkable power over the states' civil authorities, sometimes despite resistance but more often without opposition. In conditions of crisis and great vulnerability, Kirby Smith came to represent the greatest locus of power that remained in the transMississippi Confederacy. As defeat approached, his role expanded as if he were the administrator of an internal empire. He was something unique in our history: an American proconsul on American soil.

Although the trans-Mississippi region was never a crucial theatre of the war, events went so badly in the first year of conflict that Confederate officials had to reconsider their whole approach to the region. Initially the states in this region belonged to different military departments whose boundaries were soon contracting. In Missouri former governor Sterling Price switched his allegiance to the Confederacy and organized 10,000 state guardsmen in the southwestern part of the state. Price, whom Jefferson Davis later called the vainest man he ever met, thereafter clung to the delusion that thousands of Missourians were just waiting for a chance to come to the aid of the Confederacy. In August he fought a successful battle against U.S. forces, but in September he was forced to withdraw into northern Arkansas. That same summer small contingents of Confederate troops marched into what the Southern government called Arizona territory. General Henry Sibley had dreams of conquering not just New Mexico but also Colorado and California. Sibley won an initial battle in February 1862, but in March his small force was defeated near Santa Fe, and his retreat from the territory ended operations in the far west. Meanwhile, early in 1862, General Earl Van Dorn had thrown 17,000 Confederate troops against a force of 11,000 federal troops at Elkhorn Tavern, near Fayetteville, Arkansas. Although this was one of the very few times that Confederate forces in the trans-Mississippi enjoyed a numerical advantage, the attack failed. Van Dorn retreated and then, acting upon orders to support Confederate troops in Mississippi, left the region. His Indian allies returned to Indian Territory and, becoming steadily more disillusioned, played little role in the war thereafter.[6]

The defeat at Elkhorn Tavern forced Confederate officials to think about a more effective organization for defense of the region. Governor Thomas Moore of Louisiana soon added to the pressure for change. Reacting to the fall of New Orleans in April 1862, Moore urged President Davis to form a new military department west of the Mississippi. These events led to the creation of the Trans-Mississippi Department on May 26, 1862, and its organization a few months later into the three districts that Kirby Smith would inherit.[7] The first commander of the department was General Thomas Hindman, whose strong and unhesitating measures accurately foreshadowed the kind of power that Kirby Smith would attain. Admittedly acting "without authority of law"—and without apology—Hindman raised troops, established manufactories, seized and burned cotton, executed deserters, and declared martial law over all of Arkansas.[8] These rough methods began to bring an increased measure of security to the area, but Richmond was not ready to approve such aggressive, extralegal initiatives. General Theophilus Holmes replaced Hindman but soon was asking to be relieved. After further setbacks in Arkansas, Secretary of War James Seddon concluded that Holmes had "lost the confidence and attachment of all" in his district and that "disorder, confusion, and demoralization [were] everywhere prevalent." Accordingly, the government placed Kirby Smith in charge of the Trans-Mississippi Department in January 1863.[9]

Smith, a career soldier who had graduated in the middle of his West Point class, made his headquarters at Alexandria, Louisiana, and began working to bolster the department's defenses. Knowing that he could not rely entirely on Richmond, Smith acted on the necessity of developing resources within his control as a means of supplying the armies. He focused on the relatively secure areas of northwest Louisiana and east Texas as localities in which he could establish and encourage war-related industries, and in this effort he benefited from extensive cooperation from the states. Their legislatures appropriated money to produce small arms, powder, cannon, gun carriages, mining operations, leather, textiles, and even telegraph wire, and Smith detailed conscripts to work in the factories as needed. Smith's army also directly operated many important factories to produce arms and equipment, and his Clothing Bureau produced so much cloth that at the surrender "Smith's soldiers were probably the best-dressed troops in the Confederate army."[10] But before these efforts could produce much benefit, the parameters within which the Trans-Mississippi Department existed changed.

The fall of Vicksburg revolutionized Kirby Smith's situation. When Union forces gained control of the Mississippi River, with superior naval and infantry power at hand to hold and exploit their prize, they cut the Confederacy in two. Substantial support for the Trans-Mississippi Department from the eastern Confederacy was not just unlikely thereafter; it became impossible. Confederate forces in the east, outnumbered and beleaguered, would call upon Kirby Smith's units for aid rather than lending him support. Ordnance and supplies for his armies would not be forthcoming from Richmond. Even shipments of the national currency and correspondence with the War Department and the president became tenuous, uncertain, and unreliable. The entire Trans-Mississippi Department found itself in a new and unprecedented relationship with the Confederacy.

Authorities in Richmond recognized that a turning point had been reached. "Immediately after the fall of Vicksburg," Secretary of War James Seddon dispatched to Smith a letter whose text has been lost. Apparently Seddon sought to impress upon Smith that he now would have to act independently and shoulder major new responsibilities that were not of a military nature. A month later Seddon began to worry about the scope of his comments and then stressed to Smith that he had written "unofficially." But we know from Smith's description of this letter that Seddon had recommended "calling to my aid the ablest and most influential men of the country, the formation of a civil and military government, and the establishment of bureaus of the War Department."[11]

What, exactly, Seddon might have meant when he referred to Smith's forming a "civil and military government" is unclear, and the secretary of war continued to back away from the implications of his words. "When it was suggested, in my former semi-official letter," Seddon wrote in October 1863,

> that you would have to exercise powers of civil administration, it was, of course, only meant such matters of an administrative character as were naturally promotive of or connected with military operations and appropriately pertained to the executive functions of the Confederate Executive.

There was "no idea," Seddon added, "of either dispensing with or trenching on the civil powers belonging to the States or to the civil administration thereof." But the secretary protested too much. Clearly he had recognized—though he could not openly affirm it—that the physical division of the Confederate nation made Smith the locus and embodiment of the entire national government west of the Mississippi. Without the executive and legislative branches, and with only a few Confederate judges west of the Mississippi, the army *was* Confederate authority. Kirby Smith would have to act, quite independently, to express and maintain the authority of the Confederacy's national administration. In carefully chosen official words, Seddon stressed to Smith that he now had "the great duty of defending the Trans-Mississippi States and of holding them firm to the Confederacy." He suggested that such responsibilities required, immediately, using artillery to keep the United States from opening the Mississippi River for trade, destroying planters' stores of cotton, and removing slaves from plantations within 8 to 10 miles of the river.[12]

Jefferson Davis also recognized that an unprecedented situation called for unusual measures that could scarcely be reconciled with the constitution. Only ten days after the fall of Vicksburg, the discouraged and hard-pressed chief executive wrote to Smith that "your department is placed in a new relation." Not only would General Smith face greater difficulties after the U.S. victory, but also he now had "not merely a military but also a political problem involved in your command." Davis probably meant these words generally, but he also was specifically worried that efforts to split the trans-Mississippi region off from the Confederacy would grow. Davis was aware of dissatisfaction in the region. Like Seddon, he worried about "a feeling . . . in favor of a separate organization." To hold the west in the Southern nation, the president urged his general to consult with the governors and work with them while making his department self-sufficient and developing war-related industries. In the tone of this letter, Davis revealed his assumption that Smith would have to act with great independence. The president chose to advise, rather than to instruct, his military subordinate; he wrote as if he were talking with another executive. And he closed with an apology: "It grieves me to have enumerated so many and such difficult objects for your attention when I can give you so little aid in their achievement."[13]

For his part, Kirby Smith accepted the fact that military realities required him to exercise unusual powers, military and civil. Even before receiving the first letters from Seddon and Davis, Smith warned Adjutant and Inspector General Samuel Cooper that, "Without the assumption of extraordinary powers, my usefulness as department commander will be lost." He feared after Vicksburg that he would not be able to communicate with Richmond, and he sought instructions. But he had no doubt about his future direction.

> Whilst my whole course as a military commander has hitherto been to keep within the limits of the laws, and to refrain from the exercise of powers not strictly granted me, I feel that I shall now be compelled to assume great responsibilities, and to exercise powers with which I am not legally invested. I trust the President will support me in any assumption of authority which may be forced upon me, and which will be used with caution and forbearance.

When this letter reached President Davis, he embraced the spirit of Smith's comments and wrote on the letter, "I shall have no difficulty in sustaining any assumption of authority which may be necessary. Able heads of departments should be selected, and large discretion allowed."[14]

Smith continued to pledge his good intentions. In September he assured Davis that, "I feel great hesitancy and repugnance in assuming any powers not clearly expressed or implied by my position as department commander." He hoped that his "acts will be reviewed with leniency" in light of the "troubles and difficulties" against which he was struggling. And he promised to take new powers "only when impelled by necessity." But Smith's troubles and difficulties were very near, whereas Richmond was far away. A few days before he penned this letter to President Davis, Smith had named a man as tax commissioner for the state of Arkansas, citing "the authority conferred upon me by His Excellency the President of the Confederate States." He also instructed this appointee to send copies of all his reports to military headquarters, in light of the poor communication with Richmond and the absence of a Treasury Department agent. A few weeks later Smith learned by letter that a treasury officer was supposedly on the way. To Jefferson Davis he announced that except for that letter "I should ere this have taken the matter into my own hands. If I do not hear from Richmond, I will be compelled to establish here both a sub-bureau of the Treasury and Post-Office Departments, and will have to raise a loan from the people on certificates, pledging the faith of the Government to redeem them in interest-paying bonds."[15] Smith was as bold in approaching these civil matters as he was cautious in military operations.

Over the next several months Kirby Smith proceeded, with administrative energy and determination, to establish separate, trans-Mississippi versions of most of the War Department's functional offices and bureaus. A western copy of Richmond's war department came into being, with such offices as Inspector General, Adjutant General, Ordnance, Quartermaster, Subsistence and Commissary, Conscription, Medical, Niter and Mining, and Transportation. Historian Robert Kerby records that sixteen executive and military agencies, in all, came into being, staffed by troops and officers draw from field units. These facts distressed many commanders, and General Richard Taylor bitingly complained that Smith's staff was larger than "that of Von Moltke during the war with France," but Smith had little alternative. To complete his separate organization, he ordered that all reports that would normally be required in Richmond should instead be sent to his headquarters, either in Shreveport, Louisiana, or Marshall, Texas.[16]

As the war continued and Smith's independent actions mounted, the attitude of Richmond authorities became more complex. Jefferson Davis' caution began to assert itself, probably due both to political considerations and to constitutional scruples. Secretary of War Seddon, however, took a more realistic and ruthless view. As early as May 1863 Seddon had favored giving Smith great latitude to deal with the demands of his situation. In order to buy supplies in Mexico for the army, Smith's quartermasters needed cotton. Since they could not compete on the open market with private cotton buyers, who were paying in specie, Major and Quartermaster S. Hart sought permission to impress cotton from its owners. Kirby Smith promptly authorized this action, sending word to Hart that he could make impressments "whenever you may deem it necessary and indispensable for carrying on the operations of the Government." But Hart sought reassurance from Richmond as well. "Unless the department takes all the cotton in this State [Texas] and controls the entire transportation to convey it to the Rio Grande, the army cannot be supplied," Hart wrote to James Seddon. This appeal received consideration and comment from Secretary of the Treasury C. C. Memminger, President Davis, and Seddon.[17]

Memminger took a conservative position, reading Congress' law on impressments carefully and narrowly. The Congress had authorized the army to seize all kinds of private property "whenever the exigencies of any army in the field are such as to make impressments . . . absolutely necessary." Only an immediate and *military* necessity, Memminger argued, could justify impressments. Taking cotton in order to raise money was not a military necessity. Thus, although cotton could be piled up on the decks of a ship to absorb rifle bullets, it could not be seized to buy food, clothing, or ordnance for the soldiers. To justify his bold plan, Kirby Smith would need a new law from Congress. President Davis endorsed Memminger's opinion, saying that it "seems to me conclusive." But Seddon urged a more expansive view. Arguing that the law regulating impressments included the power "to impress any property when deemed necessary for the good of the service," Seddon also noted that Smith's quartermasters would not be having trouble if the treasury secretary could "manage to keep his notes at some fair relation to approximation to specie." In fact, Memminger was not even sending an adequate amount of currency to the trans-Mississippi west.[18]

When Davis did not reply to these points, Seddon could do nothing, so the desperate quartermaster soon renewed his appeals. Hart reported that he was "gravely embarrassed for want of funds" and could not pay for cotton "as it is being ready to deliver." Other officials, even including Quartermaster General A. C. Myers, gave support to Hart's plea, noting that for six months merchants in Brownsville and Matamoras had supplied Kirby Smith's army upon the government's promise that it would deliver cotton to them. Now the government had no way to pay its suppliers. In such dire circumstances, Seddon urged President Davis to give attention to "the great importance and even necessity of commanding the export of the cotton" in Texas. But Davis, who was always very reluctant to exceed legal or constitutional limits, withheld his approval. Writing that "I have never been willing to employ such means except as a last resort," Davis simply avoided the pressing question of whether there was any alternative left to Smith's quartermasters.[19]

James Seddon continued to be supportive of Smith, giving him as much latitude as possible in coping with the problems of his department. And Smith forged ahead, creating his own Cotton Bureau in August 1863 in order to impress the cotton that he needed. When Quartermaster Hart then complained to Richmond that his orders to do all the purchasing of cotton in upper and western Texas had been vitiated, Seddon backed Smith strongly. To the general Seddon declared that, "The matter is felt to be justly and necessarily subject to your judgment," and to Quartermaster Hart the secretary of war explained that, "the discretion on the whole subject, embracing even your continuance in your present duties, must be and is vested in General Smith."[20]

With these events, patterns that would continue through the remaining months of the war were set. Authorities in Richmond recognized that Kirby Smith's situation was unprecedented and required extraordinary measures, and much was done to accommodate him, but there were limits beyond which Jefferson Davis would not go. When those limits were reached, Smith often simply did what he felt was necessary, for he was in effect the final authority in his far off department. And he knew it. In a private, family letter, he wrote that he was responsible for a "vast empire, the weight of whose government both civil & military is thrown on my shoulders."[21]

In September 1863 Smith argued to Richmond that "the appointing power in cases provided for by law should be delegated to the commander of this department." Here he raised an issue on which he and the president would not agree. Jefferson Davis' reply, communicated through James Seddon, was that, "The power to appoint cannot be delegated." But Davis and Seddon suggested a simple evasion—that Smith make temporary appointments or promotions of officers and send his actions to Richmond for approval. The president, Seddon promised, has a "disposition to . . . sanction the promotions of all judicious appointees."[22] What was judicious to Smith, however, did not always seem wise or necessary to Jefferson Davis. In June 1864 Seddon informed Smith that Davis had not approved a number of appointments of generals, because the president alone had that power, and he believed that too many general officers were being named for a department whose troop strength was modest. This was not the only occasion on which Richmond overruled Smith on appointments, but it often took months for such an outcome to be determined.[23] In the meantime, Smith followed his own inclinations.

On other subjects Jefferson Davis tried to be helpful, and Seddon always was supportive. Davis wanted the Treasury Department to issue funds in the trans-Mississippi region, so that Smith would not be dependent on uncertain shipments of currency, but that department never came close to meeting Smith's needs. In December 1863 Davis recommended legislation to Congress to provide "for the exercise of temporary authority" in the trans-Mississippi "until regular action can be had at the seat of government."[24] Davis was well aware that communication with Smith was difficult; in 1864 he wrote to the general that he was *trying* to send him all laws and general orders. He added,

> I am in hopes that you will hereafter be kept well advised of the action of the legislative and executive departments. As far as the Constitution permits, full authority has been given to you to administer to the wants of your department, civil as well as military. An officer of the Treasury Department has been appointed for the Trans-Mississippi.

Significantly, when Davis commented negatively on Smith's impressments of cotton, he merely wrote, "In my opinion there is no authority in law . . . for the purposes designed by you."[25] There was no milder way for the president to signal his disapproval.

Seddon did his part to strengthen Smith's authority and keep up his morale. In a letter of June 1864, he discussed Smith's position and explained to the general that he was trying not to give advice on policy because he preferred "to leave matters very much to be regulated by your own experience, better knowledge, and sound discretion." Seddon asserted that he would "content myself with giving to your measures and administration a liberal support and sanction." For that reason the secretary of war opposed the idea of appointing an assistant secretary of war for the Trans-Mississippi Department. Even though such an official, Seddon explained, was "intended to be subordinate to you," the title alone might undermine Smith's authority. "My own judgment was and is," Seddon concluded, "that you should, in your capacity as commander of the department, combine with your strictly military duties somewhat of that relation (as far as our Constitution allows) to the Department and the President."[26]

Clearly General Smith shared that judgment, and given the growing threat of U.S. forces and the distance between Shreveport and Richmond, he was free to take strong action with little effective interference from the Davis administration. The military situation did nothing to lessen his resolve. In July 1863 federal troops won a clear victory at the Battle of Honey Springs, the largest and last engagement in Indian Territory, and then turned toward Little Rock. Within a couple of months Union general Frederick Steele would seize Little Rock while his fellow officer, General James Blunt succeeded in occupying Fort Smith. The Confederacy's hold on Arkansas was now reduced to a band across the southern portion of the state. In September and October, Smith's forces had better luck in blunting federal offensives along the coast of Louisiana. Determined artillerymen under Lt. Dick Dowling managed to damage and drive away a naval force that attempted to sail up the Sabine River, and Richard Taylor had success against federal troops that were attempting to advance northward up the Bayou Teche toward Opelousas. Because that area had been "repeatedly overrun by the two armies" and stripped of supplies, the federal commander spread his forces out to enable them to forage, which allowed Taylor to attack and drive them back toward the coast. Nevertheless it was apparent that Taylor's and the other Confederate forces were outnumbered and vulnerable, and efforts by Governor Moore to raise more troops produced "barely enough men to serve a single cannon."[27]

With citizens in the district feeling both hard-pressed and insecure, the challenge to Smith's assumption of civil authority would arise closer to home. From some of the state leaders in the trans-Mississippi would come major opposition to his policies. Their theoretical warnings, uttered in the summer after Vicksburg fell, matured into direct confrontations over state rights and the power of civil authorities vis-à-vis the military. Nowhere in the Confederacy was the conflict between the military and civil authorities more clear or direct. And yet nowhere, ultimately, was the submission of civil authority to the military more complete.

After the fall of Vicksburg, Kirby Smith recognized that the altered situation increased his need to work harmoniously with state leaders. Not only were there new challenges ahead, but he also worried about the "despondency and hopelessness" that were affecting the population. "I determined," he explained to Jefferson Davis, "upon calling together the executives, judges, and representatives of the several States, that by obtaining their support and cooperation, and by invoking the power of the States and acknowledging the supremacy of the civil laws, confidence might be restored, and the people feel that a Government remained to them capable of administering to their wants and necessities." As historian Robert Kerby has point out, it was questionable that any conference called by the military authority would increase people's confidence in the supremacy of civil law. But state leaders recognized that a crisis had been reached, so they, too, felt the need to meet and confer. On August 17, 1863, in Marshall, Texas, Smith and a top echelon of state leaders from the trans-Mississippi met and considered their future. All four states sent representatives. By this time Missouri scarcely had a Confederate government aside from Governor Thomas Reynolds, but he was in attendance. Governor Harris Flanagin of Arkansas, much of whose state was occupied by federal forces, sent as his representative Senator R. W. Johnson and two other prominent officials. From Louisiana came Governor Thomas Moore, an army official, and two judges, and Texas sent both Governor Francis Lubbock and Governor-Elect Pendleton Murrah, plus two others.[28]

Kirby Smith shaped the meeting by submitting a six-point agenda for consideration. Smith's points addressed various conditions in the region and put on the table "the extent of the civil authority to be exercised, referred to in the letter of the Secretary of War, July 14." In response, the state leaders divided into three committees that met, debated the issues, and drew up written reports that spoke to a number of problems. Their reports noted, for example, that the trans-Mississippi had never received more than "a meager share" of arms and munitions to fight the war. "As to the temper of our people," wrote these leaders, "we are compelled to report some disaffection and disloyalty and more despondency in all the States of the department." This was a considerable admission from men who were trying to rally the populace and were determined to put the best face on a serious problem. On the question of the extent of civil authority that Kirby Smith would exercise, the statements of these leaders were somewhat inconsistent.[29]

One of the committees sent a shot across the bow of Kirby Smith's prospective ship of state by declaring the importance of states' rights and civil authority. "It could not have been the intention of the Secretary of War," wrote the group chaired by Judge Edwin Merrick of Louisiana, "to advise the commanding general to exercise civil authority which belongs to the States. . . ." Secretary of War Seddon must have intended, Merrick reported, that Smith merely exercise such powers "as are now exercised by other officers at Richmond . . . according to existing laws, and that nothing should be changed, except the agents by which the operations of the Government in respect to this department are carried on." Although this was, in itself, a considerable admission, the committee chaired by Governor Reynolds of Missouri embraced the military's role in civil affairs more enthusiastically. "The safety of our people," wrote Reynolds,

> requires that he [General Smith] assume at once and exercise the discretion, power, and prerogatives of the President . . . and his subor-

dinates in reference to all matters involving the defense of his department. . . . [W]e believe that all may be done without violating the
spirit of the Constitution and laws of the Confederate States, and
without assuming dictatorial powers.[30]

These statements indicated that the region's political leaders may not
have forgotten states' rights and the primacy of civil authority, but they
seemed ready to accede to unusual powers wielded by a military commander. Only the imminent peril and fragile condition of the Trans-
Mississippi Department could explain such an attitude. The governors
certainly were aware of the demoralization in their region, and as their conference came to a close they joined in a declaration intended to bolster
morale. The loss of Vicksburg, they insisted, was in reality far less serious
than it seemed. Effective resistance would continue under Kirby Smith,
whom they praised as a vigorous and experienced general with "a profound
respect for law and the constitutional rights of the citizen." They urged
"every patriot" to support him zealously as he exercised the "more than
usual powers" given him by the president. Finally, they declared that, "The
enemy may dismiss all hopes that the western section of the Confederacy
will seek any destiny separate from that of our sisters east of the Mississippi." Their citizens, they insisted, were bound to the Confederacy "by
community of race, institutions, and interests" as well as common sacrifice.[31] But the strength of this assertion could not disguise the fact that it
was meant for internal consumption and intended to boost the low morale
of the region.
    As Kirby Smith reported to Jefferson Davis, the situation of the Trans-
Mississippi Department was deplorable. Smith had no money to support
the army's needs, and he estimated that he could not assemble an effective
force of more than 15,000 to face the expected operations of 80,000 U.S.
troops. Moreover, wrote Smith,

    The despondency of our people, their listlessness, their deafness to
    the call of both the civil and military authorities, the desertions from
    our ranks, checked neither by vigor nor clemency, all indicate despair
    and abandonment. Without men, without arms, with a people so de-
    moralized by speculation that submission is preferred to resistance,
    the immense efforts being made by the enemy must be crowned with
    success.[32]

These realities—grim as they were—gave Kirby Smith a fairly free hand
during the rest of the war. His policies and initiatives met with virtually no
resistance from the overrun or constantly threatened states of Missouri and
Arkansas, and his problems with Louisiana's civil government were few.
But he soon faced major confrontations with the governor and legislature
of Texas.

Smith's troubles with Texas began in the fall of 1863 as the insecure condition of that state's northern and western frontier worsened. Already a
loss of confidence in the government's ability to maintain order had led to
violence against slaves and vigilante actions.[33] Moreover, settlers in this
area of Texas had faced devastating raids by Native Americans from the
High Plains since the last half of the 1850s. Comanches as well as Apaches,
Kiowas, Lipans, and Kickapoos frequently resorted to violence to resist the
steady encroachment of settlers upon their traditional hunting grounds.
Measures against the tribes on the frontier usually proved futile, as had
been the case since colonial days. Static forts placed in a sparsely populated region could not control mobile warriors, and until a region filled up
and pushed the frontier further west, mounted patrols were usually too few
and too small to catch and deter the Native American warriors. Before secession, the U.S. Cavalry had briefly restored some calm to the area, but
thereafter Texas troops, mainly the Frontier Regiment, had been ineffective. In 1862 these raids continued and many settlers fled from Gillespie
and Clay counties, abandoning their homesteads. Moreover, the status of
the Frontier Regiment was in dispute between the state and the Confederacy. Texas took the position that these troops defended the Confederacy's
western border and therefore should be supported financially and materially by the nation. Jefferson Davis was willing to accept the units into Confederate service, but he balked at the state's insistence that these troops
should never be moved from the border.[34]

By the summer of 1863 conditions on the frontier were no better. In fact,
with the arrival from various parts of the Confederacy of many deserters
and draft evaders, who formed armed bands and hid out along the frontier, it could be said that things were growing worse. To provide security,
both Confederate forces and the Frontier Regiment were patently ineffective, as were militias or "minute companies," and Kirby Smith's efforts first
to pardon and then to round up the deserters and recusant conscripts had
failed. Residents defiantly warned that their men would not "stay in the
army . . . when they hear that their wives and little ones are being mur-
dered by the savage Indians." At this point the Texas legislature, fed up
with the Frontier Regiment, finally authorized its unconditional transfer to
Confederate service. But since some protection had to be found for the
frontier regions, Texas lawmakers passed a series of laws to reorganize and
strengthen its militia. Among the changes made was a new provision declaring that the men of militia age in fifty-four northern and western counties were exempt from Confederate conscription. These men would be the
source of a frontier militia, whose commanders were required to keep one-
fourth of their troops always on patrol.[35]

Kirby Smith promptly protested, as did General John Magruder. They
made the obvious point that no Confederate state could rightfully exempt
whole counties from the application of laws passed by the Confederate
Congress. On constitutional grounds, Smith and Magruder were unques-

tionably right. The Confederate Constitution contained a supremacy clause whose purpose was to make clear that national laws putting into operation the powers granted to the national government were superior to state preferences. Yet this confrontation did not reach the boiling point. What happened in fact was that Smith's and Magruder's forces on the frontier shrank, the Frontier Regiment went into Confederate service, and the state militia forces took over responsibility for the defense of northern and western Texas, without notable success.[36]

It is difficult to avoid the conclusion that Kirby Smith permitted Texas to win this round, even though his position clearly was valid. Something had to be done about the frontier counties. With residents outraged over their imperiled condition, it was obvious that few troops, if any, could be raised from the area. The priorities of Smith's department lay elsewhere, and the only drawback to tolerating Texas' action was the likelihood that this frontier region became more attractive to deserters than it had been before. But in practical terms he lost little by letting the state organize militia in that area to provide its protection. On matters that affected the vitality of his department more directly, Smith would not be so passive.

The issue that aroused him to determined defense of his power and interests was cotton. This staple had quickly become the lifeblood of the wartime economy and the only hope for the finances of the Trans-Mississippi Department. Despite the richly profitable cultivation of rice and sugar in limited areas of southern Louisiana, cotton had been *the* staple crop of the trans-Mississippi region. Secession and war only made cotton more valuable, as the South's policy of withholding cotton and the North's efforts to blockade ports reduced supplies. The Confederacy's Provisional Congress had outlawed trade with the United States at the beginning of the war, and a combination of several state laws and patriotic encouragement by the Confederate government had reduced exports and shifted production toward foodstuffs. As time passed, the U.S. blockade, though very porous at first, steadily became more effective, and thus the supplier of three-quarters of the world's cotton—the South—suddenly had reduced production and was shipping even less than it produced.

The demand for cotton would not abate. Not only did the textile mills of Great Britain and Europe need raw material, but the United States needed cotton to support the industrial economy of New England and to supply uniforms, blankets, and other materials for its troops. In accordance with classic economic laws, the combination of these facts led to soaring prices for cotton—a fact that was noticed with special clarity in "Kirby Smithdom." For in the whole Confederacy, the Trans-Mississippi Department possessed the most ubiquitous and attractive opportunities for exporting the staple. Along the lower Mississippi River, Union cotton buyers, speculators, and treasury agents came into frequent contact with Confederates who had access to supplies of cotton, and however illicit it was, trade began to flourish. Moreover, all along the Texas coast, blockade runners had manifold opportunities to ship cotton by ocean to foreign countries or to middlemen who would deliver it to New England. Still more impossible to interdict was the overland trade across the Rio Grande to Mexico. Across from Port Isabel at the southern tip of Texas, a wide-open town, dubbed Bagdad [sic], suddenly mushroomed where huge piles of cotton bales were exchanged and many varieties of crime flourished. Matamoras, across the Rio Grande from Brownsville, also played a major role in cotton exchange, and if circumstances interfered with the commerce in these areas, buyers and sellers merely moved up the Rio Grande and continued their business in a variety of towns as far northwest as Eagle Pass. With so much demand and so many opportunities, there was no way to stop the trade in cotton.[37]

Thus, Kirby Smith and other officials in the region saw commerce in cotton grow as government finances contracted. As commanding general, Smith needed funds to buy rifles, obtain food for the army, establish factories that could supply ordnance and equipment, pay the troops, and meet a host of other pressing needs. He faced soaring prices, a desperate shortage of Confederate money, and the rapidly spreading refusal of citizens to accept anything but specie as payment for their goods or services. The obvious and only feasible solution was cotton, and Smith acted. "As early as March, 1863," notes Robert Kerby, Smith had James Seddon's approval to "circumvent the law" by authorizing agents to trade Confederate cotton for Northern manufactured goods.[38] Then, as noted above, Smith established his own Cotton Bureau in August 1863.

The Cotton Bureau was to take charge of the acquisition and sale of cotton to serve the department's purposes, and Smith had no legal power to create it. Nor did he ever claim that he had proper authority. Instead he based the justification of his action on practical necessity. This proved to be a fairly effective argument with Richmond's authorities. Perhaps they kept in mind the depressing particulars of reports that reached them from officials in the Trans-Mississippi Department. For example, in November 1863, the department's assistant adjutant and inspector general wrote that the department lacked arms, with 10,000 stand "needed immediately" and 30,000 needed in all. Ammunition was scarce. "The troops have not been paid since the 30th of April last, nor are there funds to pay them." Another report in February 1864, declared that 30,000 stand of small arms was an "absolute necessity" and that the department's troops "have been paid up to August 30, 1863." Perhaps as a consequence only 31,780 of the 73,268 soldiers on the rolls were actually present for duty.[39]

Whatever the reason, James Seddon reacted mildly to Smith's assumption of powers. Initially, in October 1863, he merely suggested that Smith could benefit from dropping the name, Cotton Bureau, and carrying out its functions within his Quartermaster Bureau. The next year, in August 1864 (more than three months after Jefferson Davis had shared his "opinion" that the law did not support Smith's action), Seddon referred to the controversies and "complaints" that had followed the Cotton Bureau and informed Smith that Davis had decided to place the procurement of cotton under the Treasury Department, "to which less of popular jealousy will probably attach." In name this decision put an end to the Cotton Bureau, but in fact, concludes historian Robert Kerby, "nothing . . . really changed. The Cotton Bureau continued to function . . . impressments continued to flourish."[40]

The reaction of Texas officialdom, however, was not nearly so mild. Political pressures from outraged planters combined with the ideology of states' right to produce a major confrontation between Texas and the Confederacy's trans-Mississippi commander. Impressment of any property was always unpopular throughout the Confederacy, and in Texas, where inflation was raging, cotton prices were high, and buyers were available, planters' resentment over the loss of their most fungible asset burgeoned. At the end of 1863, the Texas legislature reorganized its Military Board and issued new bonds that Governor Murrah could use to obtain supplies for Texas troops. Murrah then announced a state-sponsored plan to obtain cotton in return for the bonds. There were several highly attractive features to Murrah's initiative. In return for exchanging half of their cotton for the state bonds, planters would be credited with market prices for that portion of their crop and, in addition, the state would transport the other half of their crop as state property—immune from impressments—to Mexico. There it would be returned to the planter, who then could sell it to the highest bidder. By comparison, when Kirby Smith's officers impressed cotton, they could pay only the prices authorized by law, which were as little as one-third of the market value, and the Confederacy did not transport any cotton for the planters to sell. Obviously the army could not compete with this state plan, and Smith's agents soon discovered that much of the cotton crop had already been sold to the state.[41] Murrah was about to put the Cotton Bureau out of business.

Smith quickly contacted the governor and began a process of negotiation that stretched over four months. Smith mixed a consistently respectful and diplomatic tone with some bold moves of his own and ultimately employed a lightly veiled threat based on military realities. At the beginning of April 1864, he asked Governor Murrah to modify his plan, admitted that his department had not managed the cotton business properly before he established the Cotton Bureau, and patiently pointed out that Texas' plan would hurt the army. Because General Nathaniel Banks' federal army was beginning its campaign up the Red River, Smith felt he could not meet in person with Murrah, but he sent an emissary to try to resolve the conflict. At this point the Texans remained adamant. Murrah rejected Smith's arguments, and the legislature passed a resolution that hotly denounced impressments, Smith's impressing officers, and the taking of any goods at less than market value.

Smith retaliated with tough talk of his own. By this time he had received Congress' law of February 6, 1864, that gave the national government power to control exports and to demand that half of all exports would serve the war's needs. Even though Smith did not have all the details of the new legislation, he announced that half of the cotton sold had to go to his Cotton Bureau and that he would control export licenses strictly. If planters refused to sell at the government's prices, he promised to impress it. In this way he was going to use national law and his military power to control the cotton trade and obtain the supplies that he needed. Tempers flared in response to this, with Murrah denouncing the threat to his state's sovereignty and Smith charging that Texas' policy would severely damage the army.[42]

Despite the exchange of heated words, Smith wrote two respectfully worded but determined letters to Governor Murrah on July 4 and 5, 1864. In these he pledged his cooperation whenever possible and protested that his training as a soldier did not equip him to work deftly in the civil realm. He recited the extreme difficulties he faced as commander in the trans-Mississippi. Patiently he explained why the Texas plan vitiated his efforts to supply the army. Then, in what may have been the most effective of his arguments, Smith observed that Murrah's actions meant that the troops "are now without the arms, clothing, hospital or ordnance stores for an effective campaign. Their condition . . . fills me with the most anxious concern, and in case of invasion . . . the most alarming apprehensions." Finally, after pledging to obey the courts if they were to rule that he could not impress, Smith said that he would take his case to the people of Texas. They would learn from him, Smith quietly indicated, that Murrah had made it impossible to support their husbands, sons, and brothers who were risking their lives in the field.[43]

Surprisingly, these arguments won the day, as Murrah suddenly capitulated. After a meeting with Smith, the Texas governor issued a public address to his citizens in which he echoed Smith's arguments that only impressments could provide for the soldiers' needs and allow the army and their region to survive. Giving up any further application of his plan, he urged every patriotic planter to cooperate with General Smith and offer up his cotton to the impressment agents.[44] On other occasions and in other battles east of the Mississippi, Jefferson Davis ultimately prevailed in struggles between unpopular Confederate laws, on the one hand, and belligerent assertions of state sovereignty, on the other. But never did Davis have the satisfaction of seeing his opponent surrender in this way.

Perhaps the desperate condition of the trans-Mississippi explained this and other victories for Kirby Smith. For although the department remained highly vulnerable, only the military had stood between its citizens and sub-

jection in 1864. That spring federal forces launched a two-pronged offensive aimed deep into Louisiana's interior. General Nathaniel Banks, with
27,000 troops and substantial naval support, pressed northward along the
Red River while General Frederick Steele, with 12,000 men, attacked
southward from Arkansas. The two wings of this pincer were to converge
on Shreveport. Predictably, the small Confederate forces had to fall back,
but Richard Taylor was determined to fight. Ignoring Kirby Smith's repeated counsels of caution, Taylor positioned his men in a good defensive
location near the town of Mansfield and attacked. The ferocity of the Confederate soldiers and their unexpected boldness routed the federal troops.
But after this battle and another attack a few miles to the south, Taylor's
entire force had shrunk from 12,000 to only 5,000 men. The Red River
helped save him from danger, as low water nearly grounded the federal
flotilla and made Banks feel fortunate to escape southward toward New
Orleans. Learning of this retreat, and hampered by a shortage of rations,
Steele also withdrew toward Little Rock after meeting some determined
Confederate opposition. Narrowly and surprisingly, the Confederate army
had defended the district against superior federal forces but not against
physical destruction. Governor Allen of Louisiana called the interior of his
state a "scene of desolation," and General Taylor declared that "The destruction of this country by the enemy exceeds anything in history."[45]

The Trans-Mississippi Department remained vulnerable and demoralized. Despair grew among hard-pressed citizens on the home front. In Texas
internal divisions had already caused W. P. Ballinger, a prominent political
leader, to confide to his diary that secession had been "the work of political leaders" without strong support from "the *mass of the people* without
property," and the military situation only aggravated people's misery.[46] The
contagion of hopelessness spread rapidly to the army. Later in 1864, when
the War Department ordered General Taylor and infantry from Texas and
Arkansas to cross the Mississippi River and support operations in the East,
there was a widespread refusal to comply. Governor Flanagin of Arkansas
and a senator from that state warned that "our troops will not go; they
will throw down their arms first." Texas troops also began to desert in
greater numbers, and "at least one 'open mutinous outbreak under arms' "
occurred. General Taylor recognized that he could move any substantial
number of troops across the Mississippi only at the cost of a mutiny, and
therefore he cancelled a crossing in which he had had little confidence any-
way.[47] The defenders of the trans-Mississippi district were few and weak,
but they were all that stood between the citizenry and further destruction.

As commander of these forces, Kirby Smith continued to take strong actions even as the structures of ordinary social organization continued to
weaken and fall away. He and his officers confronted the courts during
1864 and made naked claims to power. In essence, they asserted the military's right to take whatever steps it felt was necessary, regardless of the

Richard Taylor. General Taylor had not attended West Point, but he proved to be a bold, aggressive, and successful commander in the Trans-Mississippi West. (Courtesy of Library of Congress)

law, to fight the enemy. Without hesitation or apology, Smith trampled on state authority, and again he got away with it. He likewise confronted Confederate authority and demonstrated his readiness to defy the courts. Both instances involved individuals who were charged with treasonous actions.

In Texas late in 1863 the army arrested five individuals that it believed were engaged in treason against the Confederacy. A few months later their attorney went into state court and filed motions seeking their release from military confinement. A key fact in this case was that the military's arrests had taken place when no suspension of the writ of *habeas corpus* was in effect. Even later, as court proceedings in *Ex Parte Richard R. Peebles, and Others* went forward and the Confederate Congress passed legislation that authorized Kirby Smith to suspend the writ and move against treason, he never exercised such authority. Throughout most of the legal proceedings the military defended its actions simply by arguing that its action was necessary.

When the case went before the supreme court of Texas, the justices ordered that the army should turn the prisoners over to civil authorities and show why they should be held. In response, representatives of Kirby Smith and General Magruder presented convincing proof of treason and then forcibly seized the accused from the local sheriff. An outraged court ordered that the sheriff should regain custody of the accused and demanded that the arresting military officer show why he should not be held in contempt. When that officer explained that he had acted under orders, the court warned him that unconstitutional orders were illegal and condemned the actions of the military authorities. The justices decried "military control" over the civil authorities and described it as "a vital blow at the constitution and the principle upon which our government is organized."[48]

Thus the civil authority of the Texas courts came into direct confrontation with military power. The court next required General Magruder to show why he should not be held in contempt, an action suggesting that it would also defend the fundamental rights of the prisoners. What happened instead amounted to capitulation by the Texas authorities in both arenas. General Magruder now tried to defend himself before the court by invoking the law passed by Congress that allowed suspension of the writ of *habeas corpus*. On that point the supreme court found, accurately enough, that no suspension had ever taken place, because Kirby Smith had not availed himself of the law. It then criticized Smith for taking the law into his own hands, but it declined to punish Magruder, since he was Smith's subordinate, and it did no more than refer the matter to Governor Murrah. "The situation of the country," said the court, "forbids our attempting to punish [Magruder] by imprisonment." Then, when it took up the status of the prisoners, the court chose empty gestures over any meaningful defense of individual rights. Officially it insisted that the prisoners had to be turned over to civil authorities, but simultaneously one of the justices hinted that if the army would surrender the prisoners, they would be released and then left to the army's tender mercies. Precisely that occurred, and General Magruder promptly expelled them into Mexico without further semblance of legal proceedings.[49]

The Confederate district court was somewhat less cooperative with the military but failed to uphold its own authority in a meaningful way. A man named Andrew McKee had been working as a major purchasing agent in Kirby Smith's Cotton Bureau when it was discovered that he was aiding the enemy. The military arrested McKee, tried him before a court-martial, and sentenced him to death. McKee's attorneys made a strong case for his release based on two undeniable facts: McKee had never been commissioned by the War Department or Congress and thus was not actually a member of the military; and the writ of *habeas corpus* had not been suspended, so the military had no right to arrest him. After angry debates between the Confederate states district court judge for West Louisiana and the commanding general of that subdistrict, the court compromised and then went back on its word. The presiding judge insisted that the military hand McKee over to him but promised to see that McKee faced civil charges. Acting on that promise, the army surrendered McKee only to find that the judge allowed him to post bail. McKee fled and escaped punishment, but the court could not be said to have upheld the majesty of the law. In fact, throughout the trans-Mississippi district at this time more and more residents were taking the law into their own hands and ignoring both police and courts.[50]

In the last months of the war, defeat and the futility of continued resistance became more and more real to all the soldiers and civilians in the Trans-Mississippi Department. A final raid into Missouri by General Sterling Price failed to accomplish anything, as Price proved that he understood nothing about cavalry operations, and as Missourians demonstrated once again that they were not on fire with enthusiasm for the Southern cause. Deadly skirmishes between Union and Confederate forces along the Rio Grande quietly came to a stop, as soldiers on both sides recognized that further killing would have no impact on the war's outcome. Meanwhile trade with the enemy and with Mexico accelerated as individuals looked out for themselves and patriotism became irrelevant.[51] With every passing day there seemed to be less reason to maintain the fiction that the Confederate states had a future.

In these darkening circumstances, Kirby Smith undertook his last initiative into an area that is normally off-limits to military personnel under the U.S. tradition of civil-military relations. Considering means to stave off the Confederacy's demise, Smith turned to international diplomacy, and though he was cut off from Richmond, Smith settled on a strategy that paralleled that of Jefferson Davis himself. Smith could not know in January 1865 that the president had just sent Duncan Kenner to France with a proposition to end slavery in hopes of bringing France and Britain into the war. Yet Smith settled on the same strategy and took the same kind of action. He sent General Camille Polignac, a Frenchman fighting for the Confederacy who had led the attack at Mansfield, Louisiana, back to his native country with a letter to Ambassador John Slidell. In his letter Smith held out assurances that the planters of his district were ready to abandon slavery, and he also suggested that the emperor's recently established government in Mexico would benefit from the recognition and cooperation of the Confederacy.

Perhaps this desperate, last-minute foray into diplomacy constitutes the best possible evidence that Kirby Smith was a conscientious and loyal proconsul, for acting on his own and without information from his commander, he replicated the foreign policy of the Confederate government.[52]

Yet the fact remains that the civil-military traditions of the United States do not allow for a general who conducts a foreign policy on his own, or acts in place of the Congress and the president, or imposes his will through military power (or the threat of military power) on courts, states, and other civil authorities. "Kirby Smithdom" was a huge exception to the values that have usually been practiced in our country, and Smith's exceptional actions went beyond anything done by Abraham Lincoln or Jefferson Davis at the same time. In a steadily deteriorating situation, Smith wielded a kind of imperial power within his own country as the agent of the state. He was an American proconsul on his own soil. In this regard there is little comparison with the influence that military leaders exerted—through more customary channels—on policies of the Confederate government.

6

Military Men and
Civil Policy-making

In the U.S. tradition of civil-military relations, certain principles of civilian control have vital importance. Among these are the ideas that elected civilians must head the government and that they must control the military and direct it as an instrument of government policy. Such control includes civilian direction of the military departments, civilian determination of key decisions on funding, war, and overall policy, and protection by the courts of individual rights. Confederates, as we have seen, inherited these traditions and praised them, but they also tolerated enormous exceptions to them, especially in unusual circumstances such as those that prevailed in the trans-Mississippi west. The conditions there made "business as usual" almost impossible, regardless of the desires and intentions of civilian and military leaders.

A better measure of the strength of these traditions, however, is the behavior of military men in circumstances that more closely approximated the normal. Here we have seen that Confederate behavior was broadly comparable to that in the North and in previous U.S. experience. Yet, two factors in the South's experience make a closer examination worthwhile. One of these is the pronounced thirst for status and glory among Southern leaders who often were part of a small and highly interconnected elite. The generals in the "western concentration bloc" were exceptionally well connected to influential civilians in Congress, and they carried on a sustained campaign to influence strategy and decisions.[1] Northern commanders certainly had political connections as well, as exemplified in McClellan's nomination for president by the Democratic Party. Yet the number and density of personal and family ties among Southern politicians and generals were remarkable. In the campaign of the western concentration bloc the egos of some had the potential to breach important barriers between military and civilian responsibilities. What did the struggles for influence by Generals Johnston, Bragg, Beauregard, and their allies reveal about civil-military relations?

Another factor of great importance was the increasingly decisive weight that military considerations came to exert on all Confederate policy. As the fortunes of war dragged the new nation toward defeat, the voice of the military acquired greater power and resonance. Because the life of the Confederacy became so dependent on events on the battlefield, the needs of the army and General Lee became more influential. Eventually General Lee played a crucial role in one of the most profound debates ever conducted in the Confederacy. The passionate arguments over the use of slaves as soldiers cut to the heart of Confederate purpose and did much to define the new nation's identity in history. In that debate, the army and General Lee became prominent figures in decision-making and exerted great influence. Both Lee's stand and the eventual disposition of this issue revealed a great deal about the South.

Leaders of the Confederate military typically honored the traditions of civilian control over military affairs. As military men they informed the government of their needs, organized their forces, drew up plans or proposals, and followed the orders they were given. Both Jefferson Davis and Abraham Lincoln had reason to regret, on many occasions, that the giving of orders did not guarantee their prompt execution, but Southern generals carried out their instructions as faithfully as commanders in the field generally do. Key innovations in policy usually originated with the civil authorities. For example, the architect of the Confederacy's conscription law was George Wythe Randolph, secretary of war, acting with the support of the members of Congress (and in consultation with General Lee).[2] Likewise, Congress extended governmental authority over the railroads, authorized seizures of property, and enacted measures like the tax-in-kind in order to support the armies. Sometimes pressing military need drove congressmen to make these decisions, but the civilian authorities had unquestioned power to withhold their approval or choose among alternate solutions.

It is noteworthy, however, how many Southern generals maintained close relations with members of Congress, keeping up a frequent correspondence and lobbying for actions they saw as desirable. Sometimes their goals were personal. Joseph E. Johnston, for example, certainly used his close relationship with Senator Louis Wigfall of Texas to promote his hopes for high command, and Congressman James L. Pugh of Alabama allied himself with Braxton Bragg, championing Bragg's reputation while also asking Bragg's support of his recommendations on lesser military appointments.[3] Other military men used their ties to politicians to promote

strategic concepts or specific military actions that they believed were promising. The most significant example of this pattern was the activity of the
western concentration bloc that historians Thomas Connelly and Archer
Jones have described.

This bloc was an informal grouping of generals and legislators, many of
whom had close personal and familial ties. Though connected in many
ways, these individuals did not form an organization that regularly pursued specific goals or an agreed upon plan of action. Nor did the members
of this bloc always agree with each other; instead, rivalries and personal
animus sometimes pitted one individual against another. Joseph Johnston,
Braxton Bragg, and P.G.T. Beauregard often aspired to the same command
responsibilities, and Bragg's subordinate generals in the Army of Tennessee
turned against him and urged his ouster. Nevertheless, the many ideas and
recommendations of this bloc functioned over time to promote and keep
before the government two strategic ideas.

One was operational. Inspired by Napoleonic concepts, the generals in
this bloc favored risking an offensive concentration of troops in the trans-
Appalachian west. Rather than defending, or trying to defend the western
territory as a whole, they were eager to take the initiative—to strip troops
from one area in order to mass superior forces against one of the federal
armies and then attack. Once their offensive produced a successful advance,
they wanted to turn their forces diagonally to slash the supply lines and
communications of another enemy army. Thus, in Napoleonic fashion they
hoped to wreak havoc on the federal forces. Their second common concern was geographical. Convinced of the importance of the Confederate
heartland, they wanted the government to give high priority to the defense
of the area from Nashville to Chattanooga and to Atlanta.[4] This corridor
led in a southeasterly direction toward some of the most productive industrial and military plants of the Confederacy. In a forward strategy, the
invasion and recapture of Kentucky could serve as an effective means to
protect this corridor.

The roster of individuals associated with the western concentration bloc
was impressive. It included eleven generals, among them Joseph E. Johnston, P.G.T. Beauregard, Braxton Bragg, James Longstreet, Wade Hampton, John C. Breckinridge, and Leonidas Polk. A number of influential
Confederate legislators also were involved, including South Carolina's
William Porcher Miles, the chairman of the House Committee on Military
Affairs, Louis Wigfall of Texas, Charles Villeré of Louisiana, and William
Ballard Preston of Virginia. Even more impressive was the dense web of
consanguine and marital ties that linked most of these men. Their inter-
twined personal and family histories made them well known to each other.
For example, General Johnston was related in a variety of ways to the Pre-
stons and through them to Wade Hampton and General John B. Floyd;
General Breckinridge had family ties or connections through marriage to

no less than four of his fellow generals: Johnston, Floyd, Hampton, and William Preston.[5]

During the war this bloc brought forward and advocated at least seven plans for offensives in the west. They had an early success in the summer of 1862, when conditions favored their emphasis on the heartland. Many Confederates wanted to regain Kentucky, and overly optimistic reports from a variety of sources suggested that the citizens of that state would flock to the Confederacy's support if they had the opportunity. After conducting a successful cavalry raid in June 1862, General John Hunt Morgan predicted that as many as 30,000 men would volunteer "at once" in response to an invasion. Even General Lee favored action at this time, advising that "it would produce a great effect." When the coordinated invasions of Kentucky and Pennsylvania took place that fall, however, the results were discouraging, as Kentuckians failed to rise and take up the arms that Bragg's army had carried along to furnish to them. Confederate forces had to retreat and leave the state.[6] Thereafter, the western concentration bloc had to struggle for attention and fight to put its aims back on the national agenda.

Beauregard, who was always generating ambitious proposals and carrying on an extensive correspondence, in September 1862 advocated a junction of Southern forces to carry the battle into Kentucky and even beyond into Missouri. He followed that up in December 1863 with a plan to marshal a force at Knoxville or Dalton, Georgia, to attack Grant at Chattanooga and then pursue "to the banks of the Ohio and Mississippi." The next month, a number of Kentucky generals, who were then making a deep impression on Richmond's social scene, argued for a two-pronged offensive, with Johnston advancing from Dalton while Kentucky troops that were to be brought together from various Southern commands would reenter their state through the Cumberland Gap. Shortly thereafter both James Longstreet and Leonidas Polk developed proposals for invasions of Kentucky. These ideas succeeded in attracting attention within the administration, and even General Lee seemed enthusiastic when he sought Johnston's comments on some of these proposals. An administration plan that was scouted in the winter of 1864 would have given Johnston the alternative of invading Kentucky or fighting in middle Tennessee as a prelude to moving forward.[7]

All these efforts had an effect on administration priorities, for Jefferson Davis became more focused on the importance of Tennessee and Kentucky and operations in that region. The lobbying of the western concentration bloc was certainly a factor, but so too was the course of the war, for events crowded in on the Richmond administration. With the fall of Vicksburg and the approach of the 1864 elections in the North, it became more and more important to stop Federal advances in the west. Then General Longstreet became so enthusiastic about invading Kentucky, in cooperation with forward movements by Johnston's army, that he devised a series of plans and argued for them in Richmond. Lee's willingness to detach Longstreet for offensive action in the West further influenced Davis in favor of the bloc's priorities. In the end, the necessary resources—especially mules and wagons—for major offensive action proved to be lacking, but the proposals and lobbying and pressure by the western concentration bloc had changed the administration's strategic thinking.[8]

In this campaign to focus greater attention on the west, Confederate generals had operated both within the military chain of command and outside it, through their friends and allies in politics and their social contacts in Richmond. Use of the latter channels may have bent the rules a little, but it was predictable and not surprising. Legislators and other influential figures always had a keen interest in the security of their state and looked for ways to increase the efforts to protect and defend their areas. It was inevitable that discussions between them and military leaders about how to make their regions safe or regain lost territory would occur. Such contacts did not seem to trouble Jefferson Davis or his military advisers, and the specific ideas for military action always came back to the War Department for analysis and decision.

But the danger that a well-connected and ambitious general could challenge the authority of civilian leaders was real, and it materialized in the case of the egotistical General Beauregard. Forgetting the limits on his role as a military man, Beauregard at one point ventured into areas of foreign policy that belonged solely to the president. In October 1862, when Beauregard had been in command of the Department of South Carolina and Georgia for only a month, he wrote to three governors: Joseph Brown of Georgia, Francis Pickens of South Carolina, and John Milton of Florida. What he proposed to them was a major step in foreign or war policy. "Why should not Governors of Southern States," Beauregard asked, "offer to meet those of Northwest States, at Memphis, under flag of truce, to decide on treaty of peace, to be submitted to both Governments?" Beauregard had submitted this idea to neither the president nor the secretary of war. Acting on his own, he contacted the three governors directly, and then sent the same message to Congressman William Porcher Miles, chairman of the House Committee on Military Affairs. Beauregard's error went beyond arrogating to himself a prominent role in foreign policy. The plain meaning of his words was that these states would act independently, ignoring the authority of the central government in foreign affairs. If they arranged a "treaty of peace," they then would present the Confederate government with a *fait accompli*.[9] It is difficult to imagine a more inappropriate action.

Apparently what saved Beauregard from serious consequences over this matter was the reaction of the governors. According to historian T. Harry Williams, *they* raised the concern that their states would be interfering in matters entrusted to the central government. But Pickens and Milton were initially enthusiastic, and Pickens was sufficiently interested to share Beauregard's idea with the governor of Tennessee. Within a couple of weeks, however, Pickens had changed his mind: "I cannot see how [your plan] can be practically carried out, and have grave doubts as to any favorable results," the South Carolina governor wrote. Although Pickens expressed confidence that the Northwest would eventually leave the United States, he also pointed out that, "If Bragg's army had remained on the Ohio in force much might perhaps have been done in this way, but he has retreated, and that has weakened our cause greatly in the Northwestern States." Bragg's retreat was a potent fact, and Congressman Miles also told Beauregard that his plan was unworkable. In response, Beauregard tried belatedly to cover his tracks. He asserted that he had meant for a peace conference to be held with the approval of the Confederate government and said, "I place as much faith in *diplomacy* to end a war as in drawn battles. . . ."[10] But no claim of good intentions could disguise the fact that Beauregard had exceeded his authority.

In this area, the contrast between Beauregard and Lee was striking. Always prudent and tactful, Lee rarely allowed himself to address matters that lay outside his military responsibilities. On those few occasions when he felt a need to offer advice, Lee took care to bring his thoughts directly and privately to Jefferson Davis. On June 10, 1863, Lee expressed the hope that Davis would "excuse" a long letter that dealt with an important subject: peace sentiment in the North and how best to respond to it. Lee made it plain at the beginning of his letter that once he shared his thoughts, he would leave the matter entirely in the president's hands. If his views met with approval, Lee said, "you will best know how to give effect to them." And to excuse further his foray into this area, Lee suggested that his subject was "not unworthy" of Davis' attention "nor inappropriate to be adverted to by me, in view of its connection with the situation of military affairs."[11]

After making this elaborate plea for Davis' indulgence, Lee had much to say. His estimate of the military prospects of the Confederacy was far from hopeful and very different from the president's public rhetoric. Putting the problem bluntly, Lee wrote: "We should not conceal from ourselves that our resources in men are constantly diminishing, and the disproportion in this respect between us and our enemies, if they continue united in their efforts to subjugate us, is steadily augmenting." These sobering facts compelled what Lee saw as two simple conclusions:

> Under these circumstances, we should neglect no honorable means of dividing and weakening our enemies. . . . [T]he most effectual mode of accomplishing this object . . . is to give all the encouragement we can, consistently with truth, to the rising peace party of the North.[12]

Thus Lee's thoughts were running in the same general direction as those of Beauregard several months before.

Lee then expressed his concern that "writers and speakers among us" were responding to "the demonstration of a desire for peace at the North" in the wrong way. The reaction of "journalists and others," as he diplomatically put it, was such "as to weaken the hands of the advocates of a pacific policy on the part of the Federal Government, and give much encouragement to those who urge a continuance of the war." Here Lee was making full use of his powers of courtesy and indirection, for what troubled him was a dedication to independence expressed in such unqualified terms that it essentially ignored the Northern peace advocates. This was, in fact, the stance of Jefferson Davis, not just of certain unnamed "speakers" or "journalists."[13] The Confederate president was adamantly committed to independence and believed that a strong display of determination was most likely to discourage the North. He also was keenly aware of declining morale in the South and unwilling to do anything that might feed war weariness or nourish a desire to give up the fight. Thus his message to the North was one of defiance and strength.

Lee urged a different tactic. The Confederacy should not, he argued, "make nice distinction between those who declare for peace unconditionally and those who advocate it as a means of restoring the Union, however much we may prefer the former." To do so was to overlook the realities with which Northern peace forces had to contend. Advocates of peace in the North had to make "concessions" to the desire to restore the Union. Such an "inducement" was "essential to the success of their party," Lee argued. Therefore, it was wise to encourage those Northerners who talked about peace, and it was unwise to turn one's back on them because they also talked about reunion. "When peace is proposed to us," Lee declared, "it will be time enough to discuss its terms." Then, echoing Davis' claims about the strength of Southern will, he asserted that "the desire of our people for a distinct and independent national existence will prove as steadfast under the influence of peaceful measures as it has shown itself in the midst of war."[14]

This carefully worded letter masqueraded as a suggestion to the president, but in fact General Lee was pushing his argument as strongly as his instinct for tact allowed. The economy and directness of his language showed that his convictions on these matters were strong. His description of the likely prospects for Southern arms was grim. And as he closed, he bore down on a final point that was almost a tacit demand. Even if Davis were to find his views "inexpedient or impracticable," Lee stated, "I think you will nevertheless agree with me that we should at least carefully abstain from measures or expressions that tend to discourage any party whose purpose is peace."[15] This was Robert E. Lee's way of trying to influence

policy—through channels, behind the scenes, and with considerable deference. In this instance it had little effect.

It was ironic, then, that before the war was over Lee took a very public position of advocacy on one of the most divisive issues ever to arise
within the Confederacy. When Jefferson Davis proposed the use of slaves
as soldiers, all eyes turned toward Lee. This reserved and proper soldier
was asked to enter a fierce public controversy, one that engaged the deepest passions and prejudices of Confederates. Lee not only answered, but he
also advocated emancipation with a directness and specificity that went
well beyond anything Jefferson Davis had said. Thus, in this debate that
went to the heart of Confederate purpose and challenged the cornerstone
of Southern society, the general in chief of the army played a pivotal role.
Moreover, other generals and soldiers in the army were prominent and influential, not only in raising the issue but also in voicing support for Lee's
recommendation. The army was at the center of the whole controversy over
the future of slavery. Nothing better illustrated the sweeping influence that
the military exerted on civilian life in the Confederacy.

The military's involvement with the question of slavery's future began in
the winter of 1863–64. In many parts of the Confederacy, this was a time
of discouragement and reassessment. The simultaneous defeats at Gettysburg and Vicksburg in July 1863 had shaken the foundations of Confederate morale, and no military breakthrough was in sight. Discouraged
Southerners were asking themselves how much longer they could sustain a
war that was going badly and draining their already thin resources. At the
end of 1863 a few newspapers and politicians in the deep South were beginning to ask, is not it necessary for the Confederacy to begin to use its
slaves in military operations? The numerically superior forces of the North
now were gaining additional black troops as a result of Lincoln's Emancipation Proclamation. The *Montgomery Weekly Mail* concluded that, "We
must either employ the [N]egroes ourselves, or the enemy will employ them
against us." The *Weekly Mail* was even willing to accept emancipation in
order to raise black troops, and a few other voices spoke out in agreement.
Discussion of this portentous question was beginning.[16]

In the winter quarters of the Army of Tennessee, a number of high-
ranking officers were talking seriously among themselves about the army's
setbacks and its prospects for the future. The leader of this group was
Major General Patrick Cleburne, an Irishman who had emigrated to the
South and distinguished himself first in civilian life and then in battle. There
was no question about Cleburne's valor or dedication to the cause. But ob-
jectively, the outlook for the South's armies was discouraging. As Cleburne
waited for the beginning of the spring campaigns, he knew that the federal
forces were growing stronger while the Southern army was becoming
weaker. He therefore drafted a thorough but concisely argued document
that was to be submitted to his commander, Joseph E. Johnston. Fourteen

officers signed their names to Cleburne's proposal on January 2, 1864. In addition to Cleburne, two of the officers were generals and six were colonels.[17]

Cleburne's analysis of the situation was sober and alarming. He wrote:

> We have now been fighting for nearly three years, have spilled much of our best blood, and lost, consumed, or thrown to the flames an amount of property equal in value to the specie currency of the world. Through some lack in our system the fruits of our struggles and sacrifices have invariably slipped away from us and left us nothing but long lists of dead and mangled. . . . [W]e are hemmed in to-day into less than two-thirds of [our territory], and still the enemy menacingly confronts us at every point with superior forces. Our soldiers can see no end to this state of affairs except in our own exhaustion.

His prescription for a remedy was clear. "We propose . . . that we immediately commence training a large reserve of the most courageous of our slaves, and further that we guarantee freedom within a reasonable time to every slave in the South who shall remain true to the Confederacy in this war."[18]

Cleburne tired to advance this proposal as an idea that was consistent with a position already enunciated by Jefferson Davis. The president had said that "no effort must be spared to add largely to our effective force as promptly as possible." But the Confederate president had focused his comments on increasing *white* troops by such measures as ending substitution, modifying the exemption law, limiting details, bringing back to the ranks those who were "improperly absent," and using more black Southerners in support roles. Cleburne proceeded to show that none of these measures could be effective. Those who had supplied substitutes or were absent without leave would not make good soldiers, even if they were forced into the ranks. Many of those who were currently exempt or detailed would have to remain in their nonmilitary pursuits in order to assure that essential needs of the country were met. Thus, any gains from these measures were likely to be modest, and the Confederacy would still be without a "reserve to meet unexpected disaster or to supply a protracted struggle." After another year of fighting with white soldiers only, the South would again face a great disparity of force and an enemy that was growing stronger. A more fundamental step was required.[19]

The enrollment of black troops, Cleburne argued, would make the Southern armies "numerically superior," with "a reserve of any size we might think necessary." Citing slave revolts in Santo Domingo and Jamaica, he showed that slaves can fight and argued that the South's black men would fight well, with their "sympathies" enlisted by the "hope of freedom." Moreover, such a measure would fill Southerners with "pride and singleness of purpose" due to "the very magnitude of the sacrifice itself." It would help the Confederacy diplomatically and deprive the North of its self-congratulatory motive of crusading against slavery. Without that motive, "what is left?" he asked, except "a bloody ambition for more territory" and other selfish aims that could not inspire continued sacrifice. In regard to those who might resist the loss of slavery, Cleburne used patriotism and the logic of avoiding defeat: "[E]very patriot," he declared, "will freely . . . give up the [N]egro slave rather than be a slave himself."[20]

These were striking arguments, powerfully made, but even more remarkable was the candor with which these generals discussed the internal problems associated with slavery. Ignoring the South's time-worn boasts about the desirability and stability of its peculiar institution, they acknowledged a very different reality—that "the [N]egro has been dreaming of freedom" for years and that "it would be preposterous . . . to expect him to fight against it with any degree of enthusiasm." Indeed, they admitted that slavery was the Confederacy's "most vulnerable point" and "an insidious weakness." Not only did the army have to disperse its forces to protect slaveholders' property against raids, but "all along the lines slavery is comparatively valueless to us for labor, but of great and increasing worth to the enemy for information." With the South maintaining slavery and the North fighting to end it, "every household [was] surrounded by spies" anywhere that a federal army approached. Southern armies faced "an omnipresent spy system, pointing out our valuable men to the enemy, revealing our positions, purposes, and resources, and yet acting so safely and secretly that there is no means to guard against it." Moreover, slavery undermined white support for the war effort. "Wherever slavery is once seriously disturbed," these officers argued, "whites can no longer with safety to their property openly sympathize with our cause." "Fear of their slaves" and a desire to protect their property made these slaveowners "dead to us, if not open enemies." Though slavery had once been a source of strength for the Confederacy, it "has now become, in a military point of view, one of our chief sources of weakness."[21]

Cleburne's document acknowledged that "the slaves are dangerous now" and would be potentially more dangerous once armed as soldiers. Therefore, it was imperative to "give the [N]egro not only his own freedom, but that of his wife and child, and . . . secure it to him in his old home." Some immediate improvements, such as legalization of slave marriages and families, were needed "as an earnest of our intentions" and evidence of "our sincerity," with emancipation to follow "within such reasonable time as will prepare both races for the change." Having made these highly unconventional, if not revolutionary, arguments, Cleburne and his fellow officers asked General Johnston to obtain a rapid consideration of their proposal, since the training of black troops would take time.[22]

Johnston recognized immediately how controversial this proposal would

Patrick Cleburne. General Cleburne took the lead among officers in the Army of Tennessee in arguing that slavery was weakening the Confederacy and that slaves should be armed and freed. (Courtesy of Library of Congress)

be, and he refused to send it to Richmond on the grounds that "it was more political than military in tenor." But another officer, who found the proposal scandalous, shared its contents with Jefferson Davis, and the president decreed an end to discussion even before it could begin. Davis' motivation at this point, in January 1864, was both diplomatic and political. His goal for the coming year was to organize a stubborn military resistance

that would stimulate the growth of war-weariness in the North and lead
to the victory of a presidential candidate who would give the Confederacy
its independence. To achieve that goal, he could risk neither failure on the
battlefield nor divisive controversies on the home front. Therefore, he
judged it "injurious to the public service that such a subject should be
mooted, or even known to be entertained" by the government or high-
ranking officers. He directed the secretary of war to write to Johnston and
ask him to suppress the entire matter. Johnston did so, and his officers
obeyed; knowledge of this well-reasoned but radical document stayed
bottled-up within the army.[23]

But within a year this issue would resurface, for much had changed before the end of November 1864. By then Sherman had conquered Atlanta
and was marching to the sea, spreading destruction through Georgia's
heartland. Grant had hammered relentlessly on Lee's army, severely reducing its strength. Lincoln had won reelection, and Davis himself had been
forced to admit publicly that "two-thirds of our men are absent—some
sick, some wounded, but most of them absent without leave." The condition of the Confederacy was growing desperate, and therefore Jefferson
Davis put into motion a new strategy. To revive and bring new strength to
the armies, he would arm the slaves. To secure their loyal support and seek
diplomatic recognition from European nations, he would promote a policy involving emancipation of black troops and their families. The army
had to have more troops, and for Davis independence was the indispensable war aim, not the preservation of slavery.[24]

Davis proceeded thoroughly but indirectly. He developed a plan that
would enlist the cooperation of the states in freeing slave soldiers and their
families, and he outlined and promoted it through his allies in Richmond,
in the states, and in the press. But Davis often left it to others to articu-
late the key elements of his plan. Perhaps he had been so battered by criticism throughout the war that he wanted to remain in the background,
but it is even more likely that he judged that his visibility at the head of
the effort could doom what was already a highly controversial idea. Thus
he first proposed to the Congress only that the government should purchase 40,000 slaves to work as laborers for the army, with freedom being
granted as a reward for "past faithful service." Saying in this address on
November 7 that he did *not* "advise a general levy and arming of the
slaves for the duty of soldiers," Davis went no farther than this remark:
"But should the alternative ever be presented of subjugation or of the employment of the slave as a soldier, there seems no reason to doubt what
should then be our decision."[25]

Within a few weeks it became apparent that the administration did, indeed, believe that the Confederacy faced this critical choice, but Davis let
Judah Benjamin, Virginia's governor William Smith, and sympathetic newspaper editors advocate his plan and work most directly for its adoption.

The administration argued that independence was the Confederacy's goal, that the army had to have more men, that slaves would make useful soldiers, and that freedom should be promised to the troops and to their families, with assurance by the states that they could stay in their homes. It would be up to the states, through "cautious legislation," to provide "for their ultimate emancipation after an intermediate stage of serfage or peonage."[26] These proposals may seem limited to the modern reader and inferior to what slaves were hoping to receive through Abraham Lincoln, but they were radical, nonetheless, in the Confederate context.

The attack on these ideas was brutal and swift in coming. On the day after Davis' November 7 address, even before the full scope of the administration's proposal was known, the *Daily Richmond Examiner* raised fundamental, racist objections. After a lengthy argument that Negroes could not be good soldiers, the *Examiner* equated Confederate purpose with slavery and the rejection of abolition.

> [T]he existence of a [N]egro soldier is totally inconsistent with our political aim and with our social as well as political system. . . . If a [N]egro is fit to be a soldier he is not fit to be a slave. . . . The employment of [N]egroes as soldiers in our armies, either with or without prospective emancipation, would be the first step, but a step which would involve all the rest, to universal abolition. . . . To our own hearts it would be a confession, not only of weakness, but of absolute inability to secure the object for which we undertook the war.

The *Examiner* went on to say that it would be willing for the government to have 40,000 slaves as laborers, but not if they were to be given their freedom. The editor insisted that "the [N]egro is in his proper situation . . . while living with the white man in the relation of slave he is in a state superior and better for him than that of freedom." With sorrow and indignation the *Examiner* suspected that President Davis had adopted "the whole theory of the abolitionist."[27]

Other initial reactions to the administration's plan were hostile, even in some journals that would later come round and support the president. The *Richmond Whig*, for example, defended the "divinely appointed condition" of the slave and held that it would be "an act of cruelty" to deprive him of his master's care. "If the slave must fight," said the *Whig*, "he should fight for the blessings he enjoys as a slave, and not for the miseries that would attend him if freed." On November 12 the *Charleston Mercury* thundered that, "The African is of an inferior race, whose normal condition is slavery. Prone to barbarism, and incapable of any other state than that of pupilage, he is at his best estate as the slave of the enlightened white man of this country." Davis' "extraordinary suggestion" was "inconsistent, unsound and suicidal." From faraway Texas, a newspaper in Galveston decried any "abandonment of the foundation principle upon which the institution of slavery rests; that is, the principle that slavery is the best possible condition for the slave himself, and the only one he can occupy consistent with the welfare of the white race."[28]

This racist belief that African Americans were inferior and slavery necessary and desirable constituted the core of opposition to Davis' plan. It would continue to drive the opposition during the remaining months of the Confederacy, and it never ceased to dominate the thinking of most of the political elite. In Charleston, the editor of the *Mercury* spilled his racist bile, charging that Davis' "insane" proposal meant that "swaggering buck niggers" would ruin the poor man and reduce "the intelligence, the refinement of the country" to want. In the Confederate Senate Virginia's R.M.T. Hunter, North Carolina's William A. Graham, and Texas' Louis Wigfall led effective opposition to any idea of emancipation. In the House various representatives spoke out against the measure, and Virginia's Thomas S. Gholson printed and distributed a pamphlet that argued, "if liberty to our slaves be really a boon—if they really be fit and qualified for liberty, and should receive it as a merited reward for military service, then we surrender the whole question." Gholson added that if this policy were to create a country in which some of the slaves were free, "Who would consent to live in it?" Georgia's Howell Cobb rejected the whole idea, saying, "If slaves will make good soldiers our whole theory of slavery is wrong." To Senator Graham the administration's ideas were "insane proposals," merely "wild schemes and confessions of despair."[29]

A conviction that it would be possible to hang on to slavery proved very persistent among the slaveholding elite, even as the specter of defeat steadily took on more solid form. The *Daily Richmond Examiner* exemplified these attitudes when it reported on comments allegedly made by General Sherman at the end of the year. Quoting remarks made to "a gentleman" in Georgia "(as affirmed by an Augusta paper)," the *Examiner* reported that Sherman had said,

> "Slavery will exist in the South after the conclusion of the peace, let the war terminate as it may"—and further, that "he (Sherman) expects to own a thousands slaves himself one of these days"—that he has really expressed himself in this manner is at least possible, and even probable.[30]

Though the *Examiner* could not confirm that Sherman actually had made these statements, the general's well-known racist views made that seem at least possible. Moreover, the paper argued that Sherman was undoubtedly correct, because even if the South were to lose, Northerners would continue the system of slavery under a different name. Slavery, the article concluded, was good for the slaves and superior to the North's industrial system.

But the Davis plan began to win some converts or at least some concessions to reality. Two Richmond newspapers that were often more sympathetic to the administration, the *Enquirer* and the *Sentinel*, were prompt to offer limited support. Within days of the president's speech the *Enquirer* pointed out that he had raised the idea of using slaves in the army "solely as a remedy to which dire necessity might eventually drive the Confederate Government." The *Enquirer* also warned that if "the people of this country exhibit an unwillingness to make soldiers of their slaves," they would give color to the false idea that the South was fighting "solely for the perpetuation of slavery." The *Sentinel* criticized Confederates who claimed they would give anything for the cause but then drew back from sacrificing slavery. "The true question," according to the *Sentinel*, "is does *necessity* require it? If it does, or if it shall, that fact answers a thousand objections." By the end of January the *Richmond Whig* was supporting a plan to double the size of the army by having the government "buy and present to each soldier in the field a young and able-bodied [N]egro man, armed and equipped."[31] As weeks passed and the military situation became more desperate, a willingness grew to give the army whatever it needed.

The influence of Robert E. Lee proved very important to this process. At first Lee offered his support only privately, behind the scenes. A few days before Davis addressed Congress, Lee had responded to a request from the chairman of the House Military Affairs Committee, William Porcher Miles, for his opinion on "the arming of a portion of our negroes." Lee's letter to Miles appears to have been lost, but a reply from Miles made it clear that Lee had given support to this idea. Miles indicated that Lee had offered a "mature and decided" opinion that black troops would be helpful and that the time had arrived when it was necessary to take this step. Congressman Miles was not convinced, however, and was reluctant to move forward.[32] But Lee's views began to be discussed openly in Richmond, as people commented on this response and as other policy makers contacted Lee to seek his counsel.

On January 11, 1865, General Lee answered the "interrogatories" of a Virginia state senator named Andrew Hunter. Lee began in a conventional vein. He asserted that he considered "the relation of master and slave, controlled by humane laws and influenced by Christianity and an enlightened public sentiment, as the best that can exist between the white and black races." He even said that he would prefer to fight with an adequate number of white troops. But Lee pointed out that military realities did not allow this choice. The South soon would be "overtaxing the capacity of our white population," and the North would "penetrate our country and get access to a large part of our [N]egro population." In reality, the choice the South faced was "whether slavery shall be extinguished by our enemies and the slaves be used against us, or use them ourselves at the risk of the effects . . . upon our social institutions." Lee favored "employ[ing] them without delay" and believed that slaves "can be made efficient soldiers."[33]

After making these comments, Lee abandoned conventional views entirely to advocate some sweeping changes. In order to motivate slave soldiers, Lee proposed "giving immediate freedom to all who enlist, and freedom at the end of the war to the families of those who discharge their duties faithfully (whether they survive or not), together with the privilege of residing at the South. To this might be added a bounty for faithful service." Then, looking at the issue even more broadly, he argued that

> the best means of securing the efficiency and fidelity of this auxiliary force would be to accompany the measure with a well-digested plan of gradual and general emancipation. As that will be the result of the continuance of the war, and will certainly occur if the enemy succeed, it seems to me most advisable to adopt it at once, and thereby obtain all the benefits that will accrue to our cause.

Expressing confidence that use of the black troops would "greatly increase our military strength" and damage the enemy, Lee urged "in conclusion that whatever measures are to be adopted should be adopted at once."[34] Thus, the Confederacy's leading general had advocated not only the arming of slaves but a general emancipation.

The extent of Lee's influence was illustrated when the *Daily Richmond Examiner* commented on his views. The *Examiner*'s opposition to using slaves as soldiers had been unwavering, but it admitted on February 16, 1865, that Lee wanted "a large force of [N]egroes to be placed at his disposal." Reiterating its opposition to emancipation, the *Examiner* stubbornly declared, "It is also very certain that [N]egroes are not intended for soldiers, and will never fight when they can avoid it." Yet the paper declined to stand up to Lee. "The country will not venture to deny to General Lee, in the present position of affairs," wrote the editor, "*anything* he may ask for."[35]

Other editors showed the same deference. The *Richmond Whig* on February 20 admitted that the "proposition to put [N]egroes in the army has gained favor rapidly . . . and is known to be favored by nearly all the principal officers." The editor of the *Whig* declared that he was not "very sanguine" about this idea and seemed still to oppose emancipation, but he believed that every support had to be given to General Lee. Moreover, Lee had advocated the measure "with a warmth he has not, perhaps, exhibited in regard to any other matter of legislation." That same day the *Richmond Sentinel* warned that, "We want more men with muskets in their hands to equalize the struggle with our enemies . . . there is no time to be lost."

Three days later, when the *Sentinel* published a new letter by Lee on the subject, its editor wrote, "With the great mass of our people, nothing more than this letter is needed to settle every doubt or silence every objection."[36]

The letter by Lee that was published had been written on February 18 and was addressed to Mississippi congressman Ethelbert Barksdale. In it the general again answered the questions of a legislator who sought his views. And Lee gave them plainly. Using slaves as soldiers was "not only expedient but necessary." He believed that "the [N]egroes, under proper circumstances, will make efficient soldiers." And in addition, Lee asserted that "those who are employed should be freed. It would be neither just nor wise, in my opinion, to require them to serve as slaves." As to the next step to take, Lee favored asking for volunteers whose owners would be willing for them to join the army. This letter soon appeared in many Southern newspapers, in addition to the *Sentinel*.[37]

At this point soldiers in the Army of Northern Virginia began to make their voices heard in support of their leader. In various units troops held a meeting, discussed their perilous situation, and adopted resolutions that they sent to the Richmond newspapers. Almost without exception these resolutions expressed a determination to fight on to independence and strong support for the recruitment of slaves as soldiers, in order to make victory possible. The "Louisiana Guard Artillery," for example, notified the *Richmond Whig* that it "endorse[d] most heartily, and from stern conviction, the policy of arming the colored population of the country—slave and free—in such numbers as may be required, with as little delay as possible." The 1st Virginia Infantry, Terry's Brigade, Pickett's Division, declared its desire for "independence and separate nationality" and announced that it "would hail with acclamation the enrolment into our armies of [N]egro troops." Similarly, the *Whig* reported that the 30th Virginia Infantry "took a vote on Saturday upon the [N]egro question, and all the companies save one . . . voted with but few dissenting voices in favor of giving the colored natives an opportunity of defending their country."[38] Those men who were still in the ranks in 1865 were determined, battle-tested soldiers who had made many sacrifices for the Confederacy, and they—more than most Confederates—were ready to change slavery in order to fight on.

The desperate military situation of the Confederacy, the appeals of the troops, and the enormous prestige of Robert E. Lee were all pushing legislators toward the enlistment of slaves as soldiers. Even the *Daily Richmond Examiner* continued—grudgingly—to yield. The arming of slaves was "a very serious step," wrote the editor,

> and directly opposite to all the sentiments and principles which have heretofore governed the Southern people. Nothing, in fact, but the loud and repeated demand of the leader to whom we already owe so much, and on whose shoulders we rest so great a responsibility for

the future, could induce, or rather coerce, this people and this army
to consent. . . . It may be under protest that we yield to this imperious necessity; but still we yield.

The decision to arm slaves was an enormous change for the *Examiner* and
for the white South. In regard to the status of black soldiers, however, the
Examiner was not ready to follow Lee's views. It denied that he was "an
authority" on the moral, social, and political implications of this measure,
and it even questioned whether he could be considered "a 'good Southerner' "—that is, one who was "thoroughly satisfied of the justice and
beneficence of [N]egro slavery."[39] Here the *Examiner* was not alone, for
many Confederate leaders were still planning, less than two months before
Appomattox, how to block emancipation and perpetuate slavery.

Ironically, the Hampton Roads conference between President Lincoln,
Secretary of State Seward, and three high-ranking Confederate commissioners greatly encouraged this resistance to emancipation. In January 1865
Richmond had been buzzing with talk of possible peace conferences. Jefferson Davis was convinced that this talk was unrealistic and based on
wishful thinking, but he also felt the mounting public pressure. Therefore
he decided to expose the impossibility of gaining independence through negotiations by allowing emissaries to talk to Lincoln. He appointed Vice
President Alexander Stephens, the chief advocate of discussions with the
enemy, John A. Campbell, assistant secretary of war, and Virginia's senator R.M.T. Hunter as a delegation to meet with Northern leaders. After
passing through enemy lines, these Confederates met aboard ship in Hampton Roads, Virginia, with Lincoln and Seward on February 3, 1865.[40]

Stephens was convinced that if an armistice were ever declared, the war
would never resume, and to achieve this result he argued that the United
States should join the Confederacy in military action against France's imperial venture in Mexico. Lincoln ignored this gambit and reemphasized
that the issue was restoration of the Union, but on other matters Stephens
and his two colleagues heard some very interesting ideas. In response to a
question from Campbell, Lincoln said that the Emancipation Proclamation
was a war measure that would be inoperative once the war ceased; he and
Seward agreed that the courts would decide, after the war, precisely who
had been freed by the proclamation and who had not. Seward then observed that the U.S. Congress had proposed the 13th Amendment to the
Constitution and suggested that if the Southern states rejoined the Union,
their votes could block its ratification. Lincoln did not comment directly
on Seward's words, but, according to Stephens, he addressed the Confederate vice president and said

I'll tell you what I would do, if I were in your place: I would go home
and get the Governor of the State to call the Legislature together, and

get them to recall all the State troops from the war; elect Senators and Members to Congress, and ratify this Constitutional Amendment *prospectively*, so as to take effect—say in five years. . . . I have looked into the subject, and think such a prospective ratification would be valid. . . . [T]he best course . . . for your public men to pursue, would be to adopt such a policy as will avoid, as far as possible, the evils of immediate emancipation.

Lincoln and Seward also indicated that they were disposed to treat Southerners with liberality on other issues and that many Northerners favored a $400 million indemnity to the South for a voluntary abolition of slavery.[41]

The Confederate commissioners returned to Richmond and duly reported that the United States insisted on reunion and the restoration of national authority before other matters might be discussed. But they were greatly intrigued by the other possibilities that their discussion had opened up, particularly the idea that it might be possible to preserve or extend the life of slavery. To Jefferson Davis the chief fact was Lincoln's rejection of Confederate independence, and he pressed the commissioners, in order "to influence the people," to add to their report that the North had "insisted on abolition and submission." All three commissioners balked and refused to do so. Judge Campbell told an associate in the War Department that he "felt very much dissatisfied about the whole thing. It *ought not* to have been dropped when it was, but terms should have been distinctly offered." Davis then drafted his own statement to Congress, which emphasized that the North had demanded a conqueror's terms, insisting upon "unconditional submission" and abolition, and this statement went before the public.[42]

But behind the scenes in Richmond, Campbell and other commissioners shared their views with powerful members of Congress. R.M.T. Hunter, who completely rejected emancipation and would refuse to support even the arming of slaves until instructed to do so by the Virginia legislature, kept up many contacts with administration officials and legislators. For his part, Judge Campbell discussed the conference with a number of people, including North Carolina's William A. Graham, to whom he gave "a minute narrative of the whole mission from beginning to end." Thus, it is likely that detailed information about the meeting became fairly widespread.[43]

On February 12, 1865, Senator Graham reported to former governor David Swain of North Carolina that the 13th Amendment had been proposed to the states "but that the dissent of ten States could still reject it." He shared his understanding that Lincoln had been "apparently anxious for a settlement" and had showed his disappointment when the Confederate commissioners did not respond to his suggestions. Whereas Lincoln had tried to demonstrate "his liberality to the South," Davis had rejected any further discussions, causing both Stephens and Campbell to despair of their president's reaction to their mission. Since slavery might be prolonged or

William A. Graham. This North Carolina Senator was well aware of the conversations at Hampton Roads and helped other legislators block any legislation that would lead to emancipation. (Courtesy of Library of Congress)

protected, Graham favored a further exploration of these issues. To Governor Vance he wrote,

> No one advises the acceptance of the terms offered by Lincoln, but the question is being considered . . . whether reunion, by which ten States may defeat the proposed amendment to the Constitution, &

retain slavery, be not preferable to the triumph of his arms, and the subjection of everything to his power. . . . The President [Davis] is not in favor with Congress.

To his wife, Graham reported with approval that Judge Campbell felt that "a mission should be sent to Washington to negotiate terms."[44] Senator James L. Orr of South Carolina also was "anxious" at this time that negotiations should be "opened with the enemy to ascertain upon what terms the war could be closed" and condemned Davis as "too obstinate and supercilious to entertain the proposition." An angry Louis Wigfall, who held Davis responsible for every problem, wrote, "We are now on the very verge of revolution."[45]

Thus, influential men in the Confederate Congress were considering whether it might be possible, even at this late date, to get better terms from Abraham Lincoln than from the policy of their own president, Jefferson Davis. For many of these men—though not for Davis—the priority was to maintain slavery. Jefferson Davis wanted to arm and emancipate the slaves in order to fight on for independence. Robert E. Lee had thrown all his support behind this goal, and many soldiers and officers had reached the same decision. But with defeat on the horizon, many slaveholders in Congress still hoped to salvage slavery, and they were ready to give up the fight in order to hold onto the peculiar institution. They demonstrated that for them, if not for all Southerners, the central purpose of the Confederacy was not to defend constitutional liberty or states' right or limited government, but to defend slavery.

Given these political realities, Jefferson Davis was fortunate to secure the passage of even part of his proposal. One March 13, 1865, the Confederate Congress finally passed, by a margin of one vote in the Senate, a bill authorizing Davis to accept slaves into the army for service as soldiers. At this date Congress' action came too late to affect the final stages of the war. Nevertheless, the measure could not have won approval but for the strong and unqualified support of Lee, the call for reinforcements by many soldiers on the front lines, and the ever deepening military crisis. The army had played a major role, from the beginning of 1864, in bringing the Southern nation to consider and belatedly adopt this radical alternative to the system of slavery. The Confederacy welcomed slaves into its army, and if the Southern nation had survived, this innovation surely would have had consequences for long-established patterns of racial subordination and oppression. A bitter William A. Graham condemned this measure as "equivalent to a dissolution of the Confederacy."[46]

But Graham and the rest of the Confederacy's lawmakers refused to consider emancipation. In fact, the bill that they finally passed explicitly and aggressively stated "that nothing in this act shall be construed to authorize a change in the relation which the said slaves shall bear toward their owners." Jefferson Davis countered this provision administratively, by having the War Department issue an implementing order requiring that, "No slave will be accepted as a recruit unless with his own consent and with the approbation of his master by a written instrument conferring, as far as he may, the rights of a freedman." But this order, on March 23, 1865, was hardly a victory for freedom or for progress in race relations. It is true that Jefferson Davis, Robert E. Lee, the most dedicated soldiers in the army, and a portion of the Confederate populace had shown that they valued independence over the preservation of slavery. But the Confederate political elite as a whole proved resistant to racial change and hostile to any measure that would disturb the South's extensive system of human bondage. Stubbornly and defiantly defending racism and privilege, they demonstrated their belief that what the *Daily Richmond Examiner* called "the essential and distinctive principle of Southern civilization" was slavery.[47]

Independence was more important than slavery to some Confederates, including a good many dedicated soldiers who had sacrificed so much and so long for their cause that they continued to spurn defeat. But their numbers were limited and their power—when Congress shaped its final legislation—nil. The logic of a massive war had transformed the South and reshaped many Southern beliefs. The hard realities of the battlefield had convinced many Southerners to build a powerful central government, militarize their whole society, suspend the writ of *habeas corpus* and restrict individual liberties, and even approve the arming of slaves, but preserving the institution of slavery remained central. Even in the face of imminent defeat, Davis and Lee were able to convince only a small portion of the leadership class to choose independence over slavery.[48]

The efforts of Davis and Lee did not bring victory, but events gave the Confederacy one last chance to rescue slavery from the jaws of destruction, and a military man played a role in keeping that possibility briefly open. On April 17 and 18, 1865, Joseph E. Johnston arrived at the Bennett farmhouse near Durham, North Carolina, to surrender his army to U.S. forces. His foe, General William Tecumseh Sherman, was a very complex individual. Although Southerners hated Sherman as the scourge of the South, he was a merciless fighter disposed to be merciful in victory and a federal patriot who was both a racist and a conservative. Although Sherman had promised Edwin M. Stanton, his secretary of war, that in negotiating a surrender he would "be careful not to complicate any points of civil policy," the general violated his pledge. In fact, he completely ignored the example that Grant had given him of a strictly military surrender that avoided all political questions.

At the Bennett farmhouse Sherman "took an instant liking" to General Johnston, "sat down convivially" with him, and "pulled out a bottle of whiskey" to share as they discussed a surrender agreement. Johnston had the benefit in their discussions of a document drafted by Confederate postmaster general John Reagan as well as the presence of John Breckenridge, who was an experienced lawyer and politician. At one point the relaxed Sherman was so impressed by Breckinridge's skill in argumentation that he "pushed back his chair and exclaimed: 'See here, gentlemen, who is doing the surrendering anyhow?'" In the flush of victory, Sherman conducted himself just as he wished to during these discussions, though he later suggested that he had been "hustled."[49]

The result was an agreement, based on the Confederates' draft document, that included valuable political concessions to the South. The Sherman-Johnston convention did not merely provide for the disbanding of the latter's army. It also promised "the recognition by the Executive of the United States of the several State Governments" once their officers had taken the oath of allegiance, a "general amnesty," and a promise "not to disturb any of the people by reason of the late war" so long as they lived peaceably and obeyed the laws. Moreover, section 5 undertook to guarantee to "the people and inhabitants of all the States . . . their political rights and franchises, as well as their rights of person and property, as defined by the Constitution of the United States and of the States respectively."[50]

These remarkable terms were far-reaching and manifestly political in character. Whether Sherman and Johnston understood "rights of person and property" as defined by federal and state constitutions to exclude slavery or not, this wording certainly could be interpreted to protect slavery. For that and other reasons, such as the recognition pledged to rebel state governments, President Andrew Johnson and the cabinet in Washington immediately repudiated Sherman's agreement. They issued instructions that Sherman must meet with Johnston again and start over. Grant went in person to Sherman's headquarters to deliver the news, and new terms of surrender, much like those of Appomattox, were soon drawn up.[51] But clearly Generals Johnston and Breckinridge had tried to seize any concessions they could obtain for the white South's institutions and beliefs.

It was tragic that Southerners such as Hunter, Graham, and so many others chose to define themselves for all time as champions of human bondage. But it was not surprising, for the white South had defended slavery tenaciously for decades. What was surprising was the readiness of many Southerners to consider unconstitutional measures, and even a resort to some form of military rule, to avert their final crisis.

7

Desperate Proposals and the Maintenance of Civil Supremacy

Before the Civil War the political leaders of the South had made a clear name for themselves. Ideologically, their record was a strong and almost completely consistent one. They professed themselves to be devoted to constitutionalism, and they insisted on strict adherence to constitutional limitations, narrowly interpreted. Through many sectional controversies and during the secession crisis, they repeatedly voiced outrage over what they saw as violations of the U.S. Constitution, usurpations of power, and improper centralization of authority. The Constitution was their talisman and states' rights their shibboleth. No violation of procedure was too small, and no debate on principles too lengthy or tiresome, to escape their careful attention. Hair-splitting and obsessed they might have seemed to many, but few questioned their determination to guard every principle and restriction of the Constitution.

At the creation of the Confederacy, Southern politicians reemphasized this dedication to strict construction of the Constitution. By seceding, Jefferson Davis argued, the South was ending the pattern of violations that had characterized the United States and preserving the government intended by the Revolutionary generation. Davis charged that the North had allowed justice and law to be trampled "under the armed heel of military authority." Similarly, the *Charleston Mercury* denounced Lincoln as a power-hungry despot and summed up history by saying that the federal government had "usurped powers not granted—progressively trenched upon State Rights." Other newspapers condemned the "total and universal moral depravity" of the North and the "blind and abominable fanaticism which defies the Constitution." Only in the Confederacy, with its strict devotion to the Confederate constitution, would the liberty of white citizens be safe.[1] The chorus of voices on this theme was loud and harmonious.

How ironic it was, then, that in the short life of the Confederacy there was abundant discussion of ideas for supplanting Jefferson Davis' constitutional authority and changing the leadership of the government. The political elite fomented such ideas, rather than the ordinary citizens who were bearing heavy burdens and suffering more directly. Such discussion began to occur before the Confederacy was even one year old, and it grew tremendously in strength and variety at the end of 1864 and beginning of 1865. Many ideas were put forward. A large number of them were patently unconstitutional, and others could only be called revolutionary and were recognized as such. Comparatively few respected the niceties of the constitution. Under stress of war, the landscape of discussion about governance and the constitution changed rapidly, in surprising and unexpected ways.

Among these remarkable and desperate proposals, ideas that involved reliance on the military were prominent. Closely linked to an utter rejection of Davis' leadership was the conviction, in some quarters, that the Confederacy needed a military savior. The interest in turning over power to some dominating general increased as the condition of the nation became more desperate. To most Southerners who entertained these ideas, Robert E. Lee was the most likely figure on horseback, although Joseph E. Johnston was mentioned as well. Perhaps the longing for a Napoleonic genius who could rescue the Confederacy from defeat was natural, to some extent, because by the fall of 1864 the Confederacy faced utter ruin. Nevertheless, such proposals were the complete negation of supposedly hallowed traditions of government. How had such a development occurred? This chapter will examine the origins and character of such ideas, explore what became of them, and analyze the reasons why the supremacy of civil authority over the military was maintained.

It is remarkable how quickly Jefferson Davis became the subject of vicious attacks. Undoubtedly some of these must have been the product of jealousy and rivalries among the political elite. Those who were eager to be more important were quick to criticize. Less than two weeks after Davis took office, Mary Boykin Chesnut, the highly placed diarist from South Carolina, recorded that, "Men are willing to risk an injury to our cause, if they may in so doing hurt Jeff Davis." Shortly after Bull Run, when most Southerners were celebrating their victory, she learned that "[Congressman Lawrence] Keitt, [Congressman W. W.] Boyce, [former U.S. senator James Henry] Hammond, and many others hate Jeff Davis." Later that summer she noted that a coalition against the president had formed and that it now included—in addition to the three South Carolinians—Georgia's Howell Cobb.[2] Another observer who agreed with Mary Boykin Chesnut was Congressman A. R. Wright from Georgia. Just after the inauguration of Jefferson Davis as president under the Permanent Constitution, in February 1862, he expressed dismay over the "vileness . . . exhibited here every day in the efforts of some of those who were first to overthrow the old Government, to shake the confidence of the people in their rulers. . . ." Some were declaring that

> the best way to get clear of incompetent rulers is for the people to rise in their might and overthrow them.
>
> It is fearful to hear the talk in Congress and out of it. If we are not careful, and meet with a few more reverses, we shall have the revolution all over again.[3]

Dissatisfaction with Davis' leadership increased as the fortunes of war became more discouraging, and in the spring of 1862 there was an upwelling of the emotions that Congressman Wright had noticed. Confederates were impatient for a victory and concerned about the massive army that General McClellan was assembling in the North. There also was growing hostility among members of Congress toward Judah Benjamin, not only for his policies and confident manner but also because Benjamin was Jewish. James L. Pugh, a member of the House from Alabama, wrote to General Braxton Bragg at this time:

> The majority of Congress are [sic] clamerous [sic] for a change of Cabinet—much complaint of Mr. Benjamin, Mallory, &c. How justly I know not, but the fact is so, the disposition is to war on the President if he retains Mr. Benjamin. There was much engineering to avoid the necessity for his removal. A duality in the war office was suggested—giving all military control to one, and all civil to the other.

Pugh believed that the aborted effort to create a post of commanding general, and then Jefferson Davis's decision to assign Robert E. Lee to duty as his chief military adviser, were both responses to the congressional attacks on Benjamin.[4]

One of the most agitated congressmen at this time was W. W. Boyce of South Carolina. Boyce felt gloomy about the South's prospects, reasoning that the North had twice as many men as the Confederacy and that "Davis has no military genius." The Confederacy's military efforts had been conducted, he told James Henry Hammond, "in the most languid manner. While the enemy were [sic] exhibiting revolutionary energy we were doing nothing. . . . Davis is puffed up with his own conceit," while "the immense patronage of the Executive renders many of the Congress servile." By April 4, 1862, Boyce judged the Confederacy to be on "the brink of ruin," and he concluded that something drastic must be done. "The only way that I see by which we might save the country would be to supercede Davis, to establish a provisional Government of the ablest men of each State, for them to have absolute powers, and to appoint the ablest man to conduct the war. . . ." Davis was not "treacherous," in Boyce's opinion, but he felt that "he is totally incompetent." With General McClellan's army approaching Richmond, Boyce lamented that, "If Davis had tried to destroy us he could not have taken a more effective course than he has."[5] McClellan's defeat and withdrawal from the peninsula silenced Boyce's revolutionary grumblings, but only for awhile.

Beginning in 1863 Boyce's dissatisfaction with the Confederate president began to focus on the possibility of encouraging peace talks. That spring he met with "a very intelligent prisoner" who had just returned from the North and who brought with him "a message from a leading man of the North West." Boyce explained to James Henry Hammond that he had learned something very important through this informal channel: "the leaders of the peace party desire peace on the basis of the independence of the South." The Confederate government seemed to be keeping its distance from these Northern dissidents because they spoke publicly of reconstructing the Union, but these words could be ignored, Boyce reported. The Northern peace party was only "talk[ing] reconstruction to get votes"; it was willing to let the South go in order to end the bloodshed. Therefore, Southern newspapers needed to stop assailing and rejecting the peace party and be more discrete. Then "the war might be ended," and once the fighting stopped, the South could "decline reconstruction." Boyce was unsure just what the administration's policy was "on this point," but he feared that it had no policy "except to 'shut their eyes & fight on.' "[6] Sensing meager support for his views at this time, Boyce took no further action, but he would return to these concerns in 1864.

The year 1864 was only the third year of Jefferson Davis' six-year term under the Permanent Constitution, but it was an extremely trying time for him and an agonizing, depressing year for white Confederates. Many Southerners had lost hope after the defeats at Gettysburg and Vicksburg in July 1863, and desertion began to rise inexorably from that point forward. In both eastern and western theatres the Confederacy's armies were under attack—falling back and shrinking in size as the months passed. On the home front civilians were feeling the full weight of inflation, shortages, and stringent government policies needed to maintain the war effort—the tax-in-kind, conscription, impressments of goods and slaves, suspension of the writ of *habeas corpus*. After "countless individual sacrifices, and thousands of deaths, many in the Confederacy saw no point in continuing."[7] While Davis' policy was to maintain the appearance of unity and determined resistance, in hopes of influencing the Northern elections, morale within the Confederacy was rapidly deteriorating. Even before the disasters of the fall, many Southerners knew that the situation of their new nation was grave, and in such circumstances risky expedients and desperate measures began to be discussed.

Early in 1864 the agitation to change Davis or his policies was taken up by politicians who were far more influential and well known than Congressman Boyce—namely Vice President Alexander H. Stephens and Governor Joseph E. Brown of Georgia. Alexander Stephens had become alienated from President Davis early in the contest, and he found both Richmond and his duties as presiding officer of the Confederate Senate loathsome, so he had absented himself from the capital for most of the war. Though his private correspondence was full of hostility to such policies as conscription and suspension of the writ of *habeas corpus*, he had generally refrained from public assaults on the government. Not so Governor Joseph E. Brown, who already had denounced conscription in the strongest possible terms and fought against many other administration policies throughout the war. At this point these two leading figures—well known both in Georgia and throughout the South and aided in the Georgia legislature by Linton Stephens, Alexander's half-brother—joined in a serious attack on the government's war policies and called for a more vigorous pursuit of peace.

Linton Stephens was the firebrand among these three. He had been ready for some months to entertain revolutionary action against Jefferson Davis. Calling the President *"mad, infatuated,"* "a bloated piece of incompetence," and "a fool," Linton argued to his brother that something needed to be done about the "tyrant." "It seems to me," Linton concluded, "the case calls loudly for a Brutus."[8] The vice president felt little or no affection for Davis and found it difficult to keep up limited communications with him, but his feelings were less personal than Linton's and were grounded more in policy. Alexander Stephens was deeply agitated about what he saw as violations of principle and constitutional rights in government measures such as impressment, conscription, and suspension of the writ of *habeas corpus*. His anger on these points knew few bounds. In correspondence with Senator Herschel Johnson his rage led him to declare that there should be a change in the executive branch. If the administration would not voluntarily retire, Stephens told Johnson, "they ought to be made to retire."[9]

Herschel Johnson admired Stephens, but he worked hard to restrain the vice president's emotions, repeatedly standing up to him about the proper steps to take while sympathizing with him over the "many errors of the administration." "If Davis were to resign," Johnson assured Stephens, "I would be well satisfied with You as the President. I believe you know how sincere this remark is." But, he pointed out, no one could guarantee that a new set of Stephens appointees would act wisely or that "a different policy, which we may advocate, would yield better results." The outcome of any leader's decisions was unpredictable, especially in a Confederacy sur-

rounded by troubles and weighed down by sinking morale. Stephens himself had heard, from the editor of an Atlanta newspaper, that "thousands
of men" were "willing to give up their slaves tomorrow and go back into
the Union with slavery abolished if it will bring peace and security to them
in their other property." Now Johnson bluntly warned Stephens that he
was venturing into dangerous territory with his talk of changing the administration. "I know of but one Constitutional mode of *making* the administration retire—that is, by impeaching the President," wrote Johnson,
and "I am not aware that he has done anything that would sustain that
process." Davis, Johnson wrote,

> has four Years yet to hold the office. Hence, we must succeed or fall
> under his lead—or else he must be deposed. . . . Are You prepared for
> that movement?—I know You are not. And yet that is the tendency
> of the Counter revolution, likely to be inaugurated. . . . I dread above
> all things counter-revolution. It means blood & carnage and anarchy
> or Despotism. . . . [10]

Johnson also was troubled by the idea that a Southern peace party might
be organized or that the mechanism of a state convention could be used to
work for peace. He saw these ideas as encouraging talk of revolution or
counterrevolution. "Of course it is the right of the people of Georgia & of
n. Carolina," Johnson wrote, "to hold a Convention & sesede [*sic*] from
the Confederacy & rejoin the U.S. I do not differ from You, as to all you
say on this subject. But I doubt the wisdom & loyalty of the man who
would propose such a Convention, for any such purpose, and I deplore the
advocacy of a Policy now. . . ."[11] These strong words of advice probably
had an impact on Alexander Stephens, for he carefully kept his positions
within the bounds of constitutional action. But he also gave his active support to Governor Brown and Linton as they challenged the administration
before the Georgia legislature.

In the middle of March 1864, at a specially called session of the Georgia legislature, Linton Stephens introduced two sets of resolutions, one denouncing the suspension of *habeas corpus* and the other urging that the
Confederacy offer negotiations for peace whenever "none can impute [our]
action to alarm." Governor Brown addressed the lawmakers, mixing patriotic assertions with fierce attacks on the administration. An invitation to
Vice President Stephens to speak was arranged, and he lent his prestige and
standing to this assault on the administration, blasting both conscription
and suspension of the writ as unconstitutional and unwise. Although he
acknowledged that suspension of the writ of *habeas corpus* might be needed
in time of invasion, Stephens somehow did not feel that the presence of
Northern armies deep within the Confederacy was adequate justification

Alexander H. Stephens. Deeply disapproving of the government he served, Vice President Stephens entertained a desire to remove Jefferson Davis and urged General Lee to assume greater powers. (Courtesy of Library of Congress)

now. He charged that Congress' act was a cover for the goal of forcing men into the army, and he warned that liberty must be retained before all other things.[12]

Stephens' blistering attack on the central government created a sensation in Georgia and was widely noted in the rest of the Confederacy as well as the North. Although the Confederacy's vice president had asserted, "I am for no counter-revolution," this very public action by one in such a high office gave encouragement, and even a hint of legitimacy, to the radical schemes of others. A dismayed Herschel Johnson wrote to Stephens,

You are wrong in view of your official position; you are wrong because the whole movement originated in a mad purpose to make war
on Davis and Congress;—You are wrong because the movement is
joyous to the enemy, and they are already using it in their press.

Enough legislators shared Johnson's dismay that the two sets of resolutions
did not easily win passage, and before they did the legislature added a declaration of its undiminished confidence in Jefferson Davis, while one house
called on the governor not to interfere with conscription.[13]

Still, these events had exposed deep fissures in Southern unity and accelerated the centrifugal forces threatening Confederate society. As historian Thomas Schott has pointed out, "Within months of the special session,
three more Confederate state legislatures (Alabama, North Carolina, and
Mississippi) passed resolutions condemning the suspension act." This was
just what Governor Brown wanted, for he had printed up copies of his
speech and Alexander Stephens' address and sent them to "every county
clerk in the Confederacy," to make sure their protest was noted. Brown
could be more confident that Richmond's lawmakers would pay attention
to the events in Georgia, and, indeed, there was a response at the capital.
North Carolina's representative James T. Leach introduced resolutions in
May denouncing suspension of *habeas corpus* and calling for the appointment of commissioners to seek a ninety-day armistice.[14]

Through the summer Southerners' longing for peace continued to grow
as the military prospects of the Confederacy darkened. Ulysses S. Grant
hammered relentlessly at Robert E. Lee's army, incurring mounting casualties that shocked the North but also exacting a painful and irreparable toll
from the Army of Northern Virginia. In Georgia, Joseph E. Johnston's
Army of Tennessee fell back steadily before General Sherman. With the fate
of Atlanta becoming daily more perilous, Southerners everywhere worried
about the impact its fall would have not only on the South but also on the
peace forces of the North. When Sherman captured Atlanta—transforming
the political climate of the North and enabling Lincoln's reelection—there
were differing and opposed reactions in the Confederacy. Obviously, the
situation of the Southern nation was growing desperate. To Jefferson Davis
and his supporters, these events proved that Southerners must fight on, re-
newing their resolve in order to gain independence rather than suffer subjugation. But to many others the fall of Atlanta was evidence that
established policies were a failure and that new measures must be tried.
The idea of independent state action reappeared, with a growing number
of congressmen pinning their hopes on some form of negotiations. Talking, they hoped, could lead to an armistice, and an armistice to peace.

South Carolina's W. W. Boyce now reasserted himself by putting public
pressure on Jefferson Davis. On September 29, 1864, he wrote a strong letter to the Confederate president, arguing for a convention of the states and

an armistice, and arranged for this letter to be published in the press. One of the most striking aspects of Boyce's initiative was the fact that he posed the alternatives facing the Confederacy as either "military despotism" or negotiations. If the Confederacy did not achieve peace, it would *have* to become a centralized military despotism, Boyce argued, in order to survive. In voicing these sentiments, he gave impetus to ideas that soon would be discussed widely. In fact, they had been germinating for some time. When Congressman Pugh of Alabama deplored the opposition to Jefferson Davis in 1862, he noted that, "Some already declare Congress is bound by no Constitution in time of war."[15]

Texas's fiery senator Louis Wigfall was another legislator who saw the logic of a military solution to the Confederacy's problems. In April 1864 he had dismissed Jefferson Davis not as a tyrant but as a "failure." He saw the president as weak and timid when strength and boldness were required. Referring to the fact that Davis had made a public declaration of religious faith, Wigfall wrote that, "The last thing a Caesar, Cromwell or Napoleon would have thought of when the gunboats were in the River would have been—joining the Church." Although Davis might do well hunting rabbits, "when the bear shows himself he takes to a tree." Therefore, Wigfall suggested to South Carolina's J. H. Hammond that perhaps a "commander-in-chief" should be appointed who would take all military matters into his hands.[16]

Now, five months later, Boyce argued that negotiations were the only way to avoid a military despotism. The Confederacy should cultivate the peace forces within the North's Democratic Party, whose platform, he correctly noted, had "resolved that if they attained power they would agree to an armistice and a convention of all the States, to consider the subject of peace." Since the Confederate Congress would not convene before the federal election took place, it was necessary that the executive branch reach out to the Northern Democrats. Boyce appealed to Jefferson Davis to act and to offer some "favorable response from our Government." If Davis failed to promote peace, Boyce predicted, the military would become all powerful.

> The Republican form, especially the form of a Confederacy of free States, is not the best adapted for war. In fact it is a peace establishment. The form best adapted to war is a national military despotism. The republic at war is gradually passing into military despotism. As the war continues and the pressure of the enemy increases, this transition is accelerated. A republic forced to the wall by a powerful enemy must end in despotism.

Boyce cited examples from European history to illustrate his point, but he also asserted that proof was already at hand. Although Southerners had tried to create a central government "with the minimum of power to function," had not Davis' government "done everything that a centralized military despotism could do? Indeed if you were appointed military dictator, what greater powers could you exercise than you do now?" Boyce asked.[17]

Boyce's proposal did not sway Jefferson Davis, and his letter even sparked some fierce criticism of the congressman among his constituents. But in some quarters it gave new life to the notion that a strong military figure was needed—a generalissimo who would tackle the South's problems boldly, effectively, and with more genius and less restraint than the president. This idea of turning to a military man with extraordinary powers, as a means to ensure the survival of the Confederacy, became one of the most intriguing and widely discussed topics of conversation in Richmond by the end of 1864.

The city's newspapers took a leading role in agitating for a change in leadership and especially for a change that would put the country's fate in the hands of a military savior. The *Daily Richmond Examiner*, which had often criticized Jefferson Davis, concentrated its fire on him late in December. After ridiculing aspects of his proposal to bring slaves into the army, the *Examiner* laid all the blame for the Confederacy's perilous military position on the president. "Every military misfortune of this country," the paper charged, "is palpably and confessedly due to the personal interference of Mr. Davis." The nation's "means of defence" were "being thrown away" due to "the fancies and caprices of one unlucky man" who mistakenly thought he was a military genius. With defeat and occupation looming over Richmond, this attack stirred up the frustrations and dissatisfactions that were abundant in the capital and encouraged talk of a change. On Christmas day, rebel war clerk J. B. Jones noted in his diary that "a large number" of people "censure the President for our many misfortunes, and openly declare in favor of Lee as Dictator."[18]

Turning power over to General Lee now became the latest hopeful idea, something that despairing Confederates could seize as a possible solution to their problems. On December 27 the *Daily Richmond Enquirer*, a paper generally more sympathetic to President Davis than the *Examiner*, came out in favor of making Robert E. Lee commander of all the armies of the nation. While stopping short of blaming the president for mistakes, the paper commented that he had been "deceived" in his decision to replace Joseph E. Johnston as head of the Army of Tennessee. The *Enquirer* believed, on the other hand, that Lee had given wise advice and that his prestige as commander of all the armies could inspire troops in the trans-Mississippi to come to the aid of the eastern Confederacy "when the voice of the President might not be able to induce [them] to cross the river." If Congress and Davis would make Lee "*generalissimo* of all the armies," their action "would revive the confidence of the country." That same day the *Examiner* reported a rumor that Lee had been appointed as commander in chief, but the paper also expressed doubt about the report because it could not believe that "Mr. Davis is capable of an act so sane and wise." The next day J.B. Jones reported in his diary that "It is still believed that Gen. Lee is to be generalissimo, and most people rejoice at it." On December 29 the *Examiner* argued that the only way to lift the "gloomy impression upon the publick mind" was to appoint Lee as a "new officer—a commander-in-chief—who shall exercise supreme control over the armies and military affairs of this Confederacy." Two days later Jones, the War Department clerk, wrote that

> There is supposed to be a conspiracy on foot to transfer some of the powers of the Executive to Gen. Lee. It can only be done by revolution, and the overthrow of the Constitution. Nevertheless, it is believed many executive officers, some high in position, favor the scheme.[19]

Evidence that members of the executive branch favored these ideas is lacking and much of what Jones heard was probably no more than rumor, but it is a fact that there was discussion of such matters in Congress. An ally reported to President Davis that Senator Louis Wigfall, as he traveled through Georgia on his way to Richmond, had contacted Linton Stephens. His purpose was to communicate

> a plan he had on foot for taking all the military power out of the hands of the President on account of incapacity. His scheme is to get [Governors] Brown & McGrath [*sic*] & Vance to call a convention or the three States to unite in a call for a convention for the purpose.

Historian George Rable adds that Wigfall wanted to make Joseph E. Johnston "military dictator—a ludicrously unsuitable role for a general who so often dodged responsibility." Mary Boykin Chesnut also recorded that Senator Wigfall was declaring, "Make Joe Johnston dictator and all will be well."[20] But Wigfall's solution gained few adherents. General Johnston himself was not interested in such an unpromising and difficult appointment, and few thought of Johnston as the nation's military savior. Those interested in such ideas continued to focus their hopes on Robert E. Lee.

As 1865 began, time clearly was running out for the Confederacy, and those who favored desperate and extraconstitutional measures to save the nation recognized that they would have to act soon. J.B. Jones reported that some momentum for a change was building, but he also foresaw problems:

> The disaffection is intense and wide-spread among the politicians of 1860, and consternation and despair are expanding among the

people. Nearly all desire to see Gen. Lee at the head of affairs; . . .
[but] the President is resolved to yield the position to no man during
his term of service. Nor would Gen. Lee take it.[21]

Jones had put his finger on two formidable obstacles that lay in the path
of those who wanted to supplant President Davis or discard the constitution. Neither Lee nor Davis were going to cooperate with such a scheme.
Nevertheless, both the newspapers and some political figures continued
their agitation through the month of January. From South Carolina, for example, came the *Charleston Mercury*'s demand that Congress impeach
Davis. "Is there no high toned gentleman in the land, like General Lee, or
General Joseph E. Johnston," asked the *Mercury*, "who could be raised by
Congress to the position now held by this incompetent man, tried now for
four long years, and always found equally wanting in capacity and in patriotism?"[22] Such efforts caused Jefferson Davis' greatest crisis with Congress and culminated both in a major blow to the president's stature and
influence and in a new role for General Lee.

On January 8, 1865, R. L. Montague, a Virginia congressman, told J. B.
Jones that "there was a strong party in Congress (which he opposed) in
favor of making Gen. Lee generalissimo without the previous concurrence
of the President." Montague also reported that members of the Georgia
delegation to Congress were threatening to withdraw their state from the
Confederacy and reenter the Union, unless Lee assumed control of all military affairs. Another government officer and diarist, R.G.H. Kean, noted
on the same day that a Senate committee had been investigating the woe-
ful state of the government's finances and supply operations but would be
able to do nothing practical "except a vote to express the now almost universal 'want of confidence.'" Kean continued:

> One solution which I have heard suggested is an entire change of the
> Executive by the resignation of the President and Vice-President. This
> would make [R.M.T.] Hunter, as president of the Senate, the presi-
> dent, would really make Lee commander-in-chief, and would go far
> to restore lost confidence.

To keep up the pressure for change, the *Examiner* came out the next day
with a call for state conventions and a joint convention of all the states to
establish a general in chief and make other changes in the government.
Davis, declared the paper, was "utterly weak and narrow" and mistaken
in his belief that he had military ability.[23]

Jefferson Davis had endured enormous criticism throughout the war. He
could ignore verbal attacks, but he could not safely ignore action. By the
middle of the month, Congress—and also the Virginia legislature—were
ready to translate the wild talk and feelings of despair into some form of

R.M.T. Hunter. This well-connected Senator fought vigorously against the proposal to arm the slaves until the Virginia legislature instructed him to vote in favor of the measure. (Courtesy of Library of Congress)

action that a legislative majority could support. On January 15 the Confederate Senate overwhelmingly passed and forwarded to the House a resolution urging Davis to make Lee general in chief and to put Joseph Johnston in charge, once more, of the Army of Tennessee. Two days later the Virginia legislature unanimously resolved that "the appointment of General Robert E. Lee to the command of all the armies of the Confederate States would promote their efficiency and operate powerfully to reanimate the spirits of the Armies, as well as of the people. . . ." That same day the *Examiner* published "another article," as J. B. Jones noted, "call-

ing for a convention to abolish the Constitution and remove President
Davis."[24] The *Examiner* demanded that Lee be given the "whole military
power of the Confederacy, independent by legislative enactment of all control and restriction and interference—with authority to assign Generals and
other officers to command, transfer armies, and to give unity of plan and
aim to the whole operations of the war." Lee, the *Examiner* soon added,
must have "absolute military power."[25] At this point, Jefferson Davis mar-
shaled his self-control and subordinated his pride to deal with the discontent. Drawing on the deep mutual confidence that characterized his
relationship with Robert E. Lee, Davis took steps to resolve the situation.

On January 18 Davis wrote to General Lee and extended to him all the
possible options for assuming greater military responsibilities. Saying that
he had heard that Lee had changed his opposition "to the extension of your
command, while retaining command of the Army of Northern Virginia,"
Davis "renew[ed]" the proposition that Lee should assume responsibility
for "the South Atlantic States, together with Virginia and North Carolina."
In addition, Davis offered two "larger sphere[s]:" command of all Confederate armies east of the Mississippi; or, "if you think it practicable," to
"resume your former position of Commander of all the Armies of the Confederacy." With each of these offers went the assurance that Lee would continue to be in "immediate command" of his troops in Virginia, for Lee had
made it plain on many earlier occasions that he was not willing to leave
the Virginia theatre. But Davis now asked him to become general in chief
as well.[26]

Lee at first demurred. Not only was he determined to act with propriety and stay within the bounds of the military's traditional role, but he also
felt that Davis' proposal was unworkable in practice. After politely declining the president's offer, Lee explained that "If I had the ability, I would
not have the time." There were myriad details to oversee in commanding
the Army of Northern Virginia, and he would not be able to add effective
supervision even of troops in the south Atlantic states. Leading his army
in Virginia, Lee said, "engrosses all my time," and yet he still was unable
to do all that he needed and wanted to do as commander of those forces.
Lee felt the proposal was not practical.[27]

But pressure for some kind of change continued to build, and the pressure came in sharp, staccato fashion. On January 18, the same day that
Davis wrote to Lee, the Virginia legislature passed another resolution, this
time demanding that the entire cabinet resign. This struck particularly hard
with James Seddon, who refused to continue after such harsh, though implied, criticism from his own state. Seddon submitted his resignation and
soon left the cabinet, to Jefferson Davis' regret. The president still had to
act on the issue of military command, as the Confederate House was moving toward concurrence with the Senate's resolution on January 19. Although the House vote took place in secret session, J. B. Jones used his

contacts in the capital to record that the vote was very lop-sided—62 to 14.[28] Then on January 20 the speaker of the Confederate House, Thomas S. Bocock of Virginia, visited the president. He brought with him the entire Virginia delegation, and together they urged major changes in the cabinet. The next day Bocock wrote to explain further "one important reason" for this visit. "There has been some discussion," he warned Davis

> among the members of Congress in relation to the propriety of declaring by resolution that the country wants confidence in the cabinet as an administration. If such a resolution should be offered, and it is, I assure you, by no means improbable, we are satisfied that it will pass the House of Representatives by a vote of at least three-fourths of the members present.

Bocock added that his desire was to prevent such a confrontation with the executive branch and emphasized his "kindest regards."[29]

"What will result from this?" asked J. B. Jones after the House vote. "Is it not a condemnation of the President and the administration that displaced Gen. J[ohnston]?" What resulted was action by President Davis. When Davis reviewed Bocock's letter, he saw that it was "a warning, if not a threat," and though he was greatly displeased, he knew he would have to act.[30] Therefore, he moved ahead on two fronts: the legislative and the administrative. He took steps to respond to the Congress and to Virginia's lawmakers, knowing that he could count on the ultimate agreement and cooperation of the man with whom he had always worked so harmoniously, General Lee.

Davis replied quickly to a committee of the state legislature, giving them details about Lee's attitude and assuring them "that he is and ever has been willing to bestow larger powers on Gen. Lee." In fact, Davis wrote that whenever Lee agreed, "I will deem it promotive of the public interest to place him in such command." The *Richmond Sentinel*, which usually supported Davis, published this correspondence, an act that defended the president while it simultaneously put gentle but effective pressure on Lee. Davis also must have communicated with key members of the national legislature to shape legislation that would be acceptable to him and Lee. Only four days after the House vote, the Confederate Congress passed a bill that established the office of general in chief, who would have "command of the military forces of the Confederate States." By February 1, 1865, Davis had named Lee to this post, and the General Orders announcing this action were issued on February 6.[31]

These events nearly spelled an end to Confederates' discussions about supplanting Jefferson Davis and installing a military commander invested with extraordinary and extraconstitutional powers. The president had weathered the most serious potential threats to his authority, but there was no disguising the fact that the month of January 1865 had been painful and had cost him a great deal politically. The arrangement that eventually modified Lee's position was the least objectionable outcome of this crisis. Congress' support for Joseph E. Johnston, however, had been an extremely bitter pill for Davis to swallow. Moreover, the extensive talk about "no confidence" votes, replacement of the entire cabinet, and military dictatorships was very damaging. Davis himself complained about the "trials to which the Congress has of late subjected the Executive," and he felt that the Senate had tried "to destroy the confidence of the people in me."[32]

In implementing the new law establishing a general in chief, Robert E. Lee continued to demonstrate the tact and sensitivity that had nourished his entire relationship with Jefferson Davis. Rather than brandishing his new powers, Lee moved deliberately and with respect for the president's position. Saying that he had assumed his new duties "in obedience to orders issued from the Adjutant and Inspector General's Office," Lee told Davis "I know I am indebted entirely to your indulgence and kind consideration for this honorable position. I must beg you to continue these same feelings to me in the future and allow me to refer to you at all times for counsel and advice." Lee then went on to say that he hoped he could relieve Davis from some of his "constant labor." Even as he spoke about his resolve to hold commanders responsible for their performance, Lee indicated that he did not intend to act independently and wholly apart from Davis. If commanders failed or neglected their duties, Lee explained, "I must ask for their removal." Lee then suggested another and final proclamation of amnesty for deserters, with the understanding that there would be no clemency in the future. The need to return men to the armies was overwhelming.[33]

Jefferson Davis fully reciprocated the respect that Lee had shown him. In response to Lee's letter, he sent a warm note that was signed "as ever your friend." Davis praised Lee's patriotism and devotion to duty, lauded him for the heavy burdens he was carrying, and added these generous words: "The honor designed to be bestowed has been so fully won, that the fact of conferring it can add nothing to your fame." In regard to Lee's request for an amnesty, Davis signaled both support and a calm intention to maintain the powers belonging to the chief executive. "Your proposition to issue a proclamation" of amnesty "is approved," Davis wrote. But then, after making a helpful suggestion or two, he in effect vetoed the idea of announcing that there would be no further acts of clemency, for Davis insisted that he only granted pardons when there was new and compelling evidence that would have changed the court's findings.[34]

In short order Davis supported two other important requests from Lee. After reading Lee's harrowing description of the inadequate supplies for the Army of Northern Virginia, Davis cashiered Commissary General Lucius Northrop. Then Davis "complied" with Lee's request that Joseph Johnston be returned to command in southern Virginia and South Carolina. Davis gave this support to Lee despite his conviction—which he had just set down on paper in a lengthy analysis—that Johnston was unfit for such responsibility.[35]

For his part, Lee continued to reject the idea that he now had Napoleonic powers or even total control over the army. When Alexander Stephens urged him to act on his own and put Johnston in command, Lee replied, "I do not consider that my appointment as Genl in Chief of the Armies of the Confederate States confers the right which you assume belongs to it, nor is it proper that it should. I can only employ such troops & officers as may be placed at my disposal by the War Department. Those withheld or relieved from service are not at my disposal."[36] Lee would make his wishes known to Davis, who complied in this instance, but Lee refused to claim authority over the president in military affairs.

Early in March General in Chief Lee apparently took a large step that was intended to influence policy, yet, once again, he was scrupulous to respect the president's authority and acted with Jefferson Davis' full confidence. A federal general, E.O.C. Ord, had met with James Longstreet and suggested that their commanders, Grant and Lee, might now be able to end the war through military negotiations. Lee and Longstreet had a meeting with Davis, and after hearing Longstreet's report, Davis gave Lee considerable discretion. If Lee thought a conference might be useful, "you will proceed as you may prefer," wrote Davis, "and are clothed with all the supplemental authority you may need in the consideration of any proposition for a military convention. . . ." The next day Lee and General John B. Gordon had a long conversation about the army's prospects. According to Gordon, Lee agreed that it was fruitless to continue the struggle any longer. But he insisted that he must go to Richmond and present these arguments to Davis, since ending the war was a political matter. The next day Lee went to Richmond, probably to urge peace. But Lee found Davis still determined to fight on and "very pertinacious" about independence. Moreover, word soon arrived that Grant had refused to meet, thus rendering both the idea of a conference and the question of what would be said moot.[37]

The discussion of desperate proposals was not quite exhausted, for in March 1865 Congressman James T. Leach of North Carolina offered resolutions that supported Lee's appointment as general in chief and then proposed that Lee "be invested with powers to treat for peace."[38] But Leach had been so early and outspoken an advocate of peace that he was isolated in the Congress and without influence, and his proposals produced no result. Moreover, it was obvious by this point that military defeat was imminent. Most Confederate politicians seemed resigned to being carried along to that dreaded outcome, since they could identify no effective steps to avert it.

What, then, is the significance of these desperate and often unconstitutional proposals? What did this remarkable episode in the life of the Confederacy reveal? Notably, these events demonstrated that the tradition of civilian supremacy over the military was strong within the Southern army. Politicians and newspaper editors were the source of the ideas about putting a military man in control. These civilians generated schemes for what they would like the military to do, but the army was not part of the discussions. No evidence suggests that any general or high-ranking officer in the Confederate army wanted to seize power from the civilian government. The men who generated military scenarios and schemes, ineffective as these were, all had civilian credentials.

Among the generals, Robert E. Lee did much to maintain civilian supremacy. His actions and his words consistently manifested great respect for the principle of civilian control. At no point did Lee show any interest in using the vast prestige that he possessed by 1865 to advance himself or broaden his role beyond that of a commander who was subordinate to civilian authorities. Certainly Lee deserves credit both for his actions and for the example they set, but it is also noteworthy that the rest of the Confederate high command behaved in a similar manner. Joseph E. Johnston may have been one of the most ambitious Southern generals; he enjoyed considerable popularity, and he was very well connected with prominent politicians. Moreover, he knew that he had a fairly influential champion in Senator Louis Wigfall. Yet Johnston displayed no ambitions that went beyond a traditional military role and did not dream of being a Napoleon. The Southern general who was most attracted to Napoleonic battle plans— P.G.T. Beauregard—also reinforces the point. It would be difficult to identify another general officer who had a larger ego or was more given to envisioning himself at the center of dramatic and heroic movements than Beauregard. He, too, had abundant political contacts and allies. Yet Beauregard, at this juncture, confined his ambitions to the military arena and was not hungering to seize power from civilian authorities.

These plans and proposals failed for a number of reasons, and the lack of interest or support for them within the Confederate military was one of the most important. But they also came to nothing because they were unsound, unrealistic, and unwieldy. The problems of the Confederacy—however much critics liked to blame Jefferson Davis—were not primarily ones of executive leadership. The Southern government struggled against a host of serious difficulties, and few if any scholars feel that a different president could have made a magical difference. Weaknesses in morale, finance, transportation, diplomacy, human and material resources, and the overall political culture all weighed heavily on the Confederacy. Jefferson Davis was far from being a perfect leader, but the judgment of Herschel Johnson was probably correct: "I know of no man among us, from the ranks of the extreme Sesessionists [sic], who would have conducted affairs half so well."[39]

Moreover, there was an imaginary quality to most of these ideas. They were constructed of dreams. Facing dissolution and defeat, proud Southern politicians were grasping at straws, casting about for some panacea that could suspend reality and change everything. The *Richmond Examiner* was ignoring reality and whistling in the dark when it blamed every military problem on Jefferson Davis and insisted that General Lee could set everything right. Depressed by what was coming and unwilling to believe that their prewar confidence had been so misplaced, the advocates of these desperate measures engaged in wishful thinking and ignored the complications entailed in their supposed solutions. This was especially true of those who gave the most thought to respecting constitutional principles and procedures. All Confederates would have agreed that any state had the right to call a convention, and that the states could exercise their sovereignty to secede or to change the entire form of government. But state conventions and a convention of several states required a long and complicated procedure. How could such assemblies take place while the Confederacy maintained government functions and the morale of soldiers and civilians in the midst of an enormous war? Most politicians sensed that these ideas were unworkable or unrealistic and so withheld their support. What is remarkable is the amount of consideration they received.

These strange events at the end of the Confederacy say a great deal about the leadership class of the South and about the situational basis of Southerners' cherished theories of government. The Confederacy's politicians and editors revealed through their actions what their principles were made of, how they viewed themselves, and what they truly valued. Most discovered during the war, and again through these events, that states' rights constitutionalism had been their tool rather than their profound religion. The idea that the only safeguard for liberty was rigid adherence to all provisions of the constitution proved less compelling in wartime than during sectional conflict. The belief that the central government must be weak and the states paramount gave way before the realities of fighting a war that involved the total society.

Survival in the enormous and exhausting struggle with the North required strong measures and massive change. Given the vehemence of their prewar rhetoric about states' rights and constitutional liberty, it is amazing how many Southern politicians quickly abandoned their rigid principles. Many accepted an unaccustomed flexibility as necessary and unavoidable, while a surprising number went even farther to talk about desperate expedients such as military rule. Georgia's Herschel Johnson, who was himself among those who bowed to reality and accepted the necessity of great change, wrote at the end of 1863, "I confess I am amazed at the lightness with which State sovereignty & constitutional obligation are treated by influential members of Congress—those too, who in former days were Sticklers upon those points."[40]

The Confederacy did not lack for politicians and newspapers that made loud protests about states' right and constitutional limits, but many of these figures either acted extralegally or were inconsistent in their stands. For example, Georgia's Joseph E. Brown took many strong actions in his state—such as seizing valuable commodities such as salt and declaring a draft—that he would not have tolerated from Jefferson Davis. Brown's legal authority for some of these actions was scant or nonexistent. The *Charleston Mercury* also was not wholly consistent; though it thundered about states' right, the *Mercury* became more supportive of some of Jefferson Davis' actions as the nation's crisis deepened. Very few Southerners maintained the purity of their supposedly sacred doctrines. Alexander and Linton Stephens stand out for remaining radical and consistent in their theories, but contemporaries saw that they were unrealistic. Few could agree with Vice President Stephens that Southerners would rush to arms, without conscription, as they experienced deep invasion and the rending of their social fabric. The protests of the Stephens brothers may have won a sympathetic hearing, but they did not attract many supporters, as few believed that the Confederacy really could do without the draft or a suspension of the writ of *habeas corpus*. The shibboleths of states' right and limited government had been useful in defending slavery and sectional interests, but they were not helpful to the Confederacy.

Ironically, Jefferson Davis, who was pilloried early in the war for using the powers that the constitution gave him, proved to respect it much more than many who decided that they had to displace him. The desperate proposals of congressmen such as Louis Wigfall and journals such as the *Richmond Examiner* provide a commentary on the political culture of the slaveholding South. The competition for recognition and "honor," the thirst to assert and distinguish oneself above one's peers, was a social contagion that inflamed the body politic. It had produced belligerence, extreme positions, fistfights, canings, knife fights, and duels before the Civil War.[41] In the Confederacy this factor combined powerfully with the awareness that Confederates were inscribing their names in history's permanent record to encourage much posturing and self-aggrandizing behavior. Egotistical politicians called attention to themselves through radical talk; what South Carolina's Henry James Hammond called Big Man Me-ism afflicted and weakened the political culture.[42] These facts surely contributed to the vicious criticism of Davis and the extensive discussion of a military savior. Being balanced, reasonable, and wise did not win much attention in Confederate politics, and thus a new nation struggling for its survival had more than its share of extreme critics, overblown rhetoric, and grand-standing politicos.

Finally, this episode shows once again that some Confederates were willing to take any steps to preserve their slave-based social system. The *Richmond Examiner* put all its faith in General Lee, but it did so *despite* his advocacy of emancipation, which had no part in the *Examiner*'s vision of the Confederate future. This newspaper could insist optimistically, against all evidence, that, "The military condition of this country was never so prosperous as it was at midsummer" in 1864, before Jefferson Davis ruined everything by replacing Joseph Johnston as commander of the Army of Tennessee. And the *Examiner* didn't hesitate to claim that giving power to Lee would be "a remedy for all discontent." "If Lee is the commander-in-chief of the whole military power of the Confederacy," wrote the paper, "the full force of this people will re-appear." Determined to fight on, the *Examiner* would not give up. In fact, judging from its pages, an innocent reader in some foreign land might have concluded in February 1865 that the Confederacy was winning the war.[43]

But the *Examiner* excoriated and ridiculed the idea of freeing the slaves in return for their military service. Davis' proposal was "absurd and suicidal." Impressing slave property was one thing, but freeing slaves was another: "Impressed mules and horses do not necessarily become citizens; and if Caligula made his horse a consul, the example has not been followed by rational Governments." Indeed, the *Examiner* insisted that slavery would continue after the war, even if the North was victorious and chose to call the institution by another name. For slavery benefited the slave, was superior to the North's labor system, and constituted "the essential and distinctive principle of Southern civilization." Moreover, "[N]egroes are not intended for soldiers, and will never fight when they can avoid it." Only military necessity and the country's dependence on Lee's military genius "could induce, or rather coerce" Southerners to acquiesce in his request for black troops.[44]

Nor did the congressional advocates of desperate measures show much support for emancipation. Some may have been willing to swallow emancipation if their military hero, General Lee, demanded this step, but they would not publicly advocate it. Such advocacy was left to Jefferson Davis, Robert E. Lee, and a few members of the Davis administration. The leadership class of the South, as a whole, would consider replacing the president or handing power over to a generalissimo, but it would not countenance emancipation.

8

Citizens and Soldiers

The experience of Southerners in the Confederate era was marked by tumult, suffering, and complexity. Citizens and soldiers alike had their lives turned upside down by military events, for the war rapidly came to dominate everything. Like a tidal wave, it smashed the accustomed structures of society and flooded the land with drastic and unwanted change. The most respected historian of the South, the late C. Vann Woodward, argued that "the collective experience of the Southern people" is unique in the nation's history because Southerners have known extended periods of "poverty . . . frustration, failure, and defeat."[1] Enduring these in abundance during the Civil War, they also had to adjust to unprecedented change and to something else almost unknown in the national experience: a substantial measure of social disintegration. First the war reorganized their lives and their society, and then it subjected the Confederacy to stresses that increasingly broke it down and ate away at its unity. While some Confederates fought bravely on, others saw the structures of authority and stability crumble around them. Soldiers and civilians had divergent and difficult experiences, but both were subject to the coercive power of war. The pattern of their experiences helps us to place civil-military relations in the Confederacy in perspective.

War severely altered the lives of Southern soldiers, whether they served in the army for only part of the conflict or endured through Appomattox. The roughly 900,000 Southern whites who served at one time or another in the Confederate army represented, in a generous estimate, approximately 74 percent of the region's white males of military age.[2] As in most wars, it was the young who risked their lives in disproportionate numbers. Bell Wiley's study of a sample of 11,000 infantry privates, whose names were taken from army descriptive rolls, showed that 18 year olds were the largest single group, comprising more than 8 percent of the total. Young men in the 18 to 29 age range predominated, making up almost 80 percent of the sample, whereas boys under 18 years of age were only about 5 percent of the total, and men over 40 only a little more than 4 percent. Wiley's sample may have reflected patterns in the early part of the war more accurately than its later stages, but the initial enthusiasm for the cause gripped men of all ages in 1861, and he concludes that, "The overwhelming bulk of the Southern Army from beginning to end appears to have been made up of persons ranging in age from 18 to 35." Another study based on a random sample of 1,010 Mississippians found that 73 percent of the young men aged 18 to 24 joined Mississippi units, with lower rates of participation in older categories. Eighty-nine percent of the men in this study enlisted in 1861 or 1862, leaving only "eleven percent to join in the war's final years." That percentage may not have held constant for all parts of the Confederacy, but as General Patrick Cleburne had pointed out in 1864, recruiting from the older age categories never produced more than modest results. Once in the army, three-quarters of the troops filled the ranks of the infantry, with 20 percent serving in the cavalry and only 5 percent in the artillery.[3]

Every man who entered the army found, of course, that his life changed completely. The vast majority of Southern soldiers came from farms and sparsely populated rural regions in which they lived close to home and encountered relatively few people. On the farm they made their own decisions and ordered their lives with little interference from other individuals or from government. Army life, by contrast, threw them into close contact with hundreds and thousands of men, many of whom were complete strangers. Army discipline dictated their movements and subjected them to a level of control that was foreign and usually unpleasant. The new recruits were sent to camps of instruction where from 5 A.M. roll call to lights out at 9 P.M. all their activities were prescribed. At the head of their duties was the infamous repetition of "drill, then drill, then drill again. Then drill, drill, a little more drill. Then drill, and lastly drill." It relieved the monotony of this tiresome and dusty activity very little to know that many new officers were learning the commands and movements along with the troops. But this routine served to accustom the troops to the unwelcome discipline that was essential to the army.[4]

Many aspects of army life have proved unpopular through the centuries, but two practices that tended to support morale in the Confederate ranks were the organization of most brigades according to their state of origin and the election of officers. When volunteers enlisted, especially early in the war, they usually formed units drawn from a particular locality, and thus many soldiers were able to serve with neighbors or men they knew. A regiment was supposed to consist of 1,000 troops, with three to five regiments comprising a brigade commanded by a brigadier general. Recognizing the strength of local attachments, the Confederacy usually formed its brigades from regiments of the same state. In fact, Confederate law adopted this principle (although generals were not always cooperative), and the practice of brigading by state often encouraged local pride and *esprit de corps*. In addition, troops in the Southern army had the right of electing their lower-level officers. Initially this often meant that individuals who were politically or socially prominent in a particular locality prevailed in unit elections, but as time went on those who had earned the soldiers' confidence and respect through their courage and character won election as officers, regardless of prewar status.[5]

In a region as large as the South, individuals naturally had a variety of motives for going to war. The analysis of enlistments in Mississippi, which some contemporaries had called a "storm center of secession," tended to confirm that "enlistments were relatively constant across occupations, landholding, and family size, but they rose as the personal stake in white supremacy increased." For example, whereas 65 percent of the 1,010 men in the sample enlisted overall, "only half of those born outside the slave states" did so; and whereas "only 56 of 100 men without any personal property were likely to enlist, . . . 71 of 100 who owned $11,000 in personal property would join the army." Yet there were many variations, even in Mississippi. The rate of enlistments from riverfront counties was lower than average, even though many of those counties had large slaveholdings. Apparently the river "brought the war's dangers to the doorsteps of those who lived along it, and . . . packing one's bags was a common reaction."[6]

Extended analysis of the reasons that Southerners went to war is beyond the scope of this study, but several key generalizations can be made that are consonant with the patterns of the Mississippi findings. There was a connection between social class or socioeconomic status, on the one hand, and commitment to the cause, on the other. Although this connection was nearly invisible in the wave of enthusiasm that swept over the South in the spring and summer of 1861, it had affected voting during the secession crisis and would surface far more significantly as the war progressed. The voting behavior of counties with many slaves differed from that of counties in which there were few slaves amid an overwhelmingly white population. Contemporaries noticed that nonslaveholding small farmers dominated in most of the counties that opposed secession or were very reluctant to secede. Moreover, as the sociologist Seymour Martin Lipset has shown, between the presidential election of 1860 and state balloting on secession, voters in these differing counties moved in opposite directions that reflected their class interests.

Andrew Jackson's Democratic Party, known as the party of the common man, had always been popular among small farmers and nonslaveholders, and that fact helped John Breckinridge, the southern Democratic, states'

right presidential candidate, do well in counties with few slaves. In 1860
Breckinridge won in 64 percent of those districts. Many wealthy slaveholders, by contrast, had traditionally been Whigs, and for that reason
Breckinridge won a lower percentage of the counties with many slaves—
only 52 percent. However, these patterns reversed in the balloting on secession. In the seven states that Lipset studied, 72 percent of the counties
with many slaves voted in favor of secession, whereas only 37 percent of
the counties with few slaves supported prosecession delegates to their state's
conventions. Thus, as the possibility of war increased, support for radical
action diminished in those areas with few slaves. Analysis of voting statistics also shows that many nonslaveholders sat out the elections to choose
delegates for a secession convention.[7] Some doubts were germinating about
the extent to which a war would serve the interests of those who were not
wealthy or owned no slaves.

The nonslaveholders and yeoman farmers, however, saw themselves as
Southerners, and their class-related concerns were buried in the excitement
and upwelling of regional loyalty that accompanied the start of the war.
When months of complicated political developments eventuated in armed
conflict, individuals had to choose sides and commit to a course of action.
Initially there seemed to be general and broadly based support for the
southern cause. An unknown number of Southerners were ideological na-
tionalists, eager to establish the Confederacy. Many others, whatever their
social class or political loyalties, felt that their region was being invaded
and their security, lives, culture, and status threatened. They had little difficulty deciding to defend their homes, their states, and their region once
the shooting started. In the upper South, the many Unionists who had
worked and struggled for some solution to the crisis resolved to fight as
Southerners and quickly joined the Confederacy.[8] Local politicians, mothers, and attractive young women called for volunteers to show their patriotism and courage. Young men in towns and counties throughout the South
rushed to show that they were no less brave and no less manly than their
neighbors by joining the army. In the summer of 1861 the secretary of war
wrote that the Confederacy "could bring into the field and maintain there
with ease 500,000 men were arms and munitions sufficiently abundant."[9]

As time passed and the high-water mark of regional loyalty and enthusiasm receded, other motives for joining the army became more significant.
Only one year into the conflict the atmosphere had changed, as most Southerners who had enlisted for one year's service were ready to go home, and
"the initial flood of volunteering had ebbed to a mere trickle." Conscription then forced soldiers to stay in their units, while it compelled others
who had not initially volunteered to become soldiers or attempt to qualify
for an exemption. "Conscription produced only about 82,000 soldiers" directly, but indirectly it brought into the armies a number larger than the
total of those who served as conscripts. "Many eligible boys volun-

teered . . . to avoid the stigma of being labeled as conscripts, as well as to receive enlistment bonuses, choice of units, and the comparative pride that came with entering service on one's own free will." Others who were affluent and eligible for conscription arranged to pay another man, a substitute, to go in their place. General Bragg estimated that 150,000 Southerners sent substitutes, but historians are more disposed to accept Secretary of War Seddon's estimate in November 1863 of "not less certainly, than 50,000." Most commanders felt that conscripts and substitutes generally made rather poor soldiers, but they became part of the Southern ranks nevertheless.[10]

The realities of service in the Confederate army had opposite effects on different individuals. They pushed many men, psychologically, toward disappointment, disaffection, and desertion. Regimentation, physically demanding tasks, and widespread sickness made daily life substantially less than pleasant. A soldier was always subject to military discipline, including the ultimate penalty of execution for disobedience; one soldier reacted to these facts by telling his family that he longed to "get out of this miserable Army again and be free once more." Sickness felled many previously healthy men, and more men died from disease and accidents in the Civil War than as a direct result of wounds. Long periods of boredom and monotony in camp alternated with moments of intense pressure and danger in battle. The lack of privacy, loneliness, and separation from loved ones back home exacted a price from people's spirits. "The dirt of a camp life knocks all its poetry into a cocked hat," wrote one volunteer, and after he had campaigned with Stonewall Jackson, he reflected on harsher facts to which he had become accustomed. "We had no tents . . . but slept on the ground, in the woods or open fields, without regard to the weather. . . . I learned to eat fat bacon raw. . . . Without time to wash our clothes or our persons, and sleeping on the ground all huddled together, the whole army became lousy more or less with body lice." Comfort, cleanliness, and good food have rarely characterized any army.[11]

These were routine problems, but a number of factors made their impact even greater in the Confederate armies. A soldier's pay soon meant little as inflation robbed his meager compensation of almost all of its value. Moreover, in many parts of the army paydays were long delayed or never arrived at all. Similarly, food and rations were poor, and their quality and quantity decreased as the war went on. A soldier in the Army of Northern Virginia lamented that he and his comrades were "half-fed, badly clad, and *almost entirely* barefooted" in the month of January. Such conditions made him comment that "No man in this whole army . . . can say, with truth, that *any* part of his previous life was not preferable to his life here." In addition, the weapons of the Civil War era inflicted brutal wounds, for the sizeable lead balls that soldiers fired destroyed flesh and shattered bones. For those who initially survived a wound, infection often brought a painful death. For many others the new level of accuracy that came with the era's rifles resulted in unprecedented carnage on the battlefield. "Any one who goes over a battlefield after a battle," wrote one man, "never cares to go over another. . . . I don't care if I am never near another fight again during the war. It is a sad sight to see the dead and if possible more sad to see the wounded; shot in every possible way you can imagine." A fellow Confederate testified, "I have heard such sounds, and seen such sights, as to make my flesh almost crawl when I think of them. Such suffering, agonizing and terrible in the extreme, I never had the least idea of before. . . . The woods were alive with dead men. . . ."[12]

For the Confederate soldiers, these problems were cumulative and progressive. "While the morale of soldiers seems always to have been better than that of civilians," observed Bell Wiley, "the army experienced a growing defection of spirit as the conflict went on."[13] Certainly this was due in large part to reverses and defeats on the battlefield. As the Confederacy lost men, territory, and resources, reasoning men would tend to grow discouraged about their prospects. But this "defection of spirit" arose even more from dissatisfaction with government policies and deep concerns over the plight of loved ones at home. The connection between spirit in the army and the state of morale on the home front was quite intimate and direct.

In raising its army the Confederacy seemed, to many, to have adopted policies that favored the rich. In 1861 the government initially accepted volunteers for twelve months and provided them with their equipment. But as shortages developed, the War Department required men to enlist for three years of service unless they could provide their own equipment. Wealthy individuals benefited from this policy, but the poor could not. This rule "aroused a widespread cry of protest," and the man who presided at Mississippi's secession convention wrote to President Davis, "I leave you to imagine the consequences" among "poor laboring men, who own no slaves and live in non-slaveholding communities." The conscription law in 1862, which allowed an exemption for those who managed twenty slaves, was even more controversial. "Never did a law meet with more universal odium," declared one congressman. "Its influence upon the poor is most calamitous," he added, and the General Assembly of North Carolina formally protested its "unjust discrimination." Moreover, substitutes, which were allowed until 1864, quickly became very expensive, so that only the wealthy could afford them, and even Secretary of War Randolph complained that this "regular business" had "led to great abuses." Some felt that "its [sic] a notorious fact if a man has influential friends—or a little money to spare he will never be enrolled." These facts inevitably depressed the morale of many soldiers.[14]

Anxiety for their families had an even greater impact on many soldiers. Newspapers and public officials were lamenting inflation, speculation, and rapidly spreading poverty even before the end of 1861, warning that "want and starvation are staring thousands in the face" and that "the poor . . .

will be unable to live at all." Despairing letters from home confirmed these alarming reports and tore at the hearts of many soldiers. Confederate generals knew that much desertion arose from the problems of families struggling on the home front. "What man is there that would stay in the armey and no that his family is sufring at home?" wrote one man. Mary Boykin Chesnut, who recorded in her diary the scene in which a woman in a "cracker bonnet" yelled at her husband, urging him to desert, was only one of many observers who knew that suffering on the home front eroded Confederate strength.[15]

For all these reasons, huge numbers of Confederate soldiers deserted. The Confederate government became seriously concerned about desertion in the summer of 1862, when the total force present for duty had fallen from 259,000 to 224,000 (out of approximately 327,000 enrolled), despite the adoption of conscription. The employment of increased numbers of provost marshals and requests to the states to use more vigor in arresting deserters brought the rolls up to 360,000 present (out of 498,000) by the spring of 1863. But from that point onward the number of men on duty fell while the number of desertions spiraled upward and could not be brought under control.[16] Major reverses on the battlefield, such as Gettysburg and Vicksburg, had a major impact, and so too did the continuing deterioration of life for those at home. Economic suffering grew, while the federal armies and bands of deserters made life more insecure and demoralization spread.

In June 1863 the acting chief of the Bureau of Conscription warned of a new "determination to avoid and even resist future service." The next month Assistant Secretary of War John A. Campbell wondered if "so general a habit" as desertion should be considered a crime. In November Secretary of War Seddon reported that "the effective force of the Army is generally a little more than a half, never two-thirds" of those on the rolls and concluded that at least one-third of the army was absent without permission. Despite the application of harsh measures to slow desertion, the number of men present plummeted from 278,000 at the end of 1863 to 195,000 in the middle of 1864. By September of that year Secretary Seddon was lamenting that "desertion is committed almost with impunity." The number of men present in the ranks fell to 160,000 (with only 126,000 ready for duty) at the end of the war. Six months before the end Jefferson Davis had publicly acknowledged that "two-thirds of our men are absent . . . most of them absent without leave." In the final days before surrender, even General Lee noted that a "want of confidence seemed to possess officers and men," and that his dedicated army "began to disintegrate."[17]

But the other side of this reality is the incredible persistence and heroism of those who stayed in the armies. While some soldiers became discouraged and disaffected, others developed a more intense dedication to their cause. Tens of thousands of Confederates kept up the fight despite the fact that they faced profoundly discouraging circumstances and ever longer odds. For many individual soldiers, one's personal identity became bound up with the army and its fate. In some cases this was the product of pride. Men who served with remarkable commanders like Jackson and Lee took great pride in the achievements they had helped to bring about. For example, one member of Jackson's "foot cavalry," who wrote home during the Valley Campaign, described the army's victory at Winchester as "one of our greatest victories . . . for we have lost so few men and accomplished so much." He added, "There has been a good deal of grumbling at General Jackson about marching us so much, but this tune has changed now, and they think he is one of the greatest men that have ever lived."[18] Such élan gave the soldiers new determination to endure hardships and fight on. In other cases their devotion grew out of painful experience. Shared suffering and shared sacrifice deepened bonds to comrades and increased what is now called "unit cohesion," while it also strengthened the soldiers' commitment to the Confederacy.

After fighting so long and valiantly, the determined veterans of the Army of Northern Virginia, especially, were unwilling to see their sacrifices go for naught, and their valor was an inspiration to many Southerners. "Robert E. Lee and his soldiers," argues Gary Gallagher,

> functioned as the principal focus of Confederate nationalism for much of the war, and young slaveholding officers who matured during the 1850s stood out as perhaps the most highly nationalistic component of the Army of Northern Virginia. Through battlefield victories, reenlistments, and letters to the home front, the officers and men of Lee's army served as an engine propelling national loyalty among civilians and soldiers throughout the Confederacy.[19]

Some of the strongest dedication to Confederate nationalism could be found among Lee's veterans. It is notable that in the winter of despair of 1864–65 many of his troops spoke out strongly in favor of continued sacrifice for the goal of independence. As debate raged over the arming and freeing of slaves, the public resolutions adopted by units of Lee's army were rare, unqualified endorsements for this radical step.[20] Indeed, in 1865 there probably was no group in the Confederacy more committed to fighting on than those battle-tested soldiers who had stayed in the ranks. At great personal price, they had remained true to the cause while others fell away, and they wanted their years of sacrifice to have meaning.

It may also be true that, for many Southerners, Lee and his army "came to embody Confederate national identity after the second year of the war." And there were "thousands" who "exhibited a strong identification with their country and ended the war still firmly committed to the idea of an independent southern nation."[21] But no account of the Confederacy and its civil-military relations can be complete or faithful to the truth that does not acknowledge the rising tide of disaffection and social disintegration that threatened to inundate the Southern nation. Except for the destruction and chaos that plagued the Southern backcountry during the Revolution, our nation has never known the level of disorganization, disorder, and lawlessness that developed in the Confederate South. Whereas soldiers' experiences unfolded within the structure of the military, many civilians watched their world's familiar patterns and routines crumble.

Some disruptions affected all civilians no matter where they lived in the South. Inflation, shortages, and the absence of skilled laborers, for example, forced severe hardships and changes on everyone. Although a newspaper in 1861 could humorously describe prices as "on the rise" and "away up yonder," the rampant and uncontrolled inflation that exceeded 7,000 percent soon produced cries of anguish. "How can a poor man live," asked one woman, "but worse than that a widow with some five or six children or a poor soldiers wife?" Inflation made currency almost worthless, stimulated barter, and compelled people to use whatever economic resources they had in desperate new ways. Obtaining an item of everyday use often became cause for celebration. For example, J. B. Jones, the War Department diarist, rejoiced when his wife gave him "an excellent undershirt, made of one of her dilapidated petticoats," and even Southern belles altered old clothing, recycling dresses that they had put away. Shortages of salt meant that meat could not be preserved, sugar and coffee became memories for all but the richest Southerners, and most kitchens lacked basic items such as vinegar, baking soda, spices, and white flour. When blacksmiths, millers, potters, or other artisans went into the army, many rural districts found that they were seriously inconvenienced or in danger of suffering if no one could repair farm implements.[22] At first these problems were inconveniences, but before long they meant that daily life became a difficult struggle for much of the civilian population.

Far more serious were the insecurity, destruction, and violence that plagued steadily increasing portions of the Confederacy and destroyed the predictability of living under a stable government. Southern civilians were threatened, obviously, whenever invading federal armies drew near, and as the war progressed U.S. forces captured more and more Confederate territory. The Union advances disrupted traditional society not only in the areas that were actually conquered, but also in a band of territory all along the army's lines. Southerners whose neighborhoods were merely threatened also found that the conditions of life changed drastically. Military raids or skirmishes could take place at any time, slaves ran away or became more assertive if they remained on the plantation, Union sympathizers showed their colors, and sometimes long simmering resentments against the prewar elite manifested themselves as thefts and other acts of violence.[23] Where federal forces had conquered, daily life became an experience of occupation or control by the foe's army, with many unwelcome changes, especially as the conflict turned into a "hard" war in which Union forces punished rebels, seized slaves, and captured or destroyed as much of the agricultural wealth of the South as possible. Equally damaging to morale was the fact that for some cotton planters, such as those who lived along the Mississippi River and in Texas, the new opportunities to trade illegally with the enemy proved both lucrative and alluring.[24]

Destruction and privations caused by the military also were widespread even in many areas that remained under Confederate control, and they arose from many aspects of military operations. As noted in chapter 4, state authorities repeatedly protested that conscription and military operations to round up men for the armies were depriving nonslaveholding regions of essential labor. "There will be great suffering next year, and . . . possible starvation," warned South Carolina's governor in one of these complaints. Secretary of War Seddon lamented the necessity for impressments, which were "the sorest test of [the people's] patriotism and self-sacrificing spirit." Seizures of work oxen, mules, and cows caused "great complaint among the people" and even though impressments were legally sanctioned, they occasioned warnings of rebellion over "the most scandalous outrages." In addition, both armies indulged in unsanctioned seizures, pilfering or trampling crops, slaughtering animals, and tearing up fences and buildings for firewood. One Virginian lamented that his "whole place [was] perfectly desolated," and his experience was not unusual.[25]

Although Lee's army set an example of great valor and sacrifice, there was enormous discouragement and disaffection on the Confederate home front, and this demoralization increasingly took the forms of both individual noncooperation and organized resistance. The first identifiable areas of serious disaffection were centered in the hilly and mountainous regions along the spine of the southern Appalachians, where Unionist sentiment had often been strong. But as time went on, widespread and organized resistance spread into many piedmont areas and even into lowland regions in Mississippi and Alabama.[26] As the Confederacy fought military campaigns against federal armies, it also fought a losing battle against spreading demoralization and disintegration within.

Social disorganization led to disloyalty or resistance. Many civilians who were suffering and discouraged reached the limits of their endurance and decided, in individual but significant ways, to withdraw their support from the Confederacy. Thousands concealed their property or moved it to a distant location in order to fight impressments. By 1864 one army official reported that, "In all the States impressments are evaded by every means which ingenuity can suggest, and in some openly resisted. In North Carolina our receipts are insignificant, and in Georgia and Alabama we are unable to purchase corn for want of money." Men hid from the authorities in order to evade the draft. Senator Herschel Johnson of Georgia advised Jefferson Davis in 1864 that "the disposition to avoid military service is . . . general," and the head of the Conscription Bureau reported that elected state officials—who were responding to popular pressure from exhausted and disaffected citizens—used their laws and powers to shield potential conscripts. "From one end of the Confederacy to the other, every constituted authority . . . is engaged in opposing the enrollment officer in the execution of his duties."[27]

The social consensus needed to unite the Confederacy behind the war effort was decaying rapidly. It was true that secret peace societies, such as the Washington Constitutional Union and the Heroes of America, were at work. The former began in 1862. It was centered in northern Alabama but had members in Georgia, Mississippi, East Tennessee, and possibly Florida as well, while the Heroes of America was strongest in North Carolina, southwest Virginia, and eastern Tennessee.[28] But more common and even more serious were the widespread, daily manifestations of disaffection that arose from demoralization, suffering, and despair.

Women staged food riots in Atlanta and Macon, Georgia; Salisbury and High Point, North Carolina; and Mobile, Alabama; and others raided food depots located in small towns in mountain districts. Generalized opposition to the war effort became so serious in substantial parts of Alabama, Mississippi, Georgia, Florida, and both Carolinas that supporters of the war effort felt outnumbered by its opponents, and governors supported their citizens against Confederate demands for supplies and taxes as well as troops. By 1863 leaders in these states were reporting large areas where "the disloyal stand in open defiance of constitutional authority" or where disloyal men were "in rebellion . . . robbing loyal citizens" or combining to support "reconstruction of the United States Government." Bands of armed resisters gained so much power and had so much support in some areas that county officials entered into formal agreements not to enforce the laws if only the resisters agreed to refrain from robbery.[29]

Alabama provides a good example of the extent of social disintegration. "By August 1863," declared historian Malcolm McMillan, "the home front . . . was in turmoil." North Alabama had so many deserters and gave them so much support that one town hosted a public dinner for fifty-seven deserters in the winter of 1864–65 while local law enforcement officers ignored warrants for their arrest. Meanwhile the commandant for conscription in the state reported that resistance had spread to "some of the most wealthy and enlightened counties in the state." Politically, opponents of the war were in the ascendant. Had the conflict not ended in April 1865, McMillan concluded, elections scheduled for the summer would have given the Peace party "control of the government of Alabama and brought the whole military effort to an end."

The people lost the will to fight. They longed for the reestablishment of the old Union to save them from the new despotism that took their property without compensation, conscripted them and forced them to fight against their will. . . . The vast majority of the people had reached the conclusion that there was no reason to continue a war that the Confederacy had already lost. . . . [30]

Reacting to similar conditions in his state, North Carolina's governor Vance lamented that "the great *popular heart* is not now & never has been in this war. It was a revolution of the politicians not the people."[31]

Though disillusionment and defeatism may have advanced farther in Alabama and North Carolina than in some other states, no state of the Confederacy was free of these problems. As conditions of life deteriorated, deeper sacrifices seemed to bring only more suffering and still more discouraging prospects for the Southern nation. After two years of this kind of experience of war, the will to sacrifice and to fight on faded rapidly. For a large portion of civilians and soldiers alike, morale plummeted and disillusionment spread like a virus. Both fighting men and fighting spirit were dissipating, robbing the Southern nation of the means to sustain itself.

The Confederacy could not have maintained its war effort and would not have survived into 1865 without the coercive application of power by the central government, including military power. This was, in historical perspective, the most significant way in which civil society became militarized in the Confederacy. Jefferson Davis was determined to achieve independence, and he pressed forward as a majority in Congress acquiesced in his policies. The Richmond administration dispatched thousands of agents to collect money taxes and the tax-in-kind. With greater effectiveness the government used the army to impress or buy food and supplies for the troops. Military officials worked to enforce conscription, and military units operated repeatedly within the Confederacy to round up deserters. Military commanders and provost marshals arrested traitors, outspoken critics, and other citizens who seemed dangerous or perhaps were merely uncooperative.

It was a reality of Southern life that as voluntary societal support for the war diminished, the government turned more to coercion. Under Jefferson Davis' leadership the Richmond administration strained to save the new nation. It pursued its policies with determination, marshaling resources needed to sustain the military and then using the military to support the war effort. It forced many citizens to comply, brought immense changes, and "all but destroyed the political philosophy which underlay the founding of the Southern republic."[32] In these steps the army increasingly became the government's indispensable tool. As resistance and disorder spread, the Confederacy relied more heavily on internal use of the military in order to have the means to carry on its external conflict. Thus, the militarization of Southern life involved both an extensive reorganization of people's energies to serve military purposes and direct military interventions in civil affairs.

The entire Confederate experience was deeply shaped by the military and its activities. Military necessity was at the bottom of most of the startling innovations that altered the South's economy and society. Military needs drove most of the key policies of the government. Military men had enormous influence on vital decisions, such as conscription, impressment, the imposition and execution of martial law, and the arming of slaves. Military commanders issued the orders that put thousands of Southerners under arrest, and the military sometimes ignored or overrode the authority of courts in the Confederacy. In all of U.S. history there never was a period in which the military had so deep an influence on civil society or on the lives of civilians. What, then, should we conclude about the character and significance of civil-military relations in the Confederacy?

The unpleasant realities of the South's wartime experience remind us that civil liberties and civilian dominance of the military are malleable human traditions, not immutable natural laws. No one could have imagined in 1860 that the South would change so much or that the military would gain so much influence over civil society. The Confederate experience reveals the potential of military crisis to sweep away or alter substantially all but the most fundamental values and principles. Individual rights, and even democracy itself, can become secondary or contingent values when survival is threatened. In the face of invasion and defeat, the need for safety and security threatened to remove all barriers before it, and efforts to defend the state led to significant restrictions on individual rights and liberties. In this regard, the Confederate years were not unique. For as strong as traditions of individual liberty and citizens' rights may be in the history and society of the United States, these values have often been compromised or restricted when the safety and security of the nation or its citizens were imperiled. The preservation of these rights is never guaranteed in time of danger.

Yet it also is true that in a broad sense the commitment of the South's white population to traditions of individual liberty and representative government for white men and to civil supremacy over the military remained strong. Despite the military's enormous impact on Southern society, the Confederacy became neither a police state nor a dictatorship. Jefferson Davis was willing to use military force domestically to support many changes and to aid the armies, but he clearly regarded these intrusions into civil society as emergency measures justified only by necessity. He made no efforts to expand them into a means for seizing greater executive power, and he had many vociferous critics who were unafraid to brand him a tyrant and pillory him for his actions. Like the North, the South violated its principles of civil liberty but did not wholly discard them.

The violations that did occur, however, were substantial and significant, and—in some ways—extremely surprising. Although the Confederacy remained a representative and constitutional government, it is remarkable that a considerable number of prominent men entertained ideas of nullifying their constitution and laws, somehow, and putting their collective fate in the hands of a military savior. In 1865 these congressmen, politicians, and editors were thinking what would have been unthinkable only a few years before. Nevertheless, although the talk about a generalissimo or a military dictator went surprisingly far, it remained only talk. Most legislators and editors were unwilling to discard the constitution and the ideals of representative government. Neither Jefferson Davis nor Robert E. Lee nor any other general hungered to become an emperor or a Napoleon. When defeat, failure, and the likelihood of emancipation and political reconstruction stared Confederates in the face, most favored a continuation of elected, representative institutions rather than the rule of a man on horseback. Control of the state by an emperor or strongman held little appeal for Davis, for his generals, or for most citizens.

In a more specific sense, however, the principle of civilian control over the military came close to being compromised. In the traditions of the United States this principle has meant that elected civilian officials retain ultimate power both to control military operations and to direct or remove even the most successful commanders. Early in 1865 many voices in the South spoke in favor of restricting that principle of civilian control in order to make General Lee the ultimate decision-maker on *all* military questions. Although Davis would have continued as president for civilian matters, these advocates wanted Lee to assume complete control of military affairs, in effect removing Davis from the role of commander in chief. However, the law Congress passed did not go so far. It created the post of a general who would have command of the military forces of the nation; it made no explicit change to Davis' constitutional powers, and General Lee promptly demonstrated that he saw himself as subordinate to the president and the War Department. Thus, the principle of civilian control was maintained in its full meaning, though narrowly. Once again the pressures for change in an emergency almost overwhelmed vitally important and long-valued principles.

Tragically, the inhumane principles and prejudices that buttressed a slave society proved nearly inviolable, as the Confederate Congress rejected emancipation even in the nation's direst extremity. Despite massive amounts of change, the Congress would not give up slavery. It is a measure of the extent of the crisis faced by the Confederacy that proposals to free the slaves obtained serious consideration from a portion of the leadership class. But it also is a measure of the power of slaveholding interests and the depth of racism in American society that this departure had far less support than any of the other radical innovations that altered the Confederacy, in a period when military necessity created enormous change.

Notes

CHAPTER 1: TRADITIONS FOR A NEW NATION

1. Marcus Cunliffe, *Soldiers and Civilians: The Martial Spirit in America, 1775–1865* (Boston: Little, Brown and Company, 1968), 337–41. Cunliffe is discussing Robert D. Meade's article, "The Military Spirit of the South," *Current History* 30 (April 1929), and Samuel P. Huntington's book, *The Soldier and the State: The Theory and Politics of Civil-Military Relations* (Cambridge, MA: Belknap Press, 1957), 211–21.

2. Cunliffe, *Soldiers and Civilians*, 338–39. Cunliffe also cites works by James C. Bonner, Willard Thorp, Rollin Osterweis, Ester J. Crooks and Ruth W. Crooks, and John Hope Franklin. To these should be added Bertram Wyatt-Brown's *Southern Honor: Ethics and Behavior in the Old South* (New York: Oxford University Press, 1982).

3. Ibid., 342–70.

4. Steven E. Woodworth, ed., *No Band of Brothers: Problems in the Rebel High Command* (Columbia: University of Missouri Press, 1999), chapter 10, "Homespun Generals," 131–33; Cunliffe, *Soldiers and Civilians*, 381. Both Cunliffe and Woodworth use the important work of Ezra J. Warner, *Generals in Gray: Lives of the Confederate Commanders* (Baton Rouge: Louisiana State University Press, 1959).

5. Quoted by Cunliffe, *Soldiers and Civilians*, 344. This quotation was from the June 2, 1861, issue of the *Charleston Mercury*.

6. James M. McPherson, *Ordeal by Fire: The Civil War and Reconstruction* (New York: Knopf, 1982), 190–91.

7. Richard N. Current, editor-in-chief, *Encyclopedia of the Confederacy*, 4 vols. (New York: Simon & Schuster, 1993), 4:1601.

8. William J. Cooper Jr., *Jefferson Davis, American* (New York: Knopf, 2000), 63–64, 126–27.

9. Ibid., 138, 144, 148–55.

10. Russell F. Weigley, *History of the United States Army*, enlarged ed. (Bloomington: Indiana University Press, 1984), 189–91.

11. Ibid., 192–95.

12. Steven E. Woodworth, *Davis and Lee at War* (Lawrence: University Press of Kansas, 1995), 5–7.

13. Ibid., 147–48, 153–54, 162–64, 40, 47; C. Vann Woodward, ed., *Mary Chesnut's Civil War* (New Haven: Yale University Press, 1981), 109; Varina Howell Davis, *Jefferson Davis, Ex-President of the Confederate States of America; A Memoir*, 2 vols. (New York: Belford Company, 1890), 2:18–19.

14. Macon is quoted in Hugh Talmage Lefler and Albert Ray Newsome, *The History of a Southern State: North Carolina*, 3rd ed. (Chapel Hill: The University of North Carolina Press, 1973), 336. For the larger context of emerging sectionalism, see Robert F. Durden, *The Self-Inflicted Wound: Southern Politics in the Nineteenth Century* (Lexington: The University Press of Kentucky, 1985), 9.

15. William S. Price, "Nathaniel Macon, Planter," *North Carolina Historical Review* 78, no. 2 (April 2000): 187–214 and 201–2; *Annals of the Congress of the United States*, 16th Congress, 1st Session (Washington, DC: Gales and Seaton, 1855), 225. Price points out that scholars such as Norman Risjord have identified Macon's comments about "glad faces" and warm greetings as the first appearance in Congress of the "positive good" defense of slavery.

16. *Annals of the Congress*, 16th Congress, 1st Session, 230.

17. Both are quoted in William W. Freehling, *Prelude to Civil War: The Nullification Controversy in South Carolina, 1816–1836* (New York: Harper Torchbooks, 1966), 257.

18. Thomas E. Schott, *Alexander H. Stephens of Georgia: A Biography* (Baton Rouge: Louisiana State University Press, 1988), 61, 78.

19. Ibid., 76.

20. Quoted in Paul D. Escott, *After Secession: Jefferson Davis and the Failure of Confederate Nationalism* (Baton Rouge: Louisiana State University Press, 1978), 6, 12.

21. Charles B. Dew, *Apostles of Disunion* (Charlottesville: University Press of Virginia, 2001), 77, 79, and passim.

22. Dunbar Rowland, ed., *Jefferson Davis, Constitutionalist: His Letters, Papers and Speeches*, 10 vols. (Jackson: Mississippi Department of Archives and History, 1923), 5:30, 4, 5; Charles Robert Lee Jr., *The Confederate Constitutions* (Chapel Hill: The University of North Carolina Press, 1963), 67 (Cobb quotation); William C. Davis, ed., *A Fire-Eater Remembers: The Confederate Memoir of Robert Barnwell Rhett* (Columbia: University of South Carolina Press, 2000), 48, 49, 50.

23. Lee, *The Confederate Constitutions*, 62.

24. Davis, *A Fire-Eater Remembers*, 26; DeBow is quoted in James M. McPherson, *Ordeal by Fire: The Civil War and Reconstruction* (New York: Knopf, 1982), 131.

25. Lee, *The Confederate Constitutions*, 65–68.

26. Ibid., 171, 93–96, 111–13, 115–16, 117–18, 101.

27. Ibid., 162, 181, 169, 197, 180; Emory M. Thomas, *The Confederate Nation, 1861–1865* (New York: Harper Torchbooks, 1979), 318, citing Article II, Section 2 (1).

28. Lee, *The Confederate Constitutions*, 186, 178, 182.

29. Rhett's quotation and Brown's action are documented in Escott, *After Secession*, 77–79.

30. Rowland, *Jefferson Davis, Constitutionalist*, 5:48.

31. Ibid., 5:32.

CHAPTER 2: POLICY-MAKING PRODUCES INNOVATION AND CONTROVERSY

1. Louis Smith, *American Democracy and Military Power* (Chicago: University of Chicago Press, 1951), 14–15.

2. As chapter 4 will explain in greater detail, the Confederacy allowed military forces to abridge civilian rights far more often than has been recognized previously. Military arrests and detentions were, in fact, quite numerous and seem roughly comparable to those that occurred in the North. For this understanding, scholars are indebted to Professor Mark E. Neely, Jr., and his ground-breaking work, *Southern Rights: Political Prisoners and the Myth of Confederate Constitutionalism* (Charlottesville: University Press of Virginia, 1999).

3. Smith, *American Democracy and Military Power*, 193–205 (quotation on 202).

4. Louise B. Hill, *State Socialism in the Confederate States of America* (Charlottesville, VA: The Historical Publishing Company, Inc., 1936).

5. Kenneth C. Martis, *The Historical Atlas of the Congresses of the Confederate States of America: 1861–1865* (New York: Simon & Schuster, 1994), 9–10 and 27–28. The arithmetical calculations based on the dates given by Martis for convening and adjourning are by the current author.

6. Wilfred Buck Yearns, *The Confederate Congress* (Athens: The University of Georgia Press, 1960), 228.

7. *Southern Historical Society Papers*, 52 vols. (Richmond: Wm. Ellis Jones' Sons, Printers, 1923), 44:46; see also 47:147; 51:5.

8. Richard N. Current, editor-in-chief, *Encyclopedia of the Confederacy*, 4 vols. (New York: Simon & Schuster, 1993), 2:763; 1:133; 4:1514.

9. Steven E. Woodworth, ed., *The Art of Command in the Civil War* (Lincoln: University of Nebraska Press, 1998), 6–8.

10. Current, *Encyclopedia of the Confederacy*, 1:199–201, 3:1038, 1286–87, 2:597–600; C. Vann Woodward, ed., *Mary Chesnut's Civil War* (New Haven: Yale University Press, 1981), 138.

11. *Southern Historical Society Papers*, 44:20, 23; Yearns, *Confederate Congress*, 141; *Southern Historical Society Papers*, 50:38; 51:20.

12. *Southern Historical Society Papers*, 47:148.

13. Steven E. Woodworth, *Davis and Lee at War* (Lawrence: University Press of Kansas, 1995), 49–52, 41–47; Yearns, *Confederate Congress*, 147. At the end of the battle of Manassas, as rain and darkness fell on the exhausted troops, only Davis had shown interest in pursuing the Union forces toward Washington. Beauregard had shown no inclination to undertake what was almost surely an impractical pursuit; his aggressiveness developed after the fact. Beauregard's overly optimistic ideas for prevailing at Manassas and seizing Washington can be found in his report. See U.S. War Department, *The War of the Rebellion: A Compilation*

of the Official Records of the Union and Confederate Armies, 130 vols. (Washington, DC: Government Printing Office, 1880–1901), Series I, 2:484–505 (hereinafter abbreviated as *O.R.*).

14. Steven E. Woodworth, ed., *The Art of Command in the Civil War* (Lincoln: University of Nebraska Press, 1998), essay by Craig L. Symonds, 6–9. See also the Bell I. Wiley Papers, Special Collections, Woodruff Library, Emory University, for copies of much of Wigfall's correspondence with Johnston.

15. Thomas Connelly and Archer Jones, *The Politics of Command* (Baton Rouge: Louisiana State University Press, 1973), 52–59 and chapter 3 generally. The activities and goals of the western concentration bloc will be discussed further in chapter 6.

16. Yearns, *Confederate Congress*, 143; Paul D. Escott, *After Secession: Jefferson Davis and the Failure of Confederate Nationalism* (Baton Rouge: Louisiana State University Press, 1978), 57.

17. Yearns, *Confederate Congress*, 140; J. B. Jones, *A Rebel War Clerk's Diary*, 2 vols., ed. Howard Swiggett (New York: Old Hickory Bookshop, 1935), 2:379; Yearns, *Confederate Congress*, 142, 144, 146; Herschel V. Johnson to Alexander H. Stephens, December 29, 1863, in Bell I. Wiley Papers, Special Collections, Woodruff Library, Emory University.

18. *Southern Historical Society Papers*, 44:54, 52:136–37, 124–28.

19. In fact, in certain areas such as North Carolina, the Whigs had continued to function under different names, such as the "Opposition" party or "Conservatives." For a discussion of the continuing influence of traditional party rivalries, see Thomas B. Alexander and Richard E. Beringer, *The Anatomy of the Confederate Congress* (Nashville: Vanderbilt University Press, 1972), 35–43, 318.

20. For an earlier but insightful discussion of this phenomenon, which has frequently repeated itself in the aftermath of modern colonialism, see William Nisbet Chambers, *Political Parties in a New Nation: The American Experience, 1776–1809* (New York: Oxford University Press, 1963), chapter 5 and passim. Such sentiment was widespread in the North during the Civil War as well. See Mark E. Neely Jr., *The Union Divided* (Cambridge: Harvard University Press, 2002).

21. Alexander and Beringer, *Anatomy of the Confederate Congress*, 46–47 and ff., 54–56.

22. David Donald, ed., *Why the North Won the Civil War* (New York: Collier Books, 1962), 112.

23. Alexander and Beringer, *Anatomy of the Confederate Congress*, 342.

24. Hugh Talmage Lefler and Albert Ray Newsome, *The History of a Southern State: North Carolina*, 3rd ed. (Chapel Hill: The University of North Carolina Press, 1973), 456–57; Paul D. Escott, "Unwilling Hercules: North Carolina in the Confederacy," in *The North Carolina Experience: An Interpretive and Documentary History*, ed. Lindley S. Butler and Alan D. Watson (Chapel Hill: The University of North Carolina Press, 1984), 267. See also Martis, *Historical Atlas of the Congresses of the Confederate States of America*, 107–16. Other students of Congress have noted the same pattern. See Yearns, *Confederate Congress*, 225, and Alexander and Beringer, *Anatomy of the Confederate Congress*, chapters 10–12.

25. Martis, *Historical Atlas of the Congresses of the Confederate States of America*, 117, 32, 34. (The arithmetical calculations are my own.)

26. Ibid., 27–29. Yearns and Alexander and Beringer made this general point before Martis quantified developments on a district-by-district basis.

27. See Escott, *After Secession*, 63, 88. The draft in North Carolina, which was not noted in many earlier studies, drew on existing provisions of state law and affected mainly counties from which volunteers were not forthcoming. See Paul D. Escott, ed., *North Carolina Yeoman: The Diary of Basil Armstrong Thomasson, 1853–1862* (Athens: University of Georgia Press, 1996), 322, notes.

28. Escott, *After Secession*, 64; Emory M. Thomas, *The Confederate Nation, 1861–1865* (New York: Harper Torchbooks, 1979), 152–53.

29. Thomas, *Confederate Nation*, 153, 260–61; Escott, *After Secession*, 144.

30. Thomas, *Confederate Nation*, 196. Quotations from Escott, *After Secession*, 109 and 66.

31. Thomas, *Confederate Nation*, 150, 152; Neely, *Southern Rights*, 10; Yearns, *Confederate Congress*, 234.

32. Hill, *State Socialism*, was a pioneering work in this area. For references to the extensive subsequent literature on this topic, see Thomas, *Confederate Nation*, 206–13 and *passim*, and Escott, *After Secession*, 58–59, 65, 72–73, 209–10. See also Mary A. DeCredico, *Patriotism for Profit: Georgia's Urban Entrepreneurs and the Confederate War Effort* (Chapel Hill: The University of North Carolina Press, 1990).

33. Escott, *After Secession*, 66, 68–69; James Brewer, *The Confederate Negro: Virginia's Craftsmen and Military Laborers, 1861–1865* (Durham, NC: Duke University Press, 1969).

34. Woodworth, *Davis and Lee at War*, 70–71, 154.

35. James D. Richardson, comp., *A Compilation of the Messages and Papers of the Confederacy, Including the Diplomatic Correspondence, 1861–1865*, 2 vols. (Nashville: United States Publishing Company, 1906), 1:34, 56–57; Dunbar Rowland, ed., *Jefferson Davis, Constitutionalist; His Letters, Papers and Speeches*, 10 vols. (Jackson: Mississippi Department of Archives and History, 1923), 5:101–2, 108–9. See also Judah Benjamin to Jefferson Davis, December 14 (?), 1861, in *The War of the Rebellion*, Series IV, 1:795 and Frank L. Owsley, *State Rights in the Confederacy* (Chicago: University of Chicago Press, 1925), 25–31.

36. James M. Matthews, ed., *The Statutes at Large of the Provisional Government of the Confederate States of America* (Richmond, VA: R. M. Smith, 1864), 43, 106; Rowland, *Jefferson Davis*, 5:105, 183–85; Richardson, *Messages and Papers of the Confederacy*, 1:160.

37. J. B. Jones, *A Rebel War Clerk's Diary*, 2 vols., ed. Howard Swiggett (New York: Old Hickory Bookshop, 1935), 1:198–99.

38. Rowland, *Jefferson Davis*, 5:193, 131, 354–55, 432, 462, 465–67.

39. Thomas Bragg Diary, Southern Historical Collection, University of North Carolina, 115.

40. Joseph E. Brown to Secretary of War George Randolph, May 5, 1862, in Allen D. Candler, ed., *The Confederate Records of the State of Georgia*, 6 vols. (Atlanta: Chas. P. Byrd, 1910), 3:206–9.

41. Joseph E. Brown to Davis, April 22, 1862 and May 8, 1862, and Brown to James Seddon, July 10, 1863, in Candler, *Confederate Records of Georgia*, 3:192–98, 213–14, 362.

42. Candler, *Confederate Records of Georgia*, 3:200; Jefferson Davis to Joseph E. Brown, May 29, 1862, in Rowland, *Jefferson Davis*, 5:255, 257–61, 256.

43. Joseph E. Brown to Jefferson Davis, June 21, 1862, in *O.R.*, Series IV, 1:1160–61, and in Candler, *Confederate Records of Georgia*, 3:252, 253, 258–59, 268, 280–81, 285–86.

44. Escott, *After Secession*, 86–87.

45. Ibid., 87–88.

46. Donald M. Snow and Dennis M. Drew, *From Lexington to Desert Storm: War and Politics in the American Experience* (Armonk, NY: M.E. Sharpe, Inc., 1994), 74. On the extent of central control by the Confederate government, see also Richard Franklin Bensel, *Yankee Leviathan: The Origins of Central State Authority in America, 1859–1877* (New York and Cambridge: Cambridge University Press, 1990).

CHAPTER 3: THE POLITICS OF COMMAND

1. Richard N. Current, editor-in-chief, *Encyclopedia of the Confederacy*, 4 vols. (New York: Simon & Schuster, 1993), 1:69–70; James M. McPherson, *Battle Cry of Freedom: The Civil War Era* (New York: Oxford University Press, 1988), 306–7; William W. Freehling, *The South vs. The South: How Anti-Confederate Southerners Shaped the Course of the Civil War* (New York: Oxford University Press, 2001), 61, 19. Freehling points out that the Southern whites who fought for the Union in effect "replaced every Union fatality in the first two years of the war."

2. Current, *Encyclopedia of the Confederacy*, 1:70, 339, 399; Hugh Talmage Lefler and Albert Ray Newsome, *The History of a Southern State: North Carolina*, 3rd ed. (Chapel Hill: The University of North Carolina Press, 1973), 456. The assistant adjutant general of the Confederacy declared, as a "moderate estimate," that there were 50,000 substitutes. See Paul D. Escott, *After Secession: Jefferson Davis and the Failure of Confederate Nationalism* (Baton Rouge: Louisiana State University Press, 1978), 118.

3. Samuel P. Huntington, *The Soldier and the State: The Theory and Politics of Civil-Military Relations* (Cambridge, MA: Belknap Press, 1957), 208–9.

4. William C. Harris, *Leroy Pope Walker: Confederate Secretary of War*, Number Twenty of *Confederate Centennial Studies*, ed. William Stanley Hoole (Tuscaloosa, AL: Confederate Publishing Company, Inc., 1956–65).

5. See Robert Douthat Meade, *Judah P. Benjamin, Confederate Statesman* (1943; reprint, New York: Oxford University Press, 1975); Eli N. Evans, *Judah P. Benjamin: The Jewish Confederate* (New York: Free Press, 1988); George Green Shackelford, *George Wythe Randolph and the Confederate Elite* (Athens: University of Georgia Press, 1988); William C. Davis, *Breckinridge: Statesman, Soldier, Symbol* (Baton Rouge: Louisiana State University Press, 1974). There is no published book-length study of James Seddon.

6. Current, *Encyclopedia of the Confederacy*, 3:1383–87.

7. Steven E. Woodworth, *Davis and Lee at War* (Lawrence: University Press of Kansas, 1995), 40–51, 166; T. Harry Williams, *P.G.T. Beauregard: Napoleon in Gray* (Baton Rouge: Louisiana State University Press, 1954), 96–97.

8. Steven E. Woodworth, ed., *No Band of Brothers: Problems in the Rebel High Command* (Columbia: University of Missouri Press, 1999), 7; Escott, *After*

Secession, 57–58. See Archer Jones, *Confederate Strategy from Shiloh to Vicksburg* (Baton Rouge: Louisiana State University Press, 1961), chapter 2.

9. Woodworth, *Davis and Lee at War*, 131.

10. Most criticism of Davis through the years held that he unwisely interfered too often, but Thomas Connelly and Archer Jones have argued that he should have imposed certain strategic decisions on departmental commanders who were often reluctant to jeopardize their local situation. See Thomas L. Connelly and Archer Jones, *The Politics of Command: Factions and Ideas in Confederate Strategy* (Baton Rouge: Louisiana State University, 1973), 161, 185, 189.

11. Current, *Encyclopedia of the Confederacy*, 1:71.

12. Connelly and Jones, *Politics of Command*, 159, 89.

13. Current, *Encyclopedia of the Confederacy*, 1:71; Connelly and Jones, *Politics of Command*, 89–92.

14. Connelly and Jones, *Politics of Command*, 101, 124, 126, 155, quotation from 126. For a helpful map, see Current, *Encyclopedia of the Confederacy*, 1:73.

15. Connelly and Jones, *Politics of Command*, 153. See also 153–68. On pages 108–14 Connelly and Jones criticize Davis for lack of clarity in the assignment that he gave to General Johnston in November 1862 as commander of the Department of the West, but they admit that Johnston had reason to be assured of the extent of his authority no later than February 1863. On pages 159–60 they make a strong case that General Stephen Lee, commander in 1864 of the Department of Alabama, Mississippi, and East Louisiana, failed to mount aggressive cavalry actions that could have damaged the federal offensive against Johnston's Army of Tennessee.

16. Current, *Encyclopedia of the Confederacy*, 4:1684–88.

17. Escott, *After Secession*, 64, 69–70.

18. Current, *Encyclopedia of the Confederacy*, 4:1687. See also Frank E. Vandiver, *Ploughshares into Swords: Josiah Gorgas and Confederate Ordnance* (Austin: University of Texas Press, 1952) and Charles B. Dew, *Ironmaker to the Confederacy: Joseph R. Anderson and the Tredegar Iron Works* (New Haven: Yale University Press, 1966).

19. Current, *Encyclopedia of the Confederacy*, 1:376–78, quotation on 377. See also Richard D. Goff, *Confederate Supply* (Durham, NC: Duke University Press, 1969).

20. Woodworth, *No Band of Brothers*, 151 (Toombs quotation), 131–133, quotation on 131.

21. Ibid., 142, 134.

22. Current, *Encyclopedia of the Confederacy*, 2:766–67.

23. Woodworth, *No Band of Brothers*, 142–57.

24. Current, *Encyclopedia of the Confederacy*, 3:1226–28, quotation on 1228. See also Joseph H. Parks, *General Leonidas Polk, C.S.A.: The Fighting Bishop* (Baton Rouge: Louisiana State University Press, 1962); Steven E. Woodworth, *Jefferson Davis and His Generals: The Failure of Confederate Command in the West* (Lawrence: University Press of Kansas, 1990); and Thomas L. Connelly, *Autumn of Glory: The Army of Tennessee, 1862–1865* (Baton Rouge: Louisiana State University Press, 1971).

25. Ibid., 1188–89. See also Michael B. Ballard, *Pemberton: A Biography* (Jackson: University Press of Mississippi, 1991).

26. Woodworth, *Davis and Lee at War*, 53–55.

27. Ibid., 54.

28. Ibid., 17–19.

29. Ibid., 55–58.

30. For additional information and perspective on the Confederacy's major commanders, see Gary W. Gallagher and Joseph T. Glatthaar, eds., *Leaders of the Lost Cause: New Perspectives on the Confederate High Command* (Mechanicsburg, PA: Stackpole Books, 2004), especially the essays on Lee, Beauregard, Bragg, Joseph E. Johnston, and Edmund Kirby Smith.

31. William C. Davis, *The Cause Lost: Myths and Realities of the Confederacy* (Lawrence: University Press of Kansas, 1996), 20.

32. Williams, *Beauregard*, 161.

33. Woodworth, *Davis and Lee at War*, 328; Woodworth, *No Band of Brothers*, 3. T. Harry Williams concurred that "most" of Beauregard's "schemes" were "good in theory but too ambitious for the available manpower." See Williams, *Beauregard*, 164. Connelly and Jones describe many of Beauregard's plans as "unrealistic, and some were even ridiculous." Connelly and Jones, *The Politics of Command*, 83.

34. U.S. War Department, *The War of the Rebellion: A Compilation of the Official Records of the Union and Confederate Armies*, 130 vols. (Washington: Government Printing Office, 1880–1901), Series I, 5:904–5 (hereinafter cited as *O.R.*).

35. Davis, *The Cause Lost*, 30; Woodworth, *Davis and Lee at War*, 77, 328.

36. Williams, *Beauregard*, 164; Current, *Encyclopedia of the Confederacy*, 1:148–49. For details on Beauregard's removal, see Davis, *The Cause Lost*, 25; Williams, *Beauregard*, 157–59.

37. Davis, *The Cause Lost*, 27, 26; Woodworth, *Davis and Lee at War*, 329.

38. Davis, *The Cause Lost*, 26, 28. For additional discussion of Johnston's leadership, or lack of it, in the west, see Joseph T. Glatthaar, *Partners in Command: The Relationships Between Leaders in the Civil War* (New York: The Free Press, 1994), 95–134.

39. *O.R.*, Series I, 23, part 2, 626–27.

40. Davis to Johnston, February 19, 1863, ibid., 640.

41. Ibid., 626–27 and 637.

42. Ibid., 658–59, 674, 684, 685, 698, 708, 745.

43. Davis, *The Cause Lost*, 31.

44. Ibid., 30; Woodworth, *Davis and Lee at War*, 96.

45. C. Vann Woodward, ed., *Mary Chesnut's Civil War* (New Haven: Yale University Press, 1981), 628; Davis, *The Cause Lost*, 30; Woodworth, *Davis and Lee at War*, 305.

46. *O.R.*, Series I, 38, part 5, 867–69, 875–76, 879, 882–83.

47. Ibid., 885, 888. According to James McPherson's summary, Lee began the summer campaign in 1864 with 64,000 men compared to Grant's 115,000, whereas Johnston began his campaign with 65,000 troops against Sherman's 100,000. In regard to casualties, "In three months, Sherman's army had inflicted nearly 28,000 casualties on the Confederates while suffering only 25,000 themselves. In Virginia, by comparison, while the Confederates lost about 36,000, they had exacted nearly twice that number in return." James M. McPherson, *Ordeal by Fire: The Civil War and Reconstruction* (New York: Knopf, 1982), 411–12 and 429. A glance at the map shows that the distances between Chattanooga and At-

lanta and Spotsylvania and Petersburg are roughly the same, at least as the crow flies.

48. Davis, *The Cause Lost*, 16.

49. Current, *Encyclopedia of the Confederacy*, 1:203–5; McPherson, *Ordeal by Fire*, 337–38.

50. McPherson, *Ordeal by Fire*, 338.

51. Woodworth, *No Band of Brothers*, 38, 41, 45.

52. The finest study of this relationship is Woodworth, *Davis and Lee at War*.

53. Ibid., 102.

54. Ibid., 103.

55. Current, *Encyclopedia of the Confederacy*, 1:205.

56. Woodworth, *Davis and Lee at War*, 255–57 (quotation on 257).

57. What that strategy was and how Lee and Davis viewed it have been the subject of many serious studies. For more detailed discussions, one should begin by consulting the works cited here by Steven Woodworth, William C. Davis, Thomas Connelly and Archer Jones, and James McPherson. See also Alan T. Nolan, *Lee Considered* (Chapel Hill: The University of North Carolina Press, 1991), chapter 4.

58. Dunbar Rowland, ed., *Jefferson Davis, Constitutionalist; His Letters, Papers, and Speeches*, 10 vols. (Jackson: Mississippi Department of Archives and History, 1923), 5:48.

59. James D. Richardson, comp., *A Compilation of the Messages and Papers of the Confederacy, Including the Diplomatic Correspondence, 1861–1865*, 2 vols. (Nashville: United States Publishing Company, 1906), 1:32–36.

60. Ibid., 1:71, 70.

61. The prominent military historian, Russell Weigley, recently has argued that the South should have focused its efforts on the Virginia theatre, given that Southern armies repeatedly failed in the west and given that a quick victory was the South's best chance of success. But this view overlooks political realities that could not be ignored. See Russell Weigley, *A Great Civil War* (Bloomington: Indiana University Press, 2000), xxi.

62. Escott, *After Secession*, 57.

63. Emory M. Thomas, *The Confederate Nation, 1861–1865* (New York: Harper Torchbooks, 1979), 156–57.

64. Quoted in Woodworth, *Davis and Lee at War*, 53.

65. Quoted in Emory M. Thomas, *Robert E. Lee* (New York: W. W. Norton, 1995), 226.

66. Ibid., 227.

67. Russell F. Weigley, *The American Way of War: A History of United States Military Strategy and Policy* (Bloomington: Indiana University Press, 1973), chapter 6; Woodworth, *Davis and Lee at War*, 236–41 (quotation on 241).

68. Woodworth, *Davis and Lee at War*, 157, 250. See also 227. Archer Jones disagrees with this estimate of Lee's beliefs and intentions, citing a letter from Lee to his wife on April 19, 1863. See Archer Jones, "Military Means, Political Ends: Strategy," in *Why the Confederacy Lost*, ed. Gabor S. Borritt (New York: Oxford University Press, 1992), 66–67. What Lee wrote in a family letter and how he acted in command and in the field, however, may not be entirely consistent.

69. Woodworth, *Davis and Lee at War*, 236–41, 191; Shelby Foote, *The Civil*

War: A Narrative, 3 vols. (New York: Random House, 1963), 2:530. Foote shows on page 536 that Longstreet did not even have 15,000 men, but only 12,500.

70. Woodworth, *Davis and Lee at War*, 331. For additional stimulating discussions of strategy, see Jones, "Military Means, Political Ends: Strategy"; Gary W. Gallagher, *The Confederate War* (Cambridge, MA: Harvard University Press, 1997), chapter 3; Herman Hattaway and Archer Jones, *How the North Won: A Military History of the Civil War* (Urbana: University of Illinois Press, 1983); and other books cited therein.

71. Woodworth, *Davis and Lee at War*, 331.

72. Roy P. Basler, ed., *The Collected Works of Abraham Lincoln*, 9 vols. (New Brunswick, NJ: Rutgers University Press, 1953), 7:514.

CHAPTER 4: TOWARD A MILITARIZED SOCIETY

1. Emory M. Thomas, *The Confederacy as a Revolutionary Experience* (Englewood Cliffs, NJ: Prentice-Hall, Inc., 1971). The statistics relating to the costs of the war, North and South, can be found in Mary Beth Norton et al., *A People and a Nation*, 2nd ed. (Boston: Houghton Mifflin Company, 1986), 413–14.

2. Emory M. Thomas, *The Confederate Nation, 1861–1865* (New York: Harper Torchbooks, 1979), 196.

3. See Gavin Wright, *The Political Economy of the Cotton South: Households, Markets, and Wealth in the Nineteenth Century* (New York: W. W. Norton, 1978), chapter 3, for a sophisticated and detailed discussion of these points; and Stephen Hahn, *The Roots of Southern Populism: Yeoman Farmers and the Transformation of the Georgia Upcountry, 1850–1900* (New York: Oxford University Press, 1983).

4. Paul D. Escott, *After Secession: Jefferson Davis and the Failure of Confederate Nationalism* (Baton Rouge: Louisiana State University Press, 1978), 50.

5. Ibid., 106–7.

6. Ibid., 108–9; Paul D. Escott, *Many Excellent People: Power and Privilege in North Carolina, 1850–1900* (Chapel Hill: The University of North Carolina Press, 1985), 54. The letters or newspaper articles cited in this paragraph date from March 5, 1862; July 12, 1862; January 23, 1863; September 4, 1862; September 12, 1861; and July 22, 1863, respectively.

7. Escott, *After Secession*, 109; Escott, *Many Excellent People*, 54.

8. Peter Wallenstein, *From Slave South to New South: Public Policy in Nineteenth-Century Georgia* (Chapel Hill: The University of North Carolina Press, 1987), 126–27. Wallenstein reports (p. 125) that for the Confederacy as a whole, impressments were worth two and one half times the value of all Confederate taxes.

9. Quoted in Escott, *Many Excellent People*, 53; quoted in Wallenstein, *From Slave South to New South*, 127; quoted in Escott, *After Secession*, 110–11.

10. Quoted in Escott, *After Secession*, 111.

11. From a message of the governor of Alabama, quoted in *Appleton's American Annual Cyclopedia* (New York: D. Appleton and Company, 1865), 16; Paul D. Escott, "Poverty and Governmental Aid for the Poor in Confederate North Carolina," *North Carolina Historical Review* 56, no. 4 (October 1984): 462–80 cites evidence for figures this high or higher in North Carolina.

12. Escott, "Poverty and Governmental Aid," 467–71; Escott, *After Secession*,

157–64; see also William Frank Entrekin Jr., "Poor Relief in North Carolina in the Confederacy" (master's thesis, Duke University, 1947).

13. Private O. Goddin to Governor Zebulon Vance, February 27, 1863, in Wilfred Buck Yearns and John G. Barrett, eds., *North Carolina Civil War Documentary* (Chapel Hill: The University of North Carolina Press, 1980), 98.

14. Ibid.

15. Ibid.

16. C. Vann Woodward, ed., *Mary Chesnut's Civil War* (New Haven: Yale University Press, 1981), 773; Escott, *After Secession*, 132.

17. Figures taken and calculated from *The Statistical History of the United States: From Colonial Times to the Present* (*Historical Statistics of the United States: Colonial Times to 1970*, prepared by the U.S. Bureau of the Census), introduced by Ben J. Wattenberg (New York: Basic Books, 1976), 24–37.

18. Mary Beth Norton, et al., *A People & A Nation*, 282.

19. Thomas, *Confederacy as a Revolutionary Experience*, 95; David R. Goldfield, *Cotton Fields and Skyscrapers: Southern City and Region* (Baton Rouge: Louisiana State University Press, 1982), 82; Mary A. DeCredico, *Patriotism for Profit: Georgia's Urban Entrepreneurs and the Confederate War Effort* (Chapel Hill: The University of North Carolina Press, 1990), 35.

20. DeCredico, *Patriotism for Profit*, 31, 60–63; Goldfield, *Cotton Fields and Skyscrapers*, 82.

21. Thomas, *Confederacy as a Revolutionary Experience*, 95.

22. Ibid., 95; Goldfield, *Cotton Fields and Skyscrapers*, 80.

23. See Escott, *Many Excellent People*, chapter 3; Jeffrey J. Crow and Paul D. Escott, "The Social Order and Violent Disorder: An Analysis of North Carolina in the Revolution and the Civil War," *Journal of Southern History* 52, no. 3 (August 1986): 373–402; Paul D. Escott, "The Moral Economy of the Crowd in Confederate North Carolina," *Maryland Historian* 13, no. 1 (spring/summer 1982), 1–18.

24. Yearns and Barrett, eds., *North Carolina Civil War Documentary*, 98.

25. Escott, *Many Excellent People*, 74. The overlap between those who escaped military service and those who arrested deserters was especially visible in North Carolina, because that state (along with Georgia) exempted thousands of minor state officials, such as local magistrates.

26. Ibid., 68–69. See also Escott, *After Secession*, 129–33.

27. Malcolm C. McMillan, *The Disintegration of a Confederate State: Three Governors and Alabama's Wartime Home Front, 1861–1865* (Macon, GA: Mercer University Press, 1986), 59–60, 116; Escott, *Many Excellent People*, 69; Campbell quoted in Escott, *After Secession*, 133.

28. U.S. War Department, *The War of the Rebellion: A Compilation of the Official Records of the Union and Confederate Armies*, 130 vols. (Washington, DC: Government Printing Office, 1880–1901), Series I, 29, part 2, 796, 801 (hereinafter cited as O.R.).

29. O.R., Series IV, 2:805–6.

30. Ibid., 819–20. Pillow's twenty companies of troops officially would have comprised 2,000 men, though by this time in the war all units tended to be well below full strength.

31. John G. Barrett, *The Civil War in North Carolina* (Chapel Hill: The University of North Carolina Press, 1963), 129–97.

32. McMillan, *Disintegration of a Confederate State*, 59; Escott, *Many Excellent People*, 68.

33. Escott, *Many Excellent People*, 45; Barrett, *The Civil War in North Carolina*, 195.

34. Yearns and Barrett, *North Carolina Civil War Documentary*, 104–5.

35. James D. Richardson, comp., *A Compilation of the Messages and Papers of the Confederacy, Including the Diplomatic Correspondence, 1861–1865*, 2 vols. (Nashville: United States Publishing Company, 1906), 1:82, 70, 32–36; Dunbar Rowland, ed., *Jefferson Davis, Constitutionalist; His Letters, Papers, and Speeches*, 10 vols. (Jackson: Mississippi Department of Archives and History, 1923), 5:104. It is, of course, ironic that Davis' phrase and Lincoln's "last best hope of earth" were so close to being identical.

36. This statement applies to the present author also. See Escott, *After Secession*, 178.

37. Mark E. Neely Jr., *Southern Rights: Political Prisoners and the Myth of Confederate Constitutionalism* (Charlottesville: University Press of Virginia, 1999).

38. Ibid., 2–3.

39. Ibid., 5 (Jones quotation). See Kenneth Radley, *Rebel Watchdog: The Confederate States Army Provost Guard* (Baton Rouge: Louisiana State University Press, 1989). Radley states that "the Confederate provost system . . . eventually . . . assumed a degree of control over civil life unique in American history."

40. Radley, *Rebel Watchdog*, 75.

41. Neely, *Southern Rights*, 2–3.

42. Ibid., 17; Radley, *Rebel Watchdog*, 69.

43. Radley, *Rebel Watchdog*, 65.

44. Ibid., 66–69. Quotation on 69.

45. Neely, *Southern Rights*, 17, 10; John Brawner Robbins, "The Confederacy and the Writ of Habeas Corpus," *Georgia Historical Quarterly* 55 (1971): 83–101, 96.

46. Thomas, *The Confederacy as a Revolutionary Experience*, 63; Escott, *After Secession*, 139; Emory M. Thomas, *The Confederate State of Richmond* (Austin: University of Texas Press, 1971).

47. Radley, *Rebel Watchdog*, 215, and see also 181–96.

48. Neely, *Southern Rights*, 1.

49. Ibid., 80.

50. Ibid., 80–82.

51. Ibid., 50, 85–87, chapter 9.

52. Thomas, *The Confederacy as a Revolutionary Experience*; Louise B. Hill, "State Socialism in the Confederate States of America," in *Southern Sketches*, no. 9, First Series, ed. J.D. Eggleston (Charlottesville, VA: Historical Publishing Company, Inc., 1936); Radley, *Rebel Watchdog*, 1.

53. See the informative maps in Kenneth C. Martis, *The Historical Atlas of the Congresses of the Confederate States of America: 1861–1865* (New York: Simon & Schuster, 1994), chapter 5 and 111–16.

54. For illustrative examples see Escott, *After Secession*, 137–74 and chapter 5 generally.

55. J. Roderick Heller and Carolynn Ayres Heller, eds., *The Confederacy Is on*

Her Way up the Spout: Letters to South Carolina, 1861–1864 (Athens: University of Georgia Press, 1992).

56. Escott, *After Secession*, 129, 206.

57. James M. McPherson, *Ordeal by Fire: The Civil War and Reconstruction* (New York: Knopf, 1982), 295. For a recent study of infringements of free speech during military conflicts sees Geoffrey R. Stone, *Perilous Times: Free Speech in Wartime, from the Sedition Act of 1798 to the War on Terrorism* (New York: W. W. Norton, 2004).

58. Neely, *Southern Rights*, chapter 4, especially 65–66, 71, 73–75, 77–79 (quotation). See also Jennifer Van Zant, "Confederate Conscription and the North Carolina Supreme Court," *North Carolina Historical Review* 72, no. 1 (January 1995): 54–75.

59. *Daily Richmond Enquirer*, November 19, 1864.

60. Ibid.

CHAPTER 5: MILITARY POWER AND CIVIL DEBILITY

1. Robert L. Kerby, *Kirby Smith's Confederacy: The Trans-Mississippi South, 1863–1865* (New York: Columbia University Press, 1972), 2–9, 12.

2. Ibid., 12–13; Jack B. Scroggs, "Arkansas in the Secession Crisis," *Arkansas Historical Quarterly* 12 (autumn 1953): 179–224; Ted R. Worley, "The Arkansas Peace Society of 1861: A Study in Mountain Unionism,"*Journal of Southern History*, 24 (November 1958): 445–56; Paul D. Escott, *After Secession: Jefferson Davis and the Failure of Confederate Nationalism* (Baton Rouge: Louisiana State University Press, 1978), 31; Richard N. Current, editor-in-chief, *Encyclopedia of the Confederacy*, 4 vols. (New York: Simon & Schuster, 1993), 3:1052; 1:52–53. Also see the helpful maps in Ezra J. Warner and Wilfred Buck Yearns, *Biographical Register of the Confederate Congress* (Baton Rouge: Louisiana State University Press, 1975), 303–5.

3. Kerby, *Kirby Smith's Confederacy*, 12–13, 152.

4. Current, *Encyclopedia of the Confederacy*, 4:1605–12; Kerby, *Kirby Smith's Confederacy*, 334. See also Joseph H. Parks, *General Edmund Kirby Smith, C.S.A.* (Baton Rouge: Louisiana State University Press, 1954).

5. Kerby, *Kirby Smith's Confederacy*, 23, 92–93, 329–31.

6. Current, *Encyclopedia of the Confederacy*, 3:1251; 4:1427–28, 1606–7.

7. Governor Thomas O. Moore to Secretary of War George W. Randolph, June 1, 1862, U.S. War Department, *The War of the Rebellion: A Compilation of the Official Records of the Union and Confederate Armies*, 130 vols. (Washington, DC: Government Printing Office, 1880–1901), Series I, 53:809–10 (hereinafter cited as O.R.); Current, *Encyclopedia of the Confederacy*, 4:1607–8.

8. Mark E. Neely Jr., *Southern Rights: Political Prisoners and the Myth of Confederate Constitutionalism* (Charlottesville: University Press of Virginia, 1999), 11–20, quotation on 14.

9. Current, *Encyclopedia of the Confederacy*, 1:1607.

10. Kerby, *Kirby Smith's Confederacy*, 258–61, 380.

11. James A. Seddon to E. Kirby Smith, August 3, 1863, O.R., Series I, 22, part 2, 952–53; E. Kirby Smith to Jefferson Davis, September 11, 1863, ibid., 1004.

12. Seddon to Smith, October 10, 1863, and August 3, 1863, ibid., 1038–39 and 952–53.

13. Jefferson Davis to E. Kirby Smith, July 14, 1863, ibid., 925–27.

14. E. Kirby Smith to S. Cooper, July 28, 1863, ibid., 949.

15. Smith to Davis, September 11, 1863, ibid., 1003–10; Smith to unnamed, September 4, 1863, ibid., 990–91; Smith to Davis, September 28, 1863, ibid., 1029.

16. Kerby, *Kirby Smith's Confederacy*, 143.

17. Hart to Seddon, May 16, 1863 and June 20, 1863, O.R., Series I, 53:867–70 and 873–74.

18. The text of the impressment law is cited in General Orders #37, in ibid., Series IV, 2:469; Hart to Seddon, May 16, 1863, with endorsements, ibid., Series I, 53:867–70.

19. Hart to Seddon, June 20, 1863, ibid., Series I, 53:873–74 (with endorsements by Seddon, Memminger, and Davis); Major and Quartermaster Charles Russell to Major B. Bloomfield, Chief Quartermaster, June 11, 1863, ibid., Series I, 26, part 2, 93–94; and A. C. Myers, Quartermaster General, to Seddon, July 15, 1863, in ibid., Series I, 53:882.

20. Kerby, *Kirby Smith's Confederacy*, 172; James Seddon to Kirby Smith, October 29, 1863, and Seddon to S. Hart, October 29, 1863, O.R., Series I, 53:904–5.

21. Quoted in Kerby, *Kirby Smith's Confederacy*, 1.

22. Smith to Seddon, September 12, 1863, O.R., Series I, 53:895–96; James Seddon to Smith, October 10, 1863, ibid., Series I, 22, part 2, 1040.

23. Seddon to Smith, June 15, 1864, ibid., Series I, 34, part 4, 671–74; Smith to Adjutant and Inspector General Samuel Cooper, December 3, 1864, ibid., Series I, 41, part 4, 1094, and Samuel Cooper to Smith, December 23, 1864, ibid., 1122.

24. Davis to Congress, December 7, 1863, ibid., Series IV, 2:1045–46.

25. Davis to Smith, April 28, 1864, ibid., Series I, 53:986.

26. Seddon to Smith, June 15, 1864, ibid., Series I, 34, part 4, 672.

27. Current, *Encyclopedia of the Confederacy*, 4:1609; Kerby, *Kirby Smith's Confederacy*, 243–46, 239 (quotations on 245 and 239).

28. Smith to Davis, September 11, 1863, O.R., Series I, 22, part 2, 1004; Kerby, *Kirby Smith's Confederacy*, 137, 139.

29. O.R., Series I, 22, part 2, 1005–7.

30. Ibid.

31. Ibid., Series I, 53:892–94.

32. Smith to Davis, September 28, 1853, ibid., Series I, 22:1028–29.

33. Kerby, *Kirby Smith's Confederacy*, 257; Richard McCaslin, *Tainted Breeze: The Great Hanging at Gainesville, Texas, 1862* (Baton Rouge: Louisiana State University Press, 1994).

34. Kerby, *Kirby Smith's Confederacy*, 13–15.

35. Ibid., 218–19.

36. Ibid., 219–20.

37. See ibid., chapter 4 and passim.

38. Ibid., 160.

39. O.R., Series I, 22, part 2, 1060–61, 1128–29.

40. Seddon to Smith, October 10, 1863, ibid., 1038–40; Seddon to Smith, August 3, 1864, ibid., Series I, 53:1016–18; Kerby, *Kirby Smith's Confederacy*, 207.

41. Kerby, *Kirby Smith's Confederacy*, 198–200.

42. Ibid., 200–202.

43. *O.R.*, Series I, 53:1008–15.

44. Kerby, *Kirby Smith's Confederacy*, 202.

45. Ibid., 290–318. Quotations on 318.

46. See Nancy Head Bowen, "A Political Labyrinth: Texas in the Civil War—Questions in Continuity" (Ph.D. diss., Rice University, 1974), 84–87, 89–90, 140–41.

47. Kerby, *Kirby Smith's Confederacy*, 328–39.

48. Ibid., 270–72.

49. Ibid., 272–74, quotation on 273.

50. Ibid., 274–75.

51. Ibid., 370–79.

52. Ibid., 373. Smith was also entertaining ideas of transferring his own loyalty to Emperor Maximilian in Mexico when the Confederacy fell, although there seems to be no evidence that he considered turning rebel forces over the Mexico, as the *New York Herald* suggested. See 374–75.

CHAPTER 6: MILITARY MEN AND CIVIL POLICY-MAKING

1. See Thomas Connelly and Archer Jones, *The Politics of Command: Factions and Ideas in Confederate Strategy* (Baton Rouge: Louisiana State University Press, 1973), especially chapters 3 and 5 and appendix.

2. Richard N. Current, editor-in-chief, *Encyclopedia of the Confederacy*, 4 vols. (New York: Simon & Schuster, 1993), 396.

3. Abundant examples of both of these relationships may be found in letters in the Bell I. Wiley Papers, Special Collections, Woodruff Library, Emory University.

4. Connelly and Jones, *Politics of Command*, 54.

5. Ibid., 52–59.

6. Ibid., 74–77.

7. Ibid., 83, 78–81.

8. Ibid., 144–52.

9. Alfred Roman, *The Military Operations of General Beauregard*, 2 vols. (New York: De Capo Press, 1994), with a new introduction by T. Michael Parrish, 2:450–51.

10. U.S. War Department, *The War of the Rebellion: A Compilation of the Official Records of the Union and Confederate Armies*, 130 vols. (Washington, DC: Government Printing Office, 1880–1901), 14:667 (hereinafter cited as *O.R.*); T. Harry Williams, *P.G.T. Beauregard: Napoleon in Gray* (Baton Rouge: Louisiana State University Press, 1954), 169. See also Connelly and Jones, *Politics of Command*, 84, for reference to Beauregard's other contacts, including discussions that he had concerning diplomacy and blockade running with John Slidell.

11. *O.R.*, Series I, 27, part 3, 880–82.

12. Ibid.

13. Ibid.

14. Ibid.

15. Ibid.

16. See Robert F. Durden, *The Gray and the Black: The Confederate Debate on Emancipation* (Baton Rouge: Louisiana State University Press, 1972), 30 and chapter 2, *passim*. This volume, which collects and presents much documentary evidence, is the best study of this important topic. It is also worth noting that in the Trans-Mississippi Department, Kirby Smith considered the idea of arming the slaves in September 1863. See Robert L. Kerby, *Kirby Smith's Confederacy: The Trans-Mississippi South, 1863–1865* (New York: Columbia University Press, 1972), 239.

17. Durden, *The Gray and the Black*, 62–63. Durden gives the full text of the proposal on 54–63. It also may be found in *O.R.*, Series I, 52, Part 2, 586–92.

18. Durden, *The Gray and the Black*, 54, 57–58.

19. Ibid., 56–57.

20. Ibid., 59, 61, 60, 58.

21. Ibid., 60, 59, 56, 55.

22. Ibid., 60–62.

23. Ibid., 65–66; Paul D. Escott, *After Secession: Jefferson Davis and the Failure of Confederate Nationalism* (Baton Rouge: Louisiana State University Press, 1978), 196–98.

24. Escott, *After Secession*, 219; Durden, *The Gray and the Black*, chapter 4.

25. Durden, *The Gray and the Black*, 105.

26. Ibid., chapters 4 and 5 and 183.

27. Ibid., quoted on 108–9.

28. Ibid., 110, 112–13, 119.

29. *Charleston Mercury*, January 26, 1865; Durden, *The Gray and the Black*, 138, 169, 184; Graham to David L. Swain, January 28, 1865 and Graham to Susan Washington Graham, January 8, 1865, both in Bell I. Wiley Papers, Special Collections, Woodruff Library, Emory University.

30. *Daily Richmond Examiner*, December 31, 1864.

31. *Daily Richmond Enquirer*, November 11, 1864; *Richmond Sentinel*, November 24, 1864, as quoted in Durden, *The Gray and the Black*, 121; *Richmond Whig*, January 30, 1865. Also see the *Enquirer* on December 31, 1864.

32. Durden, *The Gray and the Black*, 135–36.

33. Ibid., 208.

34. Ibid., 208–9.

35. *Daily Richmond Examiner*, February 16, 1865.

36. *Richmond Whig*, February 20, 1865; *Richmond Sentinel*, February 20 and 23, 1865.

37. For the text of the letter, see the *Richmond Sentinel*, February 23, 1865, or Durden, *The Gray and the Black*, 206–7.

38. *Richmond Whig*, February 16, 19, and 21, 1865.

39. *Daily Richmond Examiner*, February 25, 1865.

40. See Escott, *After Secession*, 221–23; Ludwell Johnson, "Lincoln's Solution to the Problem of Peace Terms, 1864–65," *Journal of Southern History*, 34 (1968): 576–86; Alexander H. Stephens, *A Constitutional View of the War Between the States*, 2 vols. (Philadelphia: National Publishing Company, 1870), 2:599–619; Thomas E. Schott, *Alexander H. Stephens of Georgia: A Biography* (Baton Rouge: Louisiana State University Press, 1988), 445–47.

41. Stephens, *Constitutional View*, 610–17. Many particulars of Stephens' postwar account were confirmed in February 1865 by others. For example, see Edward

Younger, ed., *Inside the Confederate Government: The Diary of Robert Garlick Hill Kean* (New York: Oxford University Press, 1957), 194–98, and the letters cited below.

42. Younger, *Inside the Confederate Government*, 201–2; Escott, *After Secession*, 223–24.

43. For Hunter's active cultivation of contacts in Richmond, see frequent references to him at this time in J. B. Jones' diary: J. B. Jones, *A Rebel War Clerk's Diary*, 2 vols., ed. Howard Swiggett (New York: Old Hickory Bookshop, 1935), vol 2. For the "minute narrative" given to Graham, see Graham to David L. Swain, February 12, 1865, in Bell I. Wiley Papers, Special Collections, Woodruff Library, Emory University. Senator Graham wrote to his wife on February 5, 1865, and gave her quite a full account of the conference. In this letter he stated that he had not yet spoken with Stephens or Campbell, so it seems likely that Hunter was his source. See Graham to "Dear Wife," February 5, 1865, also in Bell I. Wiley Papers.

44. Graham to Swain, February 12, 1865; Graham to Zebulon Vance, February 12, 1865, and Graham to Susan Washington Graham, February 18, 1865, all in Bell I. Wiley Papers, Special Collections, Woodruff Library, Emory University. See also Graham to Susan Washington Graham, February 5, 1865, ibid.

45. Orr (speaking of his feelings "last winter") to Governor Francis Pickens, April 29, 1865, and Louis T. Wigfall to Joseph E. Johnston, March 3, 1865, in Bell I. Wiley Papers, Special Collections, Woodruff Library, Emory University.

46. Emory M. Thomas, *The Confederate Nation, 1861–1865* (New York: Harper Torchbooks, 1979), 296; Durden, *The Gray and the Black*, 240; William A. Graham to his wife, February 26, 1976, in Bell I. Wiley Papers, Special Collections, Woodruff Library, Emory University.

47. Thomas, *The Confederate Nation*, 296; Durden, *The Gray and the Black*, 268–69; *Daily Richmond Examiner*, January 14, 1865.

48. For a study that focuses on debates and attitudes outside the Congress, see Philip D. Dillard, "Independence or Slavery: The Confederate Debate over Arming the Slaves" (Ph.D. thesis, Rice University, 1999). Dillard sought to identify public reaction in Virginia, Georgia, and Texas and concluded that the Confederate citizenry, especially in areas that were directly feeling the hard hand of war, was more willing to sacrifice slavery than the Congress.

49. Michael Fellman, *Citizen Sherman: A Life of William Tecumseh Sherman* (New York: Random House, 1995), 238–44; Gilbert Govan and James W. Livingood, *A Different Valor: The Story of General Joseph E. Johnston* (New York: Bobbs-Merrill Company, 1956), 365–66.

50. The Sherman-Johnston Convention may be found in *O.R.*, Series I, 47, part 3, 243–45.

51. Fellman, *Citizen Sherman*, 245–47.

CHAPTER 7: DESPERATE PROPOSALS AND THE MAINTENANCE OF CIVIL SUPREMACY

1. James D. Richardson, comp., *A Compilation of the Messages and Papers of the Confederacy, Including the Diplomatic Correspondence, 1861–1865*, 2 vols. (Nashville: United States Publishing Company, 1906), 1:32–36; Paul D. Escott, *After Secession: Jefferson Davis and the Failure of Confederate Nationalism* (Baton

Rouge: Louisiana State University Press, 1978), 45–46; *Charleston Mercury*, passim in the first five months of 1861, April 19, 1861, October 10, 1861; *Rome Weekly Courier*, April 23, 1861; see also *Charlotte (N.C.) Whig*, April 23, 1861, May 28, 1861.

2. C. Vann Woodward, ed., *Mary Chesnut's Civil War* (New Haven: Yale University Press, 1981), 12, 121, 138–39. See also Escott, *After Secession*, 62.

3. A. R. Wright to Francis C. Shropshire, February 26, 1862, in Bell I. Wiley Papers, Special Collections, Woodruff Library, Emory University.

4. James L. Pugh to Maj. General Bragg, March 16, 1862, ibid. Collections.

5. W. W. Boyce to J. H. Hammond, March 17, 1862, April 4, 1862, and April 12, 1862, ibid.

6. W. W. Boyce to J. H. Hammond, April 15, 1863, ibid.

7. Thomas E. Schott, *Alexander H. Stephens of Georgia: A Biography* (Baton Rouge: Louisiana State University Press, 1988), 384.

8. Ibid., 385.

9. These words are Johnson's quoting of Stephens, in Herschel V. Johnson to A. H. Stephens, March 9, 1864, in Bell I. Wiley Papers, Special Collections, Woodruff Library, Emory University.

10. Ibid.; Schott, *Alexander H. Stephens*, 384 (report from newspaper editor); Johnson to Stephens, March 10, 1864, in Bell I. Wiley Papers, Special Collections, Woodruff Library, Emory University.

11. Johnson to Stephens, March 19, 1864, ibid.

12. Schott, *Alexander H. Stephens*, 406–8.

13. Ibid., 410–11; Johnson quoted in Escott, *After Secession*, 204–5.

14. Schott, *Alexander H. Stephens*, 415; Richard N. Current, editor-in-chief, *Encyclopedia of the Confederacy*, 4 vols. (New York: Simon & Schuster, 1993), 2:912.

15. Boyce to Davis, September 29, 1864, from *Memphis Daily Appeal* (then published in Montgomery, Alabama), in Bell I. Wiley Papers, Special Collections, Woodruff Library, Emory University; James L. Pugh to Maj. General Bragg, March 16, 1862, ibid.

16. Louis Wigfall to J. H. Hammond, April ?, 1864, ibid. In August 1863 the ever volatile Wigfall had even raised questions about Davis' sanity, suggesting to Clement C. Clay that the president's "mind is becoming unsettled. No sane man would act as he is doing." See Wigfall to Clay, August 13, 1863, ibid.

17. Boyce to Davis, September 29, 1864, from *Memphis Daily Appeal*, ibid. The Democratic platform stated that "after four years of failure to restore the Union by the experiment of war . . . [we] demand that immediate efforts be made for a cessation of hostilities, with a view to an ultimate convention of the states, or other peaceable means, to the end that, at the earliest practicable moment, people may be restored on the basis of the Federal Union." Quoted in James M. McPherson, *Ordeal by Fire: The Civil War and Reconstruction* (New York: Knopf, 1982), 441.

18. *Daily Richmond Examiner*, December 21, 1864, 2, January 2 and January 9, 1865; J. B. Jones, *A Rebel War Clerk's Diary*, 2 vols., ed. Howard Swiggett (New York: Old Hickory Bookshop, 1935), 2:364–65.

19. *Daily Richmond Enquirer*, December 27, 1864, 2; *Daily Richmond Examiner*, December 27, 1864, 2; Jones, *A Rebel War Clerk's Diary*, 2:368; *Daily Rich-*

mond Examiner, December 29, 1864, 2; Jones, *A Rebel War Clerk's Diary*, 2:370–71.

20. David W. Lewis to Jefferson Davis, December 30, 1864, copy in Bell I. Wiley Papers, Special Collections, Woodruff Library, Emory University; George C. Rable, *The Confederate Republic: A Revolution Against Politics* (Chapel Hill: The University of North Carolina Press, 1994), 286; Woodward, *Mary Chesnut's Civil War*, 698.

21. Jones, *A Rebel War Clerk's Diary*, 2:372.

22. *Charleston Mercury*, February 6, 1865.

23. Jones, *A Rebel War Clerk's Diary*, 2:380; Edward Younger, ed., *Inside the Confederate Government: The Diary of Robert Garlick Hill Kean* (New York: Oxford University Press, 1957), 185; *Daily Richmond Examiner*, January 9, 1865, 2. At this time Davis also made a statement to Georgia's Confederate senators in which he argued against the idea of holding a convention to end the war. See William C. Rives to William Porcher Miles, January 22, 1865, in Bell I. Wiley Papers, Special Collections, Woodruff Library, Emory University.

24. Steven E. Woodworth, *Davis and Lee at War* (Lawrence: University Press of Kansas, 1995), 310, 309–10; Jones, *A Rebel War Clerk's Diary*, 2:390.

25. *Daily Richmond Examiner*, January 17 and January 19, 1865.

26. Dunbar Rowland, ed., *Jefferson Davis, Constitutionalist; His Letters, Papers, and Speeches*, 10 vols. (Jackson: Mississippi Department of Archives and History, 1923), 6:452–53.

27. Douglas Southall Freeman and W. J. De Renne, eds., *Lee's Dispatches* (New York: G. P. Putnam's Sons, 1915), 322–23.

28. Woodworth, *Davis and Lee at War*, 310; Jones, *A Rebel War Clerk's Diary*, 2:392.

29. Thomas S. Bocock to Davis, marked Confidential, January 21, 1864 [1865], in U.S. War Department, *The War of the Rebellion: A Compilation of the Official Records of the Union and Confederate Armies*, 130 vols. (Washington, DC: Government Printing Office, 1880–1901), Series I, 46, part 2, 1118 (hereinafter cited as *O.R.*).

30. Jones, *A Rebel War Clerk's Diary*, 2:392; Bocock to Davis, January 21, 1864 [1865] (bearing Davis' written comment), in *O.R.*, Series I, 46, part 2, 1118.

31. Jones, *A Rebel War Clerk's Diary*, 2:399; *Richmond Sentinel*, January 26, 1865; see Douglas Southall Freeman, *Lee's Lieutenants, a Study in Command*, 3 vols. (New York: Charles Scribner's Sons, 1942–44), 3:634–35.

32. Escott, *After Secession*, 221.

33. Lee to Davis, February 9, 1865, *O.R.*, Series I, 41, part 2, 1082–83.

34. Davis to Lee, two letters on February 10, 1865, in Rowland, *Jefferson Davis, Constitutionalist*, 6:478–79.

35. Woodworth, *Davis and Lee at War*, 312–13; Rowland, *Jefferson Davis, Constitutionalist*, 6:491, 491–503.

36. Lee to Alexander H. Stephens, et al., February 13, 1865, in Clifford Dowdey, ed., *The Wartime Papers of R. E. Lee* (New York: Bramhall House, 1961), 894.

37. Davis to Lee, February 28, 1865, in Rowland, *Jefferson Davis, Constitutionalist*, 6:489; Woodworth, *Davis and Lee at War*, 314–15.

38. Richard N. Current, *Encyclopedia of the Confederacy*, 2:912.

39. Herschel V. Johnson to A. H. Stephens, September 28, 1864, in Bell I. Wiley Papers, Special Collections, Woodruff Library, Emory University.

40. Herschel V. Johnson to Alexander H. Stephens, December 29, 1863, ibid.

41. See the important work of Bertram Wyatt-Brown, *Southern Honor: Ethics and Behavior in the Old South* (New York: Oxford University Press, 1982). Even the diminutive and sickly Alexander Stephens was involved in a vicious knife-fight and several near-duels. See Schott, *Alexander H. Stephens,* 92–93, 46, 52, 72, 74, 128, 218–20.

42. Emory M. Thomas, *The Confederate Nation, 1861–1865* (New York: Harper Torchbooks, 1979), 140.

43. *Daily Richmond Examiner,* December 21 and December 19, 1864, January 17, 1865.

44. *Daily Richmond Examiner,* January 14, 1865, December 20 and December 31, 1864, January 14, 1865, February 16 and February 25, 1865.

CHAPTER 8: CITIZENS AND SOLDIERS

1. C. Vann Woodward, *The Burden of Southern History,* rev. ed. (New York: Mentor Books, 1969), 25, 26, 27.

2. In making this calculation, I have subtracted the 90,000 who served from the border states of Missouri, Kentucky, Maryland, and Delaware from the total of 900,000 and compared that figure to the 1.1 million white men available in the eleven states that unquestionably seceded in 1861. All data on enrollments are estimates, because the records are fragmentary. This calculation uses a fairly high estimate for the total number of men who served at some time and a fairly low estimate for the number of Confederate soldiers from the border states. See Richard N. Current, editor-in-chief, *Encyclopedia of the Confederacy,* 4 vols. (New York: Simon & Schuster, 1993), 1:69, and William W. Freehling, *The South vs. The South: How Anti-Confederate Southerners Shaped the Course of the Civil War* (New York: Oxford University Press, 2001), 61, 19.

3. Bell Irvin Wiley, *The Life of Johnny Reb: The Common Soldier of the Confederacy* (New York: Bobbs-Merrill, 1943), 331; Larry M. Logue, "Who Joined the Confederate Army? Soldiers, Civilians, and Communities in Mississippi," in *The Civil War Soldier: A Historical Reader,* ed. Michael Barton and Larry M. Logue (New York: New York University Press, 2002), 47–48; James I. Robertson Jr., *Soldiers Blue and Gray* (Columbia: University of South Carolina Press, 1988), 19.

4. Robertson, *Soldiers Blue and Gray,* 47–49; Joseph T. Glatthaar, "The Common Soldier of the Civil War," in *New Perspectives on the Civil War: Myths and Realities of the National Conflict,* ed. John Y. Simon and Michael E. Stevens (Madison: Madison House, published in cooperation with the State Historical Society of Wisconsin, 1998), 126–27.

5. Wiley, *The Life of Johnny Reb,* 339–40; Robertson, *Soldiers Blue and Gray,* 23–24; Paul D. Escott, *After Secession: Jefferson Davis and the Failure of Confederate Nationalism* (Baton Rouge: Louisiana State University Press, 1978), 74, 102; David Donald, "The Southerner as a Fighting Man," in *The Southerner as American,* ed. Charles Grier Sellers, Jr. (Chapel Hill: University of North Carolina Press, 1960), 79. As the war went on, the size of experienced combat regiments quickly shrank to 500 or fewer troops. "Many regiments by 1863 went into battle with

fewer than 200 men." See James M. McPherson, *Ordeal by Fire: The Civil War and Reconstruction* (New York: Knopf, 1982), 168.

6. Percy Lee Rainwater, *Mississippi, Storm Center of Secession, 1856–1861* (Baton Rouge: Otto Claitor, 1938); Logue, "Who Joined the Confederate Army?" 48–51.

7. Escott, *After Secession*, 21–32; Seymour Martin Lipset, *Political Man: The Social Bases of Politics* (Garden City, NY: Doubleday and Company, Anchor Books, 1963), 374–79; Mary Beth Norton et al., *A People and a Nation*, 1st ed. (Boston: Houghton Mifflin Company, 1982), 362; Robin E. Baker, "Class Conflict and Political Upheaval: The Transformation of North Carolina Politics during the Civil War," *North Carolina Historical Review* 69, no. 2 (April 1992): 156–60. Lipset's study was based on election returns for the states of Virginia, Alabama, Georgia, Mississippi, North Carolina, Tennessee, and Louisiana.

8. An outstanding study of political sentiment and developments in the upper South is Daniel W. Crofts, *Reluctant Confederates: Upper South Unionists in the Secession Crisis* (Chapel Hill: The University of North Carolina Press, 1989).

9. Escott, *After Secession*, 50. Despite the general enthusiasm for volunteering, there were in many states certain districts or neighborhoods where Unionism remained strong. For example, see Malcolm C. McMillan, *The Disintegration of a Confederate State: Three Governors and Alabama's Wartime Home Front, 1861–1865* (Macon, GA: Mercer University Press, 1986), 128.

10. Wiley, *Life of Johnny Reb*, 124, 127; Robertson, *Soldiers, Blue and Gray*, 8–9, 38–40; Emory M. Thomas, *The Confederate Nation, 1861–1865* (New York: Harper Torchbooks, 1979), 154. Other estimates place the number of conscripts at roughly 90,000.

11. Paul D. Escott, *Many Excellent People: Power and Privilege in North Carolina, 1850–1900* (Chapel Hill: The University of North Carolina Press, 1985), 40; Norton et al., *A People and a Nation*, 4th ed. (1994), 448.

12. Escott, *Many Excellent People*, 40–41.

13. Wiley, *Life of Johnny Reb*, 127.

14. Ibid., 124; Escott, *After Secession*, 115–16, 120.

15. Escott, *After Secession*, 123–25.

16. Ibid., 125–26.

17. Ibid., 126–27, 219; Wiley, *Life of Johnny Reb*, 144; Lee to Davis, April 20, 1865, in Clifford Dowdey, ed., *The Wartime Papers of R. E. Lee* (New York: Virginia Civil War Commission, 1961), 938. Lee reported that his army "began to disintegrate" on April 2, 1865, "and straggling from the ranks increased up to surrender on the 9th." On that latter day he had only 7,892 effective infantry, but as news of the surrender became known, men began to come back in, with the result that on April 12 26,018 officers and men surrendered.

18. James W. Clay et al., *The Land of the South* (Birmingham, AL: Oxmoor House, 1989), 162.

19. Gary W. Gallagher, *The Confederate War* (Cambridge, MA: Harvard University Press, 1997), 63. Another useful study is James M. McPherson, *For Cause and Comrades* (New York: Oxford University Press, 1997), but see also Michael Barton, *Goodmen: The Character of Civil War Soldiers* (University Park: Pennsylvania State University Press, 1981).

20. See chapter 6.

21. Gallagher, *The Confederate War*, 72, 71.

22. Escott, *After Secession*, 112, 103–5. For greater detail see Mary Elizabeth Massey, *Ersatz in the Confederacy* (Columbia: University of South Carolina Press, 1952).

23. Wayne K. Durrill, *War of Another Kind: A Southern Community in the Great Rebellion* (New York: Oxford University Press, 1990); Escott, *Many Excellent People*, 61–63.

24. See Stephen V. Ash, *When the Yankees Came: Conflict and Chaos in the Occupied South, 1861–1865* (Chapel Hill: The University of North Carolina Press, 1995); Mark Grimsley, *The Hard Hand of War: Union Military Policy Toward Southern Civilians, 1861–1865* (New York: Cambridge University Press, 1995).

25. Escott, *After Secession*, 109–11.

26. See Georgia Lee Tatum, *Disloyalty in the Confederacy* (Chapel Hill: The University of North Carolina Press, 1934); McMillan, *The Disintegration of a Confederate State*; and Ella Lonn, *Desertion During the Civil War* (New York: Century Company, 1928).

27. Escott, *After Secession*, 129, 214; chapter 5 contains an extended discussion of the popular basis for opposition by the governors.

28. Ibid., 194.

29. Ibid., 128–31; Escott, *Many Excellent People*, 67, 79–80. The final quotations come, respectively, from Alabama's senator Clement C. Clay Jr., Georgia's governor Brown, and Florida's governor John Milton. The conversion of Alabama's Thomas Watts, who was the Confederacy's attorney general before he became governor, from an advocate of central power to an opponent of Richmond's policies, is instructive and is well treated in McMillan's *The Disintegration of a Confederate State*.

30. McMillan, *The Disintegration of a Confederate State*, 117–18, 135.

31. Vance to David L. Swain, September 22, 1864, Vance Papers, North Carolina Division of Archives and History, Raleigh, N.C.

32. Thomas, *The Confederate Nation*, 190.

Selected Bibliography

Alexander, Thomas B., and Beringer, Richard. *The Anatomy of the Confederate Congress*. Nashville: Vanderbilt University Press, 1972.

Ash, Stephen V. *When the Yankees Came: Conflict and Chaos in the Occupied South, 1861–1865*. Chapel Hill: The University of North Carolina Press, 1995.

Ballard, Michael. *Pemberton: A Biography*. Jackson: University Press of Mississippi, 1991.

Barrett, John G. *The Civil War in North Carolina*. Chapel Hill: The University of North Carolina Press, 1963.

Barton, Michael, and Logue, Larry M., eds. *The Civil War Soldier: A Historical Reader*. New York: New York University Press, 2002.

Bensel, Richard Franklin. *Yankee Leviathan: The Origins of Central State Authority in America, 1859–1877*. New York and Cambridge: Cambridge University Press, 1990.

Boritt, Gabor S., ed. *Why the Confederacy Lost*. New York: Oxford University Press, 1992.

Brewer, James. *The Confederate Negro: Virginia's Craftsmen and Military Laborers, 1861–1865*. Durham, NC: Duke University Press, 1969.

Candler, Allen D., ed. *The Confederate Records of the State of Georgia*. 6 vols. Atlanta: Chas. P. Byrd, 1910.

Chambers, William Nisbet. *Political Parties in a New Nation: The American Experience, 1776–1809*. New York: Oxford University Press, 1972.

Chesnut, Mary Boykin. *Diary from Dixie*. Edited by Ben Ames Williams. Boston: Houghton Mifflin Company, Sentry edition, 1949.

Connelly, Thomas L. *Autumn of Glory: The Army of Tennessee, 1862–1865*. Baton Rouge: Louisiana State University Press, 1971.

Connelly, Thomas, and Jones, Archer. *The Politics of Command: Factions and Ideas in Confederate Strategy*. Baton Rouge: Louisiana State University Press, 1973.

Cooper, William J., Jr. *Jefferson Davis, American*. New York: Knopf, 2000.

Crofts, Daniel W. *Reluctant Confederates: Upper South Unionists in the Secession Crisis*. Chapel Hill: The University of North Carolina Press, 1989.

Cunliffe, Marcus. *Soldiers and Civilians: The Martial Spirit in America, 1775–1865*. Boston: Little, Brown and Company, 1968.

Current, Richard N., editor-in-chief. *Encyclopedia of the Confederacy*. 4 vols. New York: Simon & Schuster, 1993.

Davis, Varina Howell. *Jefferson Davis, Ex-President of the Confederate States of America; A Memoir*. 2 vols. New York: Belford Company, 1890.

Davis, William C. *Breckinridge: Statesman, Soldier, Symbol*. Baton Rouge: Louisiana State University Press, 1974.

———. *The Cause Lost: Myths and Realities of the Confederacy*. Lawrence: University Press of Kansas, 1996.

———, ed. *A Fire-Eater Remembers: The Confederate Memoir of Robert Barnwell Rhett*. Columbia: University of South Carolina Press, 2000.

DeCredico, Mary A. *Patriotism for Profit: Georgia's Urban Entrepreneurs and the Confederate War Effort*. Chapel Hill: The University of North Carolina Press, 1990.

Dew, Charles B. *Apostles of Disunion*. Charlottesville: University Press of Virginia, 2001.

———. *Ironmaker to the Confederacy: Joseph R. Anderson and the Tredegar Iron Works*. New Haven: Yale University Press, 1966.

Donald, David, ed. *Why the North Won the Civil War*. New York: Collier Books, 1962.

Dowdey, Clifford, ed. *The Wartime Papers of R. E. Lee*. New York: Virginia Civil War Commission, 1961.

Durden, Robert F. *The Gray and the Black: The Confederate Debate on Emancipation*. Baton Rouge: Louisiana State University Press, 1972.

———. *The Self-Inflicted Wound: Southern Politics in the Nineteenth Century*. Lexington: The University Press of Kentucky, 1985.

Durrill, Wayne K. *War of Another Kind: A Southern Community in the Great Rebellion*. New York: Oxford University Press, 1990.

Evans, Eli N. *Judah P. Benjamin: The Jewish Confederate*. New York: Free Press, 1988.

Escott, Paul D. *After Secession: Jefferson Davis and the Failure of Confederate Nationalism*. Baton Rouge: Louisiana State University Press, 1978.

———. *Many Excellent People: Power and Privilege in North Carolina, 1850–1900*. Chapel Hill: The University of North Carolina Press, 1985.

Fellman, Michael. *Citizen Sherman: A Life of William Tecumseh Sherman*. New York: Random House, 1995.

Freehling, William W. *Prelude to Civil War: The Nullification Controversy in South Carolina, 1816–1836*. New York: Harper Torchbooks, 1966.

———. *The South vs. The South: How Anti-Confederate Southerners Shaped the Course of the Civil War*. New York: Oxford University Press, 2001.

Freeman, Douglas Southall. *Lee's Lieutenants, a Study in Command*. 3 vols. New York: Charles Scribner's Sons, 1942–44.

Freeman, Douglas Southall, and De Renne, W. J., eds. *Lee's Dispatches*. New York: G. P. Putnam's Sons, 1915.

Gallagher, Gary W. *The Confederate War*. Cambridge, MA: Harvard University Press, 1997.

Goff, Richard D. *Confederate Supply*. Durham, NC: Duke University Press, 1969.

Goldfield, David R. *Cotton Fields and Skyscrapers: Southern City and Region*. Baton Rouge: Louisiana State University Press, 1982.

Govan, Gilbert, and Livingood, James W. *A Different Valor: The Story of General Joseph E. Johnston*. New York: Bobbs-Merrill Company, 1956.

Grimsley, Mark. *The Hard Hand of War: Union Military Policy Toward Southern Civilians, 1861–1865*. New York: Cambridge University Press, 1995.

Hahn, Stephen. *The Roots of Southern Populism: Yeoman Farmers and the Transformation of the Georgia Upcountry, 1850–1900*. New York: Oxford University Press, 1983.

Harris, William C. *Leroy Pope Walker: Confederate Secretary of War*. Tuscaloosa, AL: Confederate Publishing Company, Inc., 1962.

Hattaway, Herman, and Jones, Archer. *How the North Won: A Military History of the Civil War*. Urbana: University of Illinois Press, 1983.

Hill, Louise B. *State Socialism in the Confederate States of America*. Charlottesville, VA: The Historical Publishing Company, Inc., 1936.

Huntington, Samuel P. *The Soldier and the State: The Theory and Politics of Civil-Military Relations*. Cambridge, MA: Belknap Press, 1957.

Jones, Archer. *Confederate Strategy from Shiloh to Vicksburg*. Baton Rouge: Louisiana State University Press, 1961.

Jones, J.B. *A Rebel War Clerk's Diary*. 2 vols. Edited by Howard Swiggett. New York: Old Hickory Bookshop, 1935.

Kerby, Robert L. *Kirby Smith's Confederacy: The Trans-Mississippi South, 1863–1865*. New York: Columbia University Press, 1972.

Lee, Charles Robert, Jr. *The Confederate Constitutions*. Chapel Hill: The University of North Carolina Press, 1963.

Lefler, Hugh Talmage, and Newsome, Albert Ray. *The History of a Southern State: North Carolina*. 3rd ed. Chapel Hill: The University of North Carolina Press, 1973.

Lipset, Seymour Martin. *Political Man: The Social Bases of Politics*. Garden City, NY: Doubleday and Company, Anchor Books, 1963.

Lonn, Ella. *Desertion During the Civil War*. New York: Century Company, 1928.

McCaslin, Richard. *Tainted Breeze: The Great Hanging at Gainesville, Texas, 1862*. Baton Rouge: Louisiana State University Press, 1994.

McMillan, Malcolm C. *The Disintegration of a Confederate State: Three Governors and Alabama's Wartime Home Front, 1861–1865*. Macon, GA: Mercer University Press, 1986.

McPherson, James M. *Battle Cry of Freedom: The Civil War Era*. New York: Oxford University Press, 1988.

———. *For Cause and Comrades*. New York: Oxford University Press, 1997.

———. *Ordeal by Fire: The Civil War and Reconstruction*. New York: Knopf, 1982.

Martis, Kenneth C. *The Historical Atlas of the Congresses of the Confederate States of America: 1861–1865*. New York: Simon & Schuster, 1994.

Massey, Mary Elizabeth. *Ersatz in the Confederacy*. Columbia: University of South Carolina Press, 1952.

Matthews, James M., ed. *The Statutes at Large of the Provisional Government of the Confederate States of America.* Richmond, VA: R. M. Smith, 1864.

Meade, Robert Douthat. *Judah P. Benjamin, Confederate Statesman.* 1943. Reprint, New York: Oxford University Press, 1975.

Neely, Mark E., Jr. *Southern Rights: Political Prisoners and the Myth of Confederate Constitutionalism.* Charlottesville: University Press of Virginia, 1999.

Nolan, Alan. *Lee Considered.* Chapel Hill: The University of North Carolina Press, 1991.

Owsley, Frank L. *State Rights in the Confederacy.* Chicago: University of Chicago Press, 1925.

Parks, Joseph H. *General Edmund Kirby Smith, C.S.A.* Baton Rouge: Louisiana State University Press, 1954.

————. *General Leonidas Polk, C.S.A.: The Fighting Bishop.* Baton Rouge: Louisiana State University Press, 1962.

Rable, George C. *The Confederate Republic: A Revolution Against Politics.* Chapel Hill: The University of North Carolina Press, 1994.

Radley, Kenneth. *Rebel Watchdog: The Confederate States Army Provost Guard.* Baton Rouge: Louisiana State University Press, 1989.

Richardson, James D., comp. *A Compilation of the Messages and Papers of the Confederacy, Including the Diplomatic Correspondence, 1861–1865.* 2 vols. Nashville: United States Publishing Company, 1906.

Robertson, James I., Jr. *Soldiers Blue and Gray.* Columbia: University of South Carolina Press, 1988.

Rowland, Dunbar, ed. *Jefferson Davis, Constitutionalist; His Letters, Papers, and Speeches.* 10 vols. Jackson: Mississippi Department of Archives and History, 1923.

Schott, Thomas E. *Alexander H. Stephens of Georgia: A Biography.* Baton Rouge: Louisiana State University Press, 1988.

Shackelford, George Green. *George Wythe Randolph and the Confederate Elite.* Athens: University of Georgia Press, 1988.

Simon, John Y., and Stevens, Michael E., eds. *New Perspectives on the Civil War: Myths and Realities of the National Conflict.* Madison: Madison House in cooperation with the State Historical Society of Wisconsin, 1998.

Smith, Louis. *American Democracy and Military Power.* Chicago: University of Chicago Press, 1951.

Snow, Donald M., and Drew, Dennis M. *From Lexington to Desert Storm: War and Politics in the American Experience.* Armonk, NY: M. E. Sharpe, Inc., 1994.

Stone, Geoffrey R. *Perilous Times: Free Speech in Wartime, From the Sedition Act of 1798 to the War on Terrorism.* New York: W. W. Norton, 2004.

Tatum, Georgia Lee. *Disloyalty in the Confederacy.* Chapel Hill: The University of North Carolina Press, 1934.

Thomas, Emory M. *The Confederacy as a Revolutionary Experience.* Englewood Cliffs, NJ: Prentice-Hall, Inc., 1971.

————. *The Confederate Nation, 1861–1865.* New York: Harper Torchbooks, 1979.

————. *Robert E. Lee.* New York: W. W. Norton, 1995.

U.S. War Department. *The War of the Rebellion: A Compilation of the Official*

Records of the Union and Confederate Armies. 130 vols. Washington, DC: Government Printing Office, 1880–1901.

Vandiver, Frank E. *Ploughshares into Swords: Josiah Gorgas and Confederate Ordnance.* Austin: University of Texas Press, 1952.

Wallenstein, Peter. *From Slave South to New South: Public Policy in Nineteenth-Century Georgia.* Chapel Hill: The University of North Carolina Press, 1987.

Warner, Ezra J. *Generals in Gray: Lives of the Confederate Commanders.* Baton Rouge: Louisiana State University Press, 1959.

Weigley, Russell F. *The American Way of War: A History of United States Military Strategy and Policy.* Bloomington: Indiana University Press, 1973.

———. *A Great Civil War.* Bloomington: Indiana University Press, 2000.

———. *History of the United States Army.* Enlarged ed. Bloomington: Indiana University Press, 1984.

Wiley, Bell Irvin. *The Life of Johnny Reb: The Common Soldier of the Confederacy.* New York: Bobbs-Merrill, 1943.

Williams, T. Harry. *P.G.T. Beauregard: Napoleon in Gray.* Baton Rouge: Louisiana State University Press, 1954.

Woodward, C. Vann. *The Burden of Southern History.* Revised ed. New York: Mentor Books, 1969.

———, ed. *Mary Chesnut's Civil War.* New Haven: Yale University Press, 1981.

Woodworth, Steven E. *Davis and Lee at War.* Lawrence: University Press of Kansas, 1995.

———. *Jefferson Davis and His Generals: The Failure of Confederate Command in the West.* Lawrence: University Press of Kansas, 1990.

———, ed. *The Art of Command in the Civil War.* Lincoln: University of Nebraska Press, 1998.

———. *No Band of Brothers: Problems in the Rebel High Command.* Columbia: University of Missouri Press, 1999.

Wright, Gavin. *The Political Economy of the Cotton South: Households, Markets, and Wealth in the Nineteenth Century.* New York: W. W. Norton, 1978.

Wyatt-Brown, Bertram. *Southern Honor: Ethics and Behavior in the Old South.* New York: Oxford University Press, 1982.

Yearns, Wilfred Buck. *The Confederate Congress.* Athens: University of Georgia Press, 1960.

Yearns, Wilfred Buck, and Barrett, John G., eds. *North Carolina Civil War Documentary.* Chapel Hill: The University of North Carolina Press, 1980.

Younger, Edward, ed. *Inside the Confederate Government: The Diary of Robert Garlick Hill Kean.* New York: Oxford University Press, 1957.

Index

About the Author

PAUL D. ESCOTT is Professor of History at Wake Forest University. His publications include books and articles on the Confederacy, the South, and on African American history.